MORAL INJURY RECONCILIATION

of related interest

The Forgiveness Project
Stories for a Vengeful Age
Marina Cantacuzino
Forewords by Archbishop Emeritus Desmond Tutu and Alexander McCall Smith
ISBN 978 1 84905 566 6 (Hardback)
ISBN 978 1 78592 000 4
eISBN 978 1 78450 006 1

At War with Yourself
A Comic about Post-Traumatic Stress and the Military
Samuel C. Williams
ISBN 978 1 84819 295 9
eISBN 978 0 85701 245 6

Psycho-spiritual Care in Health Care Practice
Edited by Guy Harrison
ISBN 978 1 78592 039 4
eISBN 978 1 78450 292 8

What Counsellors and Spiritual Directors Can Learn from Each Other
Ethical Practice, Training and Supervision
Edited by Peter Madsen Gubi
ISBN 978 1 78592 025 7
eISBN 978 1 78450 271 3

Hope and Grace
Spiritual Experiences in Severe Distress, Illness and Dying
Dr Monika Renz
ISBN 978 1 78592 030 1
eISBN 978 1 78450 277 5

MORAL INJURY
RECONCILIATION

A Practitioner's Guide for Treating Moral Injury,
PTSD, Grief, and Military Sexual Trauma
through Spiritual Formation Strategies

LEWIS JEFF LEE

Jessica Kingsley *Publishers*
London and Philadelphia

Epigraph on p.17—Introduction from The Doctor and the Soul: From Psychotherapy to Logotherapy by Viktor E. Frankl and translated by Richard & Clara Winston, copyright © 1955, 1965 by Alfred A. Knopf, a division of Random House LLC. Used by permission of Alfred A. Knopf, an imprint of the Knopf Doubleday Publishing Group, a division of Penguin Random House LLC. All rights reserved.

Eye-2-Eye Exercise on pp.188-89. Acceptance and Commitment Therapy: An Experiental Approach to Behavior Change, Hayes, S.C., Strosahl, K.D., and Wilson, K.G. (1999). Copyright Guilford Press. Reprinted with permission of The Guilford Press.

First published in 2018
by Jessica Kingsley Publishers
73 Collier Street
London N1 9BE, UK
and
400 Market Street, Suite 400
Philadelphia, PA 19106, USA

www.jkp.com

Copyright © Lewis Jeff Lee 2018

Library of Congress Cataloging in Publication Data
A CIP catalog record for this book is available from the Library of Congress

British Library Cataloguing in Publication Data
A CIP catalogue record for this book is available from the British Library

ISBN 978 1 78592 757 7
eISBN 978 1 78450 597 4

Printed and bound in the United States

Contents

Preface

Foundations are the bedrock of excellence. For out of the *basics*, great deeds result. This adage seems truer now than ever. Football great Vince Lombardi of the Green Bay Packers appeared to embody this belief. Not only famous for Super Bowl championship wins, but for opening pre-season training camp with hard-nosed men of the gridiron saying: "Gentlemen, this is a football." When my old boss from SEAL Team THREE Bill McCraven wrote the book titled *Make Your Bed* (2017), I was reminded of this principle. This rule finds that basic habits are the keys to profound change. Both men underscore the ideals found in this treatment guide. The basics set the stage for reversing difficulties with habits that increase endurance. Making such a rule actionable will transform one's head, heart, and life.

Investing in others is a basic principle I learned. I also learned that hard work and looking out for your neighbor were commendable moral standards. Investing in another is a sorely needed remedy amidst the overheated political climate and the one-upmanship that prevails. Concern for a fellow citizen is a character-shaping virtue that transforms the benefactor and uplifts the beneficiary.

Early on, I sensed life was about more than things or positions. And as I survey my life, it is characterized by service and wider community-building efforts. At a young age I partnered with the Muscular Dystrophy Association, then the American Red Cross, and other volunteer groups that provided initial opportunities to serve. I took advantage of those openings and worked for the good of others. My active-duty service further suggests my lifelong quest to serve. To be sure, I find high honor and great reward in giving to a worthy cause such as righting wrongs, and protecting the young, helpless, and disadvantaged. This is my calling.

The *moral injury reconciliation* approach (also known as "the *reconciliation model*") continues in a service-oriented direction. The strength of this methodology is believed found in its three-phased thematic, religious/spiritual framework. Its design aims to bind the spiritual and psychic wounds of the past and promote new thinking that affects present functioning and one's future outlook. To be sure, while some scars will remain, new strategies and the continued support of those in and out of uniform are critically needed. My incentive to help wounded men and women recover is borne out of gratitude and a want for the good of others. The moral injury reconciliation model is the result of personal experience in the helping professions, military service, and decades of religious/spiritual study.

However, before caring for those challenged by *moral injury* or posttraumatic stress, mental health providers are encouraged to gain a keen knowledge of the military landscape. An understanding of the makeup of veterans, servicemembers, and their families is an essential competency. It will weigh heavily as part of the formula for achieving positive outcomes. It is also part of the basics of this proposed treatment.

Moral injury presents when one's moral–ethical codes have been violated. Once violated, the moral injury spectrum of guilt, shame, isolation, psychic numbing, or depression steers a course toward maladaptive behaviors known as *invisible wounds*. Yet despite such an injury, the reconciliation model offers hope.

In the past, I aided the visibly handicapped. Now, I am determined to treat the inside wounds; the wounds that cripple the spiritual and emotional health of our veterans and military personnel. Without a therapeutic spirit of service, ultimately, a client's symptoms may go unattended. Hopelessness and grave physical consequences may result. Investing in others may be viewed as an investment where the caregiver joins in the spiritual transformation of the afflicted. Both patient and provider are changed.

Following is one man's progressive immersion into the unique culture of military life and the plan to continue serving the morally wounded. This plan is a spiritual care strategy for full life transformation that addresses recovery from moral injury and other trauma. This strategy is founded on religious/spiritual, psychological, and physical remedies both ancient and new. As you read, I encourage you to use my life story as a pretext for understanding the influences that shaped other veterans and active-duty personnel. While each person is unique, a common thread may be found in the life stories of those who have served or currently serving. For the military experience must be understood as a *cultural transformation* where the potential for moral injury uniquely exists. Mine is such a story.

My transformation started over 50 years ago. When I was aged about seven, my brothers and I discovered my father's drab World War II olive U.S. Army blouse respectfully folded and neatly stowed. With great deference, we would cautiously sneak a peek at this exhibit. It was complete with stripes, patches, and insignia tucked discreetly in my parents' bottom dresser drawer. Although I could not explain it, I was transfixed, however briefly, by this icon from American history of which my father was a part. As I held, smelled, and fingered the texture of the garment, I imagined this uniform somehow representing a greater good. A noble cause. It was proof of service to others. As I later realized, it was proof, too, that the military was governed by discipline, order, meaning, and higher ideals. His uniform stood for something.

Other life events steadily sparked my continued interest in military life. Together, they increasingly infused a passion to serve. One such influence was church attendance; the other was television.

We went to church often as a family. And, like many children, I was ambivalent about church matters and rambunctious. I had trouble sitting still as older women taught children's Bible lessons with flannel board figures as visual aids. On a typical church day, the transition between the children's church and the main service was punctuated by unauthorized excursions. My brothers and I would sneak out the side door, cross the street, and buy candy with our church offering. Then, we would slip back inside and find our seats before the main service started. But little did I realize the impact the religious/spiritual teachings were having. It was there I understood my calling. Later, I realized the many religious precepts had strong associations with the moral principles forming the bedrock of warrior codes as well as the foundation of many secular civil laws. At this age, an uncanny resonance between religious/spiritual doctrines and the fabric of life emerged.

Next, television notably impacted me. Television brought historic and vivid images to life. I laughed at *The Three Stooges*, enjoyed the black and white cartoons, and watched other variety programming like

The Ed Sullivan Show. But I took a different sort of interest in the news coverage presented. For instance, networks like ABC and CBS were reporting distant accounts of current events of the 1960s. And as my father switched between the *NBC Nightly News* or the *Huntley–Brinkley Report*, I found myself standing, watching intently as news coverage inspired a special level of awareness. News programming routinely featured American KIAs (killed in action) or the major campaigns of the escalating Vietnam conflict. While I could not fully grasp the import of the national geopolitical strategy of the time, I again felt such reporting was highly significant. I wanted to do something to help.

The attraction to military life further stamped my memory through other early-life events like my morning and evening newspaper routes. I began to make the connection between the televised war-news coverage and those touched by real life. I had frequent reminders as I dutifully delivered my newspapers. Those yellow-ribboned homes were welcoming the return of their soldier who was a bit older than me. I made the connection. Television was showing the real, albeit distant, state of affairs of those serving abroad. However, customers brought the personal and proximate better into focus. And as I witnessed this strain, it brought new meaning to life.

And so it was that I went playing "army" with my brothers and the other kids in our modest multiracial, but predominantly Polish, neighborhood. During this period, television also told the story of war through the popular 1960s-era television war drama series called *Combat!* Many episodes opened with actual combat footage that segued into the dramatized version of events. The program then opened with the sound effects of grenades exploding and splashing fragmented images upon the screen's backdrop. It continued on with animated rifles fixed with bayonets moving in orderly procession in advance of the announcer introducing the cast—"*Combat!*" he barked. "Starring Vic Morrow and Rick Jason"—all while the marshal music continued playing in the background.

This was my young world where the basics were learned. I grew up familiar with hard work, cold Detroit winters, and the intrigue of military service. My father's U.S. Army wool jumper was the physical reminder helping to etch the multiple other early-life influences on my mind.

Military records show my father was deployed for 13 months to the warzone of Central Burma (China, Burma, India) or what was known as the *CBI Campaign* of South and Southeast Asia. He spoke few words of his World War II experiences as a Chaplain's Assistant during the height of the war. Nevertheless, he did mention two events.

First, he shared that he developed an extreme distaste for "chicken" as he described an overabundance of this canned ration during the war. He never ate it once he returned home. Second, sometime before his deployment, he vowed he would never carry a rifle in the field. However, one day a tiger surprised him while performing assigned duties. This encounter forced him to re-evaluate his decision. Afterwards, he never left unarmed. I imagine he was surprised by many other things too. Perhaps he saw or did things that violated his religious beliefs or moral code. Or, maybe he witnessed things that people should never have to see, but were thrust into such situations by circumstances nonetheless.

Today, I believe I know why my father spoke so little of his service, since I better understand the invisible wounds of trauma and grief. Even so, however difficult his ordeal, I wanted to walk in my father's footsteps, wherever they led, because service meant something. It meant that there was something in life greater than one's self-interest, though I knew there was a price to be paid. Service comes with costs and consequences.

Nevertheless, the most convincing event that sealed my decision to join the military was my father moving the family from Michigan to Newport, Rhode Island. For it was at that moment in 1972 when I first saw the Atlantic Ocean and two Navy destroyers docked pierside that I knew my course was set. Sleek, clean, and at the ready those ships stood. That very instant affirmed there was a something bigger in life; a something far larger than me and it was in that realm I belonged. By serving others, I was unknowingly investing in the higher ideals linked to a religious/spiritual life.

On that day by the dock, that awakening was where the vertical (existential) and horizontal (community) realities crossed, filling my life with meaning and purpose. And since I was so fond of history, Newport served as an incubator that increased the intensity of my zeal for further exploration of history and eventual military service.

Newport, a tiny colonial town with a quaint, touristy appeal, was completely unlike my Detroit neighborhood. This historic setting accelerated my want to do something meaningful. I was compelled to act. Whereas I played army amongst old homes and makeshift forts in my old hometown of Detroit, I now played army in Newport's historic cemeteries, throwing snowballs while hiding behind the many headstones that were barely readable. There, the oldest recorded burial is of one John Coggeshall, Governor, 1647. History was literally everywhere.

In school, I read of the likes of Crispus Attucks who symbolized the fierce spirit of American independence. Attucks, a black man, is recognized as the first martyr of the American Revolution, killed in 1770 during the infamous *Boston Massacre*. Olympian Jesse Owens served with distinction as an American hero. As a member of the *Black Legion* so-called by the Nazi-controlled German press, he discredited Aryan ideals of supremacy on the international stage during track and field events in Berlin, 1936. And in 1941 when Pearl Harbor was attacked, Dorie Miller's wartime heroics proved inspirational. Similarly, the leadership of the Reverend Dr. Martin Luther King Jr. of *America's Civil Rights Movement* is legendary.

Despite great hardships, these and countless other unnamed men and women achieved much. They, too, remained steadfast in service for a greater cause at considerable risk. While my early focus was to help others and join the armed services, I never viewed it as a prideful, attention-seeking endeavor. I always thought it a thankless, sober enterprise, because pain and possible death was so often a consequence. However, as altruism would be required to meet the challenge, I relished the opportunity to achieve a greater good.

Soon after this 1972 relocation experience, I joined the U.S. Naval Sea Cadets Corps in Newport where I continued a more systematic military cultural indoctrination. It was at this organization where I began to anticipate the rigors of military life. The place to acquire the skills needed to not just successfully serve, but to excel. Seamanship, naval history, and drill were on the agenda. Leadership principles were taught by guest speakers, such as Admiral Stansfield Turner, then President of the U.S. Naval War College and later Director of the U.S. Central Intelligence Agency.

Training films were part of the curriculum too. Department of Defense 16-millimeter movies featured actors like Jack Webb, the stern, no-nonsense, law-and-order detective of the 1960s crime drama *Dragnet*. Webb provided firm instruction on the principles of "The Code," *The U.S. Code of Military Conduct*. The Code embodied the clear directives to uphold in the course of eventual combat or if captured by the enemy. In clear and steady voice his audience heard: "Courage, self-sacrifice, devotion to country... This is the heritage left to us by those who served before." Webb challenged his audience. I grew and learned such lessons well. They reinforced the values I would so honor a few years later. Some would protest such training as propaganda, but the Code helped many Vietnam-era *prisoners of war* maintain their *moral integrity* after repeated episodes of savage torture. Additionally, religious/spiritual doctrines encouraged steadfastness under duress, but for entirely different reasons and from an existential context.

But in 1973, Newport Naval Base closed. My father's civil service position at Quonset Point Naval Air Station was transferred to Norfolk Naval Air Station, Virginia. We moved again. So, during my junior and senior high school years, I joined the Navy Junior Reserve Officer Training Corps at my new school. I also re-joined the Sea Cadets where I looked forward to Cadet drill weekends. I even attended a two-week Sea Cadet "mini-boot camp" at Orlando Naval Training Center, Florida. So eager was I to serve that I felt the urge to drop out of school and enlist in the Navy, but I knew instinctively how poor a choice that was.

Still, my older brother routinely spoke of exciting Navy travel and teamwork. I craved this rite of passage and the promise of adventure. My anticipation swelled as my love affair with the sea grew. Shortly afterwards, I signed up under the one-year Navy Delayed Entry Program. And, roughly eight days after high school graduation, I departed for boot camp at Great Lakes Naval Training Center, Illinois.

Now, almost 40 years later, I have spent over 22 years of service as a Naval Special Warfare operator. This service includes: completion, deployments, or training with Basic Underwater Demolition Team/ SEAL (BUD/S; Sea, Air, Land or SEAL), Underwater Demolition Team (UDT), SEAL (Sea, Air, Land) Team, a SEAL Delivery Vehicle, and the former Special Boat Units (now Special Boat Teams). My duties required performing parachuting, diving, demolitions, anti-terrorist and hostage rescue training, wet submersible (mini-submarine) operations, and coordinating Foreign Internal Defense (FID) training missions. Having served, I retired from active duty in January 2004. However, the call to serve actually increased, albeit from an entirely different direction.

Since 1998, I have received continuous formal and informal religious/spiritual and mental health training, education, and experience. Currently, I serve veterans, some active-duty members, and families as a chaplain with the Veterans Administration, San Diego. I also have my private practice as a licensed marriage and family therapist serving a wide range of clients. My contact with veterans is extensive. And from combined years of military and religious/spiritual training, I have come to find that healing resources are acquired through practicing the basics. These include: spiritual awareness (insight), community, resilience know-how, and the ability to make sense of one's circumstances. Such skills are requisite features for the sustained spiritual equilibrium. They are needed to negotiate life along the trauma continuum and to accomplish one's mission and purpose in life.

I am a Cold War, post-Vietnam-era veteran. My service ended as the "War on Terror" was growing. Nevertheless, training events have placed me in numerous stressful situations, like being in a civil war-torn country where mission planning, escape and evasion, and carrying concealed weapons proved necessary. This country's civil war enlisted children and used suicide bombers (especially female combatants) long before America's introduction to such oft-used terror tactics employed in Iraq or Afghanistan. Even though such experiences cannot equate to direct-action combat operations, it has increased my belief that repeated stressors, life threat, and war alter one's spiritual equilibrium. I trained hard for war, but did not find it. Nevertheless, my new task is to rightly present a religious/spiritual framework to amend current clinical procedures. These new procedures will represent a new paradigm in clinical care that treats moral injury and the moral injury spectrum that causes untold mental distress.

To be sure, killing of any kind (especially in war) necessarily induces moral injury, however slight. While I use the term moral injury exclusively for veterans and active-duty men and women, repercussions of killing even in a civilian context is a diminishing of the soul that must be reconciled.

In theory, diminishment of the soul is an applicable universal phenomenon believed to be true for the local police officer or service member. And other pathologies notwithstanding, a diminishing of the soul is at work in all incidents of warfare, including voluntary or involuntary manslaughter. Accidents, too, will unbalance the soul. Perhaps a weakened spirit is the germ at the center of the guilt-shame constructs. The moral injury spectrum is the result of severing this spiritual bond and it will take others in community to restore the morally wounded back into the bond of kindred spirits.

Still, operating lawfully under the color of authority or a justifiable war cannot mitigate the soul's response to the taking of life. Moral foundations from religious teachings tend to confirm this invisible and common humanity shared by all. And once a life is taken, the soul is thought to suffer a spiritual diminishing, though perhaps not fully understood. Even so, an almost unshakable stress or an ill-ease may be present until arrested.

In my new career as healer, I routinely speak to veterans struggling with moral injury and other trauma. As I treat each case, I see more than the veteran sitting nearby. I see their families, too. And though the family may not be physically present, I seek to hear *their* stories too. Such stories (not unlike mine) are their histories that have shaped their lives whether they are a newly discharged veteran or an aging ex-prisoner of war from World War II. As I listen, I hear the meta-narrative, the larger overarching story. I pay attention to the events of their background, as their story contains the core values responsible for their sense of morality and meaning in life. Collectively, these stories configure our values for how one makes sense of the world. They help form the broader worldview about how things in life are supposed to work, such as "children do not get massacred at school," or "people don't crash airplanes into buildings, killing innocents."

Part of my job is to help fellow veterans *make sense* of their trauma when their moral codes are violated. I do this so that a transformed and resilient client and family comes forth. It is also part of my service (calling) toward others; part of the basics of life.

In the preceding paragraphs, I have provided a snapshot of my own progression—my account of how my culture, moral foundations, and military upbringing fashioned me. Hopefully, my short story will be used as a template to spark interest in themes for clinicians to listen for. During sessions, such themes may help detect a client's meaning-making system to connect them to other healthcare resources discussed later. Such a strategy may offer openings for useful appropriation of transitional themes or help spot a festering moral breach.

Understanding a veteran's and servicemember's story is pivotal as it generally defines the governing architecture that describes the person and what specific moral injury themes characterize their trauma. Moral injury themes are identified as: betrayal, disproportionate violence, incidents involving civilians, and within-rank violence (military sexual trauma, friendly fire). This skill should amplify what is most needed for ultimate healing and transformation. Listening with both ears may help to develop a service orientation and a spiritual resonance required to engender the necessary elements of trust which is paramount for the reconciliation process to be of use. So, let us begin.

INTRODUCTION

A well-known psychiatrist once remarked that Western humanity has turned from the priest to the doctor. Another psychiatrist complains that nowadays too many patients come to the medical man with problems which should really be put to a priest... The spiritual dimension cannot be ignored, for it is what makes us human.

Viktor E. Frankl, psychiatrist and Holocaust survivor
The Doctor and the Soul, p.xv

Following the terrorist attack on September 11, 2001, the *New England Journal of Medicine* reported approximately 90 percent of Americans turned to *religion* as a coping response (Schuster *et al.* 2001). In 2014, a *Journal of the American Medical Association* article found those placing a high importance on religion or spirituality "may confer resilience to the development of depressive illness in individuals at high familial risk for major depression" (Miller *et al.* 2014). At Harvard University's T.H. Chan School of Public Health, Boston, researchers analyzed data from 1996 through 2010 from a *Nurses' Health Study* of nearly 90,000 women. They report that those attending church at least once a week had a five-times reduced or a "significantly" lower risk of suicide when compared with those never attending services (VanderWeele *et al.* 2016). Additionally, of the "141 peer-reviewed quantitative studies that examined the relationship between R/S (religious/spiritual) involvement and suicide ideation, attempts, and completed suicide, 106 (75%) found lower suicidal ideation and behaviors with those who were more religious" (Koenig, King, and Carson 2012, p.190).

While there is much more to learn about the relationship between health and religious/spiritual matters, such evidence is remarkable. Yet there is more. For instance, in 271 of the 443 quantitative studies reviewed, 61 percent show a higher religious/spiritual involvement associated with less depression. It also predicts faster recovery from depression or that religious/spiritual interventions reduce depressive symptoms faster compared to secular treatment or controls (Koenig *et al.* 2012). And, of 278 original research studies analyzing relationships between religion/spirituality and alcohol use or abuse, after a systematic review, 240 (86%) reported inverse relationships, and of 185 studies examining the religious/spiritual–drug abuse relationship, 155 (84%) reported less drug abuse among the more religious (Koenig *et al.* 2012). Not only that, but hope for relationships may be found considering that 69 out of the 79 quantitative studies (87%) showed that religion and spirituality is related to increased marital stability and 35 of the 38 best designed studies (92%) show significant associations (Koenig *et al.* 2012).

Still other data show when religion/spirituality are features of individual lifestyle: 1) "twenty-six of thirty-two studies (81 percent) reported significant positive relationships between religiousness and optimism, and the remainder reported no association or mixed findings" (Koenig *et al.* 2012, p.129; see also Koenig, McCullough, and Larson 2001); and 2) "both qualitative and quantitative studies document associations between religious involvement and greater meaning and purpose in the United States (Mattis 2002; Fletcher 2004; Mohr *et al.* 2006) and abroad" (Koenig *et al.* 2012, pp.129–130; see also Soothill *et al.* 2002; Skrabski *et al.* 2005). It was even Freud (1929, p.8) in his *Civilizations and Its Discontents* who curiously penned: "So again, only religion can answer the question of the purpose of life. One can hardly be wrong in concluding that the idea of life having a purpose stands and falls with the religious system." Finally, "there is evidence that religious involvement—particularly religious attendance—can delay the onset of functional impairment in later life through a number of pathways, including perception of disability at any given level of objective physical illness" (Koenig *et al.* 2012, p.130; see also Idler 1987, 1995, 1997; Benjamins 2004; Berges *et al.* 2007; Park *et al.* 2008).

From this brief sample of available research, it would appear, then, that our belief systems and subsequent behaviors (or faith applications) contain high potential for individual healing and family hope. For this reason, additional space was devoted to spotlighting the positive correlations between religious/spiritual lifestyles and documented outcomes. Citing such research is a purposeful effort to detail the efficacy of religious/spiritual treatment offerings.

Unfortunately, while spiritually oriented lifestyles have been shown to be effective, they appear to have been generally undermined. By examining the history of psychology, we find one reason may be the following:

> Generations prior to Freud's time viewed humans as the maverick children of the divine, designed in God's image in a unique and special fashion. But the scientific speculation of Freud's era no longer allowed humans this unquestioned privilege. Darwin's influence cast a long, gray shadow over what had been a black-and-white divide between humans and other creatures; Freud was fascinated not with humankind's godlike visage but with the beast in men and women. The rich illumination Freud brought to our contemporary understanding of human experience often entailed pointing out the wild, primitive impulses and fantasies beneath the thin veneer of civilized conduct and demeanor. For Freud, the process of socialization involved taming the beast... For Freud, the distinctly human form of being was generated in the very process through which the primitive, bestial sexual and aggressive impulses were brought under control. (Mitchell and Black 2016, p.140)

What is also discouraging is the knowledge that there remains neglect of religious/spiritual inquiry out of which an "anti-tenure factor" developed. That is to say that the diligent study of religious/spiritual phenomena in academic circles may ruin professional credibility. For within this setting there is a "considerable bias" based on "personal views rather than objective evidence." Thus, a considerable gulf seems to remain between understanding what function religion and spirituality plays in health, coping, and resilience (Koenig *et al.* 2012, pp.5, 71–72).

REFORMED THINKING FOR OLD PROBLEMS

Despite existing professional and personal impediments, there is promise. Computer searches of key words such as "religion," "spirituality," or "religiosity" "suggest an enormous increase in attention paid to the topic by academic, medical, sociological, public health, nursing, psychiatric, and psychological journals. There has literally been the birth of an entire new field, the field of religion, spirituality, and health" (Koenig *et al.* 2012, p.4). Additionally, Hufford, Fritts, and Rhodes (2010) note a "five-fold increase in research" between 1990 and 2007, which may be seen as a testament to the growing scientific interest in the study of religion and spirituality.

Considering previous data, the moral injury reconciliation model's hypothesis is that moral injury and traumatic stress may be treated through transitional themes. Transitional themes serve as a unified treatment and may address the moral incongruence of one's actions that fail to meet moral standards. This thematic treatment strategy provides a modular composition to support a transdiagnostic (or unified) model of care (Sauer-Zavala *et al.* 2017).

A thematic component in a treatment plan allows the therapeutic flexibility of a menu-style option for the provider to offer veteran treatment. In other words, a unified treatment may be efficacious and cost-saving especially when high levels of comorbidities are present (Gutner *et al.* 2016). And instead of using a "disorder-specific" treatment for, say, posttraumatic stress disorder, the moral injury reconciliation model is intended to be a transdiagnostic treatment "designed to treat underlying vulnerabilities rather than just one disorder...focusing on commonalities across diagnosis" (Gutner *et al.* 2016). Thus, since increased rates of comorbidities in posttraumatic stress are present (Kessler *et al.* 1995; Brown *et al.* 2001), using the reconciliation model as a unified treatment approach seems appropriate.

The moral injury reconciliation model is thought to be effective for its new thinking to old problems. Using an old methodology may provide reasoned and corrective guidance consistent with belief and faith principles. Relative to moral injury, clinical evidence (above) shows that an accurate combination of such features is useful for confronting various stress and trauma-related challenges. Hope, meaning, and purpose, or the intrapersonal freedom *forgiveness* affords, abound within the several world religions' spiritual teaching milieu (Enright 2001, pp.6–7). Transitional themes are those religious/spiritual vehicles such as "hope" or "forgiveness" that assist clients in moving up and out of moral injury or other life challenges.

From the abundance of religious/spiritual literature, we may find a wealth of essential elements needed for developing life's orienting *beliefs*, or what mental health professionals may know as *schema* (Beck *et al.* 1979). Schema refers to the inherent and complex internal apparatus for perceiving, evaluating, and organizing life's experiences (Beck and Alford 2009, pp.12–13). Schema may be equated with *beliefs* or *meaning-making systems* that direct the structure for understanding how life works. Expanding the meaning-making system is the hoped-for transactional exchange transacted within the *spiritual economy*. Therefore, understanding the basics for effecting change in *spiritual awareness* (insight), beliefs, and corresponding actions (faith) is the essence of the moral injury reconciliation process.

Using transitional themes for expanding and re-orienting clients' beliefs may be a powerful healing intervention. Religious/spiritual teachings that promote anger resolution, forgiveness, and love have historically been shown to be effective foils retarding interpersonal strife and hostilities. Key components of religious doctrines employed by Mahatma Gandhi in India, the Reverend Dr. Martin Luther King Jr. in America, and Nelson Mandela of South Africa seem evident as an international focus, and change was the result.

So, how can transitional themes be integrated to initiate healing? What would this look like when treating moral injury or other trauma? Figure I.1 is a conceptual illustration of the transactional phase of the reconciliation process. A spiritual transaction takes existing moral injury or trauma (the spiritual imbalance), considers transitional themes, and through the *spiritual crucible* works out new, effectual beliefs and actions. Here, trauma and moral codes are transacted to form *reconciled* thinking for a return to spiritual balance. This is thought about how moral injury or trauma is processed within the spiritual economy for symptom reduction and behavior change.

Moral injury reconciliation's spiritual economy

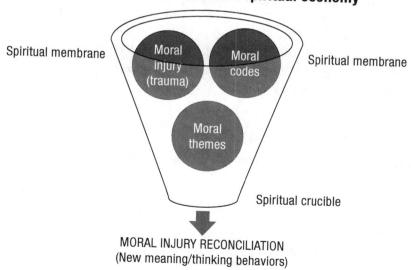

Figure I.1 The spiritual economy

THEOLOGICAL AND PSYCHOLOGICAL LINKS

Moral injury reconciliation is thought to be capable of harnessing the potential of modifying one's thinking (beliefs) through the strategic employment of transitional themes. In theory and practice, moral injury reconciliation uses a specific assortment of religious/spiritual teachings tailored to reconcile (synthesize) the veteran's or servicemember's moral injury. This spiritual framework is a model for both symptom reduction and higher functioning that works as follows. For instance, if "betrayal" is the primary lament (or presenting problem), the chaplain or provider selects a well-defined transitional theme from the religious/spiritual literature such as "forgiveness" as part of the treatment. Combined with other features of the client's care plan, meaning-making, anger resolution, behavior change, and hope-orienting transformation may result. As religious/spiritual teachings generally undergird all positive values such as courage and endurance, religious/spiritual literature can also instill a healthy self-regard and other concepts responsible for measurable life change.

Included in transitional themes are core beliefs about honesty, integrity, a divine and "ultimately" good God, or a proper understanding of forgiveness. And, at various points, religious/spiritual literature is used to affirm the sovereignty of God-honoring governments and the rule of law and its designated law enforcement agencies. Core beliefs can frame a direction for the spiritually injured and may forecast whether or not clients can reasonably expect to *move through* their lament and thrive despite their presenting problems. And the degree to which one is able to make transitional themes actionable, the more likely the sufferer will eventually flourish. The link between theology and psychology is the quest for change, and this transformation is the anticipated outcome described below.

MORAL INJURY MITIGATION

Following is a general overview of the mental healthcare treatment process. This section further describes moral injury's theory of operation and how the reconciliation model uses a religious/spiritual framework for ongoing life transformation. The moral injury reconciliation process hopes to represent a novel approach to mental healthcare treatments for the 21st century.

It is generally common to visit a psychologist who may offer prolonged exposure (PE), cognitive-behavior therapy (CBT), or other evidence-based approaches to treat posttraumatic stress. However, Yan (2016) suggests that

> strict adherence to EBT (evidence-based treatments) such as exposure therapy or cognitive-behavioral therapy in veterans with significant moral injury may not be optimal. Veterans may feel that their root problems are not distorted cognitions or arousal symptoms, but how their relationships with a higher power, their role in the universe, and the value of the lives have changed since the traumatic event. Given the significant impact of moral injury in this study, increased attention and resources on addressing moral injury will help clinicians to better meet the needs of OEF/OIF veterans. (p.456)

On the other hand, using this proposed model, spiritual care providers may conceptualize treating moral injury and other trauma. With the reconciliation model, chaplains select the appropriate transitional theme(s) from the reconciliation model's religious/spiritual framework menu. Treatment themes include: hope, humility, or forgiveness. And by appropriating such habits, these new (or recovered) gifts are akin to the spiritual disciplines that lead to what is known as *spiritual formation.*

Spiritual formation is the continuous product of new beliefs (thinking) and those progressive and consistent activities of the *spiritual disciplines* (habit training) that yield lifelong and profound change (transformation). This training in the spiritual disciplines may be likened to physical fitness, music instruction, or developing any other skill. However, the spiritual disciplines (as the name implies) are the targeted, intentional training of one's spirit for thinking and reasoning for behavior change in spiritual matters. Developing the virtues of peace, joy, love, humility, or patience would be examples. Such traits as self-control or stress tolerance are not easily mastered. So, as a veteran or servicemember adapts new beliefs to their conscious awareness, transactions (or reasoned behavior changes) take place within the *spiritual membrane.*

The spiritual membrane dwells within the spiritual economy. As used here, it is a concept for illustration purposes to help explain where moral injury or trauma resides and how it is dispatched during moral injury reconciliation treatments (see Figure I.1). In this context, we may call the environment for the intricate interplay between the transitional themes designed to transform traumatized thinking the *spiritual economy* for critical life change. It is within the spiritual economy where veterans or active-duty personnel "sort things out." This sorting is finally passed through the spiritual crucible where tension theoretically decreases and resilience increases. New functioning and thoughts displace old, dysfunctional thinking and maladaptive behaviors. The new orientation is the product of reconciled moral injury.

The spiritual economy is the locus of change. Conceptually, the spiritual economy houses the central machinery of intentional internalization of transactional themes. In theory, it sets to motion interventions associated with the reconciliation process. The reconciliation model suggests that spiritual awareness, trauma identification, and verbal expressions of the lament are initial general recovery steps. During treatment, as transitional themes are introduced by the chaplain (or therapist), the veteran's spiritual economy pits the old thinking against the new and considers transactions that suggest healing (e.g. forgiveness processing). Potential pathways for new thinking and meaning-making may be found environmentally or stored within the client's latent core beliefs (to include religious/spiritual beliefs). Such resources may be called *generalized resistance resources* (Antonovsky 1979). And for those lacking identifiable core beliefs, new ones (from various sources) may be offered by the caregiver. Figure I.2 is representative of what both the client and caregiver bring to the encounter and the desired outcome of all.

Moral injury reconciliation's client–therapist healing dynamic

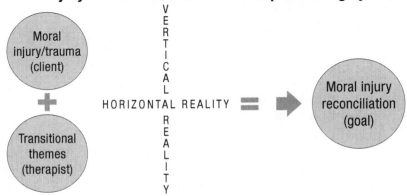

Figure I.2 The client–therapist healing dynamic

The spiritual economy is also where those in spiritual distress may amass other workable solutions for transformation such as depression or anxiety relief. The skilled appropriation of transitional themes may help reduce the effects of trauma through meaning-making and hope-generation. Moral injury reconciliation goes to the heart of why one is affected by moral injury. To this end, this model contends that moral injury and posttraumatic stress have religious/spiritual origins. Moral code violations trigger an *immediate* spiritual reaction.

PRECEPTS FOR MORAL INJURY RECONCILIATION

In view of military-borne trauma, the reconciliation model contends that life *purpose* consists of more than a blind striving towards values. Likewise, rules or laws in and of themselves are inadequate as structures to direct new thinking and higher ideals. The 2010 *Military Review Special Edition* seems to share this view as authors Imiola and Cazier state that "values are too vague by themselves to provide guidance for action" and: "Laws tell you what you must do to avoid punishment, but not what you ultimately *should do*" (p.15, emphasis original). However, *principles* convey a general path to virtue even while encouraging individual judgment to craft superior outcomes that stand-alone values or rules simply cannot do.

Therefore, moral injury reconciliation suggests a similar strategy by providing a spiritual "how-to" of sorts to attain *transformation* that lies behind one's efforts to develop virtue and eschew transgressions. And some of what is behind our determined efforts is a "will to meaning" (Frankl 1978, p.29), a hunt for significance to make sense of trauma and our world. The reconciliation model prescribes a counterintuitive if not asymmetrical journey toward wholeness after a morally injurious episode. It uses a perfect historical model; a model of one having perfected the spiritual disciplines and character formation. Once understood, this knowledge can make lives meaningful as the spiritual balance is restored.

To aid practitioners in understanding the moral injury reconciliation model, the following precepts are presented as guidance. This model arrives at transformation through the spiritual disciplines (i.e. habits for thought and behavior training). The religious/spiritual framework toils in unison to successfully reconcile the *past*, interacts with the *present*, and grows hope for the *future*.

Precept 1. Humans respond to moral injury and trauma according to their nature

The moral injury reconciliation model hypothesizes that clients respond according to their inherent *spiritual nature*. And treatment designs from religious/spiritual foundations are geared to their make-up (construction) and are thought to bring the greatest post-intervention change. Therefore, a key to understanding moral injury reconciliation is to create remedies from a *spiritual* foundation.

Precept 2. Forgiveness is an absolute condition for reconciliation

Forgiveness seems a wholly illogical exercise. Nevertheless, its transformative power is noteworthy. For example, "There is *No Future without Forgiveness*," declared former Archbishop Desmond Tutu of apartheid South Africa (Tutu 1999). Tutu's book title boldly asserted forgiveness as a transitional theme capable of healing the racial divide responsible for thousands of deaths. Strategically adopting this theme inaugurated a transformational process. Forgiveness may also provide further liberation from an assortment of comorbidities (e.g. depression) in the moral injury spectrum.

Forgiveness is a concept found in the earliest writings of sacred literature (Genesis 50.17). Similarly, "The vocabulary of forgiveness, and certainly of political and judicial pardon, was known to Plato, Aristotle, and their contemporaries as well as successors" (Griswold 2007, p.3). Forgiveness is a lynchpin bridging old and new ways of life. It is an intentional process of a changed mind that renounces old thinking and gives up self-destructive ruminations over personal hurts or thoughts of revenge. Properly understood, it demonstrates an internal transformation. Forgiveness signals an acceptance of a past wrong, be it a wrong committed upon one's person or a wrong of one's own making. This transitional theme is viewed as a clear religious/spiritual principle with adopted social conventions. Forgiveness is a difficult and complex process, a liberating construct that permits more choices for corrective behavior changes. It allows the offended to move forward in a new way of thinking not necessarily involving immediate *trust*.

Once the *initial* forgiveness thought stage is reached, it may be considered as part of the client's reconciliation. Reaching this apex holds the potential reset for whole-life transformation. To the extent one is able to forgive, life transformation and new behaviors are anticipated. Forgiveness is a transaction within the spiritual economy that involves the *will* and affirms moral agency.

Precept 3. Sacred literature as a meaning-making system

Despite varying opinions over religious doctrines, America was founded on religious/spiritual principles as evidenced by language contained in the articles of its founding. For this reason, civilians often join the military vowing to defend and preserve traditions, culture, and values through their military service. Sacred literature as a meaning-making system contains individual and societal organizing structures. Sacred literature discusses the values and promotion of relationships, community, and the benefit of many social institutions including government, marriage, and the family.

In large measure, not only does the Bible outline potential root causes of moral injury or trauma, but its remedy for recovery. The reconciliation model contains *existential* fundamentals to ground those in spiritual distress with long-held and plausible views to construct what Aaron Antonovsky (1979) might call "a sense of coherence." And being that Scripture has been pivotal in creating a meaning-making system, it is thought that religion and faith will remain key features of the human experience and foundations for moral and ethical standards.

As noted at the start of this introduction, religious and spiritual affairs are deep and abiding dimensions in life. Borne from tradition, sacred literature will likely remain of significance to a very large segment of the American population for some time to come. Currently, sacred Scripture is perhaps the leading system for: meaning-making, finding hope, forgiveness, purpose, origins, and the rudimentary steps for reconciliation in America and the Western world. Whether or not one is "spiritual, but not religious," American culture has been shaped by religious tenets. Enough goodwill and religious doctrine remains to further shape its population.

Precept 4. Identity: A caregiver's use of "self" and their personal faith journey

As it will be vital to assist a veteran in re-establishing their *identity*, it is advantageous for the provider to have a *faith identity*. It is recommended that this faith identity be well established with a firm grounding in Western values. Still, even if the provider has no such traditions, the reading of biographies may provide additional education. A therapist's familiarity with religious/spiritual issues lends added credibility and reinforces the necessary spiritual alliance between client and therapist.

Even without a faith identity, a provider may adapt existing social conventions (e.g. forgiveness, compassion, hopefulness) to effectively use the moral injury reconciliation model. The use of "self" (personal examples), social learning, and displacement stories are avenues for developing an inventory of transitional themes for working through trauma toward recovery.

Precept 5. Family systems are to be considered

While efforts to reduce traumatic symptoms and quell spiritual disequilibrium are goals of reconciliation, the family must not be ignored. Even after completion of a nine-week course such as this, caregivers are encouraged to recommend follow-on communication skills and marriage and family therapy as appropriate. Many veteran administrations have the *Warrior to Soul Mate* program available for such training.[1] As the veteran or servicemember requires reconciliation, so too will their family. Families are an integral part of the reconciliation model's spiritual care framework.

In the process of treating the family system, it is recommended that such an undertaking be initiated only after the active-duty member is discharged from active service. This is suggested to preclude re-traumatization from the moral injury spectrum influenced by the possibility of re-deployment to warzones.

Precept 6. Emotions and their importance

Our emotional inventory interacts with our life. This interplay allows life experiences to make us unique individuals. They are an inseparable part

---

1   See www.vasdhs.pairs.com/docs/w2sm_psg.pdf

of our character. Therefore, they must be accounted for. Some veterans and active-duty personnel have been shocked by the trauma of war or betrayal. As a result, some experience blunted affect and an inability to experience social bonding or pleasurable activities previously enjoyed. Moral injury reconciliation seeks to restore expressions of "self" through spiritual awareness and Emotional Intelligence psychoeducation (Goleman 2006). Knowledge and practices of interpersonal skills can prove pivotal in moral injury and trauma recovery.

Precept 7. Meaning and purpose

Central to life is meaning and purpose. Life must have stable reference points and significance. It must also have a meaning-making system available to orient one's thinking even in the face of future uncertainty or a present disaster. Oftentimes, a religious/spiritual framework has appropriate answers. A sense of order, symmetry, and routine can elevate the spirit, providing a measure of predictability. Noted author, psychiatrist, and Holocaust survivor Viktor Frankl (a student of Sigmund Freud) framed this orientation "the will to meaning" back in 1938 (Frankl 1978, p.29). Frankl considered, but abandoned, Freud's "will to pleasure" and Adler's "will to power" in favor of a more expansive expression of the human striving: "the will to meaning" (Pattakos 2010, p.66). Yet, moral injury reconciliation's religious/spiritual framework believes there is more. To capture this intrinsic drive of human nature, a "spiritual welling" is a term used to describe this pull.

Welling is one's spiritual enthusiasm to seek out meaning. It is that inner drive; the ever-questioning dimension of being. Thus, meaning in life must be found and can only be found through personal inquiry. Moral injury reconciliation finds that *story* is to be an effective device to instruct about life. Story is a tool; a medium to help make sense of the significant acts that may confound those in spiritual distress. Story may cull meaning from an otherwise lonely or disenfranchised existence. Not only is the examination of our personal story an effective tutor, but other instruments such as *displacement stories* may be of great value too. Moral injury reconciliation's religious/spiritual framework places a premium on displacement stories and social learning (vicarious learning). They allow another to "see" and internalize meaning and its associated elements while in a spiritual care holding environment. More importantly, they can provide examples of hope.

Precept 8. Faith, hope, and love

Expecting the good is the nature of hope. And hope grows through love, service, or alms-giving. These acts can be sure signs of transformation. Such behaviors are generally motivated out of a sense of gratitude (thanksgiving), wellbeing, and the want to serve others. Love is an enduring commitment to care for another; to be other-focused. As faith acts out of one's beliefs and is the active, desirable agent of love, knowledge of self and the joining in community is a basic reconciliation process function.

A transformed life is an altruistic one. Selflessness seeks the hoped-for good of others and one's self. There is perhaps no higher understanding of love than to give one's life in the service of another. Love, therefore, is the highest virtue humankind can hope to achieve. And as faith, hope, and love are prime character qualities, the greatest of these is love (1 Corinthians 13.13).

Precept 9. Humility: The prelude of tension reduction

Tension in life can help to transform through internal prompting. Tension in life may be helpful so long as it does not cross into a level of stress which can lead to dysfunction (Antonovsky 1979). In proper proportion, tension helps one grow and pushes one into new and healthy adventures. As one accomplishes set goals, self-confidence and purpose may be witnessed through objective evidence. It bears considering, however, that to reduce tension leading to stress, humility is in order.

Humility may be thought of as a lowering of one's defenses of control or perceived power. Humility breaks through internal defenses of conscious and unconscious barriers. A healthy tension can fortify one unto responsible action-taking. In this pursuit, caregivers join clients to assist and may gently push and challenge when warranted.

Precept 10. Resilience

Although the scientific study of resilience is in its infancy and there is no universally accepted definition (Southwick et al. 2015), "Humans are endowed with natural protective systems that help them adapt to change and adversity" (p.4).

Resilience is complex and refers to one's ability to "bounce back" after encountering difficulty (Southwick and Charney 2015, p.7).

Resilience is not simply about adaptation to stress, but the adroit use of available resources or what may be called generalized resistance resources (Antonovsky 1979, 1987).

Resilience may be defined as possessing the knowledge, resources, and motivations to overcome adversity. Resilience implies recovery and is characterized by properties allowing flexibility and bending: the ability of a thing to right itself. As part of the reconciliation model's holistic orientation, our physical health contributes mightily to our overall wellbeing. And being able to rebound from moral injury and other trauma includes the spiritual self-care disciplines of sleep hygiene, physical activity/recreation, and nutrition.

The reconciliation model advocates not only the favorable lifestyle habits, but persuades against negative ones like alcohol/drug abuse and risky behaviors. While avoiding harmful lifestyle choices, Southwick and Charney (2015) find that resilience is bound up in: 1) a realistic optimism; 2) in facing one's fear; 3) having a moral compass; 4) a religious and spiritual foundation; 5) social support; 6) resilient role models; 7) physical fitness; 8) brain fitness; 9) cognitive and emotional flexibility; and 10) meaning and purpose.

When one lacks resilience or mastery of one's resources, moral degeneration may follow. How moral injury develops out of a spiritual distress is explained below.

MORAL FRACTURE AND THE PATH TO MORAL INJURY

Figure I.3 is a simple block diagram depicting how moral injury manifests. With due regard to Bandura *et al.*'s (1996, 2002) work on moral agency, moral disengagement, and the theories of moral development by Kohlberg (1984), moral injury reconciliation considers work from both viewpoints. However, the reconciliation model is intended to go further. It includes ancient religious/spiritual insights and offers explanations of moral phenomenology which Kohlberg, Bandura, and others' research may not have addressed—particularly the influences of religion and spirituality. Human perceptions figure strongly in the reconciliation model. Cognitions and conduct are fundamental aspects of religious instruction used in this practitioner's guide. Historic doctrines for life transformation are used in the moral injury reconciliation model. Such teachings reveal timeless offerings of clear guidance as to the cause, course, and remedy for sufferers of moral injury and other trauma.

Moral injury pathway

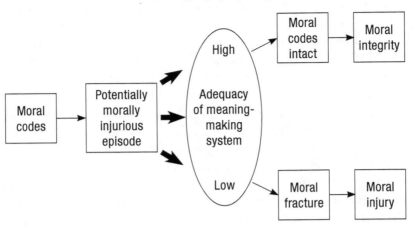

Figure I.3 Moral injury's pathway

WAR, PEACE, AND THE HUMAN SPIRIT

Despite our aversion, war is occasionally necessary. To be sure, the reconciliation model was developed anticipating this reality. And if history is any measure, conflict seems inevitable. This sentiment was suggested during then-President Barack Obama's Nobel Peace Prize acceptance speech in Oslo, Norway, in 2010. He stated:

> I face the world as it is, and cannot stand idle in the face of threats to the American people. For make no mistake: evil does exist in the world. A non-violent movement could not have halted Hitler's armies. Negotiations cannot convince al Qaeda's leaders to lay down their arms. To say that force is sometimes necessary is not a call to cynicism—it is a recognition of history; the imperfections of man and the limits of reason. I raise this point because in many countries there is a deep ambivalence about military action today, no matter the cause. At times, this is joined by a reflexive suspicion of America, the world's sole military superpower.

This is another basic of life. War causes great harm. Periods of war may be demanded to prevent an even greater evil as "peace at all costs" will actually cost the peace. Nevertheless, moral injury reconciliation is available when the country is required to go to war. By this, recovery from some wounds is available should a conflict escalate.

As some Americans seek to protect its institutions, it is reasonable to assume they are fond of its freedoms. Yet, both within and outside America, there exist ideologies and belligerents vehemently opposed to such freedoms, even to the point of mass murder. The reconciliation framework understands this fact as a clear and present danger to contemporary societies. The idea of peace must be buttressed with contingencies for war, and this includes quality physical and mental healthcare.

Ancient religious/spiritual literature has described the specific stressors of today with great precision. And in order for peaceful societies to exist, legitimate governments require forces to suppress those bent on destroying a people's way of life. Economic or other forms of suppression may be actionable through offensive or defensive political or military means. Once the command to defend or establish the peace is given, combatants face the potential of both a physical and spiritual warfare. Under such conditions, warfighters, serving to keep the peace, subject themselves to a variety of stressors including family separation and role strain. Sound religious/spiritual health is a measurable protective factor for life. The military calls this *spiritual fitness* (Hufford *et al.* 2010).

Therefore, the reconciliation model understands that in the course of war spiritual wounds may manifest. These wounds will result from a diminishing of the spirit such as when a life is taken. Such acts may be lessened by effective religious/spiritual treatments. When core beliefs are disrupted, transformed thinking and behavior alteration is necessary to accommodate the trauma so that new learning and meaning-making occur. That is to say, the reconciliation model contends that re-ordered thinking is the nature of spiritual and mental health. Spiritual wellness depends on new learning and lifelong spiritual formation strategies. This new learning includes what the clinician learns too in the joining process that fortifies the spiritual alliance.

Learning about both moral injury and moral injury reconciliation's healing pathways is critical for successfully serving the distinct veteran and active-duty populations. Accordingly, moral injury reconciliation seeks to treat the emotional-cognitive (guilt/shame, anger), behavioral (anti-social acts), and spiritual responses (lament) that threaten mental health. A key goal, therefore, is second-order change (Fraser and Solovey 2007) or simply whole-life transformation. Transformation is defined as significant, long-term, and profound change as a result of spiritual awareness and behavior alterations.

CONSTRUCTIONS

Moral injury reconciliation is a spiritual care model and framework for pastoral care. It uses aspects from cognitive behavior and cognitive processing therapy (CBT/CPT), mind–body medicine, mindfulness, and Acceptance and Commitment Therapy (ACT). Also included is Virginia Satir's communications model. Combined with religious/ spiritual transitional themes, these interventions may be capable of reconciling (assimilating) one's past, enhancing present-focused functioning, and grounding one's future through experiential hope-promoting activities (e.g. altruism). The transformative structure of moral injury reconciliation is the difficult task of *actual* reconciliation processing.

For instance, former Archbishop Desmond Tutu speaks of this difficulty. He notes:

> True reconciliation exposes the awfulness, the abuse, the pain, the degradation, truth. It could even sometimes make things worse. It is a risky undertaking, but in the end it is worthwhile, because in the end dealing with the real situation helps to bring real healing. Spurious reconciliation can bring only spurious healing. (Tutu 1999, pp.270–271)

Therefore, transformation, as theorized, occurs through a client articulating their lament and encountering the spiritual crucible to work out psychic pain. The crucible is where one is squeezed and transformed by the reconciliation process. Here, the veteran's or servicemember's specific *lament* or trauma is articulated with considerable specificity. During therapy, repeated exposure episodes in conjunction with other spiritual disciplines results in developing a thicker *spiritual membrane*. This results in new learning, stress tolerance, and resilience resources. All help to make sense of spiritual turmoil for resolving moral conflict and traumatic stress.

This outworking takes place within the veteran, servicemember, or family's spiritual economy. The lament and confession themes encountered during Movement I (self), Phase 1, prepares the stage for *forgiveness* or other transitional theme processing (as appropriate). In later sessions, the reconciliation model also reveals how therapeutic touch, community life, values, and virtues are the required progressive re-integration steps.

BECOMING A MORAL INJURY RECONCILIATION HEALER

As clinicians may adopt other psychotherapeutic modalities, mental health professionals can incorporate the moral injury reconciliation model as well. Veterans Administration chaplains seem best suited for forming the spiritual alliance to engage veterans for the delicate task of reconciliation. That is to say, chaplains may generally enjoy a higher level of inherent trust, and be attuned to transitional themes and optimal spiritual caring behaviors. And to a large degree, they may understand grief affections and available spiritual resources at a different level. Moreover, chaplains have a long service history and have been embedded with the military since 1775.

Veterans, active-duty personnel, and family members are routinely familiar with a chaplain's role. Chaplains are most likely routinely welcomed into a veteran's toxic spiritual environments and the angst of one's "dark night of the soul." And as a high level of trust will be required for this sensitive assignment, moral injury reconciliation suggests chaplains and caregivers embrace this new treatment paradigm to meet today's challenges of modern warfare.

This reconciliation process asks its co-collaborators to ready themselves in order to operate at maximum effectiveness during client contacts. To form a cohesive spiritual alliance, chaplains and other leaders are asked to reflect upon their thoughts about war in general and the current conflicts in particular. Moreover, as pastoral caregivers move into outcome-oriented chaplaincy, this may challenge a more passive, person-centered Clinical Pastoral Education (CPE) student curriculum. While intercessory prayer, sacraments, sermon preparation, and comforting the sick are elementary, directive interventions, research reviews, client outcomes, and treatment planning during results-focused care may not be. The reconciliation process is a method utilizing previously dormant mental health features that contemporary psychology often neglects—the spiritual domain of personhood.

In this practitioner's guide, I describe the historical context, key concepts, foundations, and mechanisms for change. Also briefly detailed are spiritual and moral injury assessments along with the three movements, phases, and the delivery structure for conducting moral injury reconciliation interventions. Carried out over its three movements, these interventions are presented as a counterweight to moral injury, posttraumatic stress, military sexual trauma, and grief and loss. Through the reconciliation process, spiritual despair and the downward trajectory of moral injury may be arrested so that healing starts to reverse the inside wounds that wars produce.

HOW TO USE THIS GUIDE

Principally, this guide hopes to help connect the horizontal reality of trauma with the vertical reality of the existential healing resources (see Figure I.2). In this way, distressed clients are shown how they may use their religious/spiritual resources to secure hope leading to transformation. Joining the horizontal and vertical axis is no easy task. Some who avow a religious/spiritual heritage might believe they have "lost" their faith or be all too embarrassed to admit only a vague knowledge of its tenets. Nevertheless, with chaplains at the lead, great care may be exercised to reassure those struggling with their spiritual moorings. The value of their beliefs may be found by trusting in them and intentionally applying neglected religious/spiritual applications.

In developing this guide it became increasingly clear that the reconciliation framework may be useful in a wider patient care context. This includes treating general despair, sleep disorders, anxiety, depression, hopelessness, aloneness, or loss of meaning and purpose. Bringing a person's chief complaint under the microscope of their meaning-making system (e.g. religious instruction) can put a transitional theme in league with healing pathways, resulting in new schema (beliefs) and refined within the patient's spiritual economy.

Considering the application of techniques contained herein, it is expected that care providers have an adequate level of training, education, and experience to employ prescribed interventions. That is to say, this guide should be used to alert potential caregivers that misapplied or hasty use of the following framework may forestall recovery or cause further complications. Even so, freely utilize the ideas, dialogue, narratives, or examples during interactions with clients. Incorporate your own interventions derived from the tables, charts, media suggestions, and graphs for maximum effectiveness. You may also use your own displacement stories and include your own or other professionals' practices to enhance outcomes.

It is also recommended that the preface be used as a general structure for understanding the military mindset through reflecting on one man's journey through more than 33 years of combined military life and culture. If, as a practitioner, you are unfamiliar with the military life-ways, it is suggested again that the spiritual caregiver review the preface or search out Veterans Administration websites. Use it as a general outline during the moral injury assessment and intervention processes. A core competency for treating moral injury is the caregiver's knowledge of military culture. Examples provided are scenarios for clarity of case conceptualization that should be readily translatable into actual use. Apply this guide upon first contact with client(s). This may improve the crucial spiritual alliance.

To initiate recovery, this treatment framework opens with Part I as an overview of the moral injury construct. It contains Chapters 1 through 3. Chapter 1 describes the costs and challenges of moral injury; Chapter 2 provides the background of moral injury reconciliation and its religious/spiritual foundations. Also, explanations of words and definitions are provided to help those from a psychological orientation understand pastoral care language. Key concepts involving resilience, forgiveness, the lament, and coherence are part of Chapter 2 and the work of researchers such as Aaron Antonovsky and Aaron Beck. They supply critical components undergirding the methodology of Chapter 3's foundations and mechanisms for change in the reconciliation process.

Part II begins the discussion concerning moral injury reconciliation techniques. It contains Chapters 4 through 7 where caregivers are provided necessary assessment criteria and skills for successfully interrupting moral injury, posttraumatic stress, and other trauma-related injuries discussed throughout this text. These chapters guide the practitioner through the early, middle, and later stages of therapy. Chapters 4 through 7 also contain the three sequential Movements and transitional theme phases to conduct moral injury reconciliation. Movement I focuses on self where spiritual awareness is intentionally practiced and the specific trauma is processed. Movement II aids in communication skills for the rejoining of family and community, and Movement III works toward encouraging altruism and benevolent service to restore self-good through lifelong service to others.

It is the aim of this practitioner's guide to be a potent adjunct to existing treatment strategies that address moral injury and other military traumas. Nationwide, diverse religious and spiritual beliefs are practiced and are still very much at the heart and soul of American veterans and military personnel. Religion and spirituality remain a formidable buttress against further spiritual breakdown from war exposure.

The following pages are this writer's contribution in an attempt to bridge the gap between treatments that have neglected the spiritual domain. And by utilizing sacred documents, a new model of care is available. Sacred literature re-introduces time-tested religious/spiritual components which have provided great comfort for scores of people across the globe. Scripture has been shown to be highly effective for perhaps billions of people over hundreds of years and has been the firm foundation for our veterans and service personnel in the United States for almost 250 years.

A THEOLOGICAL AND PSYCHOLOGICAL CHALLENGE

Before closing this introduction, it seems appropriate to offer a challenge to the helping professions. This call is to consolidate efforts and share knowledge so that morally wounded clients make significant progress toward their spiritual goals and become standout contributors to society. To facilitate spiritual transformation, conscious efforts to remove roadblocks between the theological and psychological disciplines is a recommended start.

However, this is not a top-down approach, but rather a bottom-up tactic that starts with building a clinical care environment. This is where the office spaces where mental health providers reside are intentionally cultivating a spiritual community amongst themselves, first. This is simply done by opening office doors and being accessible to one another; saying "good morning," bringing a snack, learning about each other, and otherwise cultivating goodwill amongst the team. For if a spiritual community does not exist amongst a mental healthcare staff, it would seem difficult to make a case that such an environment might exist where clients meet behind closed doors. Unity and working for the good of all may heighten client outcomes through albeit brief social learning examples and the modeling of spiritual wellbeing between providers. Where service or interdisciplinary silos are reduced, client healthcare outcomes are thought to improve. This practitioner's guide seeks to not only bridge chaplaincy and mental healthcare for the good of all, but to change the healing environment through sound clinical practice that includes the religious/spiritual domain.

To illustrate the primacy of religious/spiritual and mental health collaboration, for example, Chapter 1 discusses the cost of moral injury and other traumas and Chapter 2 describes moral injury reconciliation's background and religious/spiritual foundations. Such content may alert stakeholders to the need for new constructions in mental healthcare—challenging current thinking on how mental healthcare is delivered is one of my aims in writing this book. A more open and spiritually oriented treatment environment might encourage spiritual formation amongst the clinical staff. By this it is hoped that a directional change in the care of our veterans, active-duty members, and families may result. Short of embracing a new wave of robust spiritual and mental healthcare, existing current efforts may fail to consider the past, current, and future costs of care, with our veterans and servicemembers paying the fare. This is the subject of the next chapter.

SUMMARY

We are spiritual creatures by nature. Though it seems religious/spiritual matters have not been pursued with honest academic integrity, a renewed emphasis seems to have surfaced. Such a turnaround may prove beneficial in terms of client health and quality of life as well as recognizing cost savings for the healthcare industry. Transitional themes of the reconciliation model offer a vehicle for new thinking and corrective behavior change. Themes like forgiveness or hope may do much to mitigate moral injury and its spectrum. And as veterans and servicemembers are guided by the spiritual care provider using the precepts of this model, those who may have endured transgressions of moral/ethical norms may be better able to make sense of their morally injurious experience. This is because the spiritual dimensions of *self* will not have been neglected. And by using new knowledge to challenge ineffective strategies to recover after a moral injury, a spiritual transaction takes place in one's spiritual economy to push and press a final resolution through the spiritual crucible for progressive wellness.

Successful processing takes the vertical and horizontal realities into a reconciled state. And as moral injury reconciliation's healing principles guide the reconciliation process to its desired goals, the reality of war and religious/spiritual constructions are available to aid with not only symptom reduction, but wholeness and hope. Yet while the reconciliation model may supply aid to the morally wounded, there are real costs and consequences at the heart of moral injury and trauma that shall be discussed.

For, on the one hand, moral injury costs and consequences need examination so that the agony of war and the task of healing are given full attention by all clinicians. Initiating this will give hope of uncovering links between human spirituality and the religious/ spiritual experience. In this way, healing may be found. And on the other hand, spiritual caregivers must fully appreciate the responsibility of facilitating veterans' and servicemembers' spiritual transformation.

PART I

OVERVIEW AND FUNDAMENTALS

CHAPTER 1

MORAL INJURY ITS COSTS AND CHALLENGES

No one leaves war unscathed. Physical, psychological, and spiritual harm await the warfighter. The hazards of war have been well documented, and the combat setting reveals the exacting nature of military life (Figley and Nash 2007; Litz *et al.* 2009; Drescher *et al.* 2011; Maguen *et al.* 2011; Maguen and Litz 2012; Maguen and Burkman 2013; Nash and Litz 2013; Nash *et al.* 2013; Currier *et al.* 2014; Yehuda *et al.* 2014; Yan 2016).

To be sure, the military's physical environment is demanding. However, it is made more demanding with its multiple layers of regulations and within-rank, unwritten norms. Consequently, when the norms of the military culture are violated, moral injury may result. Moral injury invariably *wounds* the individual on the inside at an unseen spiritual level.

To this point, Jonathan Shay (1993, p.15) writes in *Achilles in Vietnam* that the very "structure" of the military culture

> is ultimately a moral structure, a *fiduciary*, a trustee holding the life and safety of that soldier. The need for an intact moral world increases with every added coil of a soldier's mortal dependency on others. The vulnerability of the soldier's moral world has vastly increased in three millennia. (emphasis original)

The parsing of words such as "inner moral conflict" versus "moral injury" (Litz *et al.* 2016, p.8; see also Nash *et al.* 2013) seems to hint at this "vulnerability" in the servicemember's world. Rules attempt to hold this "moral world" together. Layers of rules exemplify the depths to which the military culture regulates the climate to strike the correct tone to maintain a warrior ethos. Regulations are said to maintain good order and discipline. Upsetting the *moral* climate tips the balance thought necessary for *mission accomplishment*. Therefore, it is easy to see how a violation of moral codes is a taboo of sorts out of which profound guilt and shame may result. Such challenges affirm the sophistication of modern warfare and necessitate effective mental health treatment designs.

Given the steep cost of moral injury, the reconciliation model assumes part of this cost may be found in the associated lack of spiritually based, veteran-centric interventions. These interventions appear to be in limited supply due to moral injury being an emerging construct and the mental health field's historic marginalization of religious/spiritual issues. And since moral injury is not a diagnosed mental health disorder, but a new construct (Maguen and Litz 2012), timely religious/spiritual treatments have yet to be constructed. Moreover, moral injury may go unrecognized and remain untreated at Veterans Health Administration medical centers, as the requisite competencies for understanding military culture, the moral injury spectrum, and its sequelae may not be sufficiently understood (Yan 2016).

Being that moral injury is *dimensional* in nature (Maguen and Litz 2012), this gives moral injury a stealth-like quality, adding to the costs incurred by veterans and active-duty members. This is to say that those with moral injury may or may not manifest signs or symptoms. And, should such symptoms present, they may do so with varying degrees of severity. Therefore, the concept of moral injury is distinguished from posttraumatic stress since moral injury is not fear-based and there is no set point indicating its presence. Extreme, mild, or no symptoms may be present from one moment to the next. Thus, the moral injury reconciliation model strongly encourages initial treatments be initiated soon after active-duty discharge to address suspected injuries. For those remaining on active duty, assignments that minimize re-traumatization are encouraged to preclude clinical aggravation. Sherman (2015, p.72) has called this situation "moral rewounding." With these challenges in mind, this book was developed.

ENDURING WAR-HURTS

It is the unfortunate reality that warfighters will always be required. No matter how well meaning the social activism or fluent the debunking of "just war theory" (Meagher 2014), the United States is the leader nation with global responsibilities. While mistakes will be made and blind spots remain America's leadership abdication is not likely to produce the international stability hoped for. History shows evil to be real and unrelenting. Evil cares little of its target being war weary; that it relishes.

Dedicated men and women committed to military service are to be commended. Quality training and spiritual fitness (Hufford et al. 2010) may serve as a protective feature. Such resilience factors may mitigate many adverse effects of war. Though war may not always be avoided, a universal objection to war is more problematic. However, the absence of a clinically sound religious/spiritual framework to reverse moral injury and traumatic stress is even more unfortunate.

But how high are moral injury costs and what weakens the veteran or servicemember most? This may allow one to "operate in and control chaos." In some ways, this was a survival tactic for Josh Mantz. Captain Mantz was wounded in Iraq's Sadr City in 2007. He describes the costs he's paid to heal the moral wound of survivor's guilt. He speaks of what is sacrificed in order of function in a combat environment. For Mantz, adopting a stance of "stoic indifference" released him of the burden of an unproductive worry of returning home. However, "that restriction that comes with caring is no longer upon you anymore." Mantz continues, "But it is also the point where emotional contact is severed" (Sherman 2015, p.11). War, trauma, and killing, then, seems to transform the soul. Other warfighters describe their challenges and personal costs in the following ways.

U.S. Navy SEAL Chris Kyle is credited with 160 confirmed kills in his duties as a sniper. He writes that while in Iraq providing "overwatch" (preventing soldiers from being ambushed) on a rooftop, he observed only a woman and maybe a child or two stirring about. As ten Marines organized their line of march, the woman pulled something otherwise concealed from her clothes. It was a grenade. And with only a momentary hesitation, he notes that he pulled the trigger, killing the woman before she could complete her destructive deed against advancing U.S. Marines. "It was my duty to shoot, and I don't regret it... My shots saved several Americans, whose lives were clearly worth more than that woman's twisted soul" (Kyle, McEwen, and DeFelice 2012, pp.3–4).

Later, Kyle (Kyle et al. 2012, p.378) closes his book with the words:

I'M NOT THE SAME GUY I WAS WHEN I FIRST WENT TO WAR [sic]. No one is. Before you're in combat, you have this innocence about you. Then all of a sudden, you see this whole other side of life. I don't regret any of it. I'd do it again. At the same time, war definitely changes you. You embrace death as a SEAL, you go to the Dark Side. You're immersed in it. Continually going to war, you gravitate to the blackest parts of existence… Growing up, I wanted to be military. But I wondered, how would I feel about killing someone? Now I know. It's no big deal… But I also witnessed the evil my targets committed and wanted to commit, and by killing them, I protected the lives of many fellow soldiers.

He does, however, express that "MY REGRETS ARE ABOUT THE PEOPLE I COULDN'T SAVE [sic] – Marines, soldiers, my buddies" (2012, p.379). Such reflections are part of the moral injury spectrum (e.g. regret). Ironically, Kyle was later killed in America on a pistol range by a fellow veteran, Eddie Routh, who was believed to be suffering from posttraumatic stress disorder. Kyle was attempting to help Routh using weapons training as a form of healing. This is a cost of freedom.

Treating moral injury is challenging because it is an invisible wound. Veterans, active-duty members, and families pay a price for the invisible wounds received if correctives are not available. In nearly all present-centered or evidence-based treatments (CPT, PE, ACT), the religious/spiritual domains are generally absent or given only brief mention as a goal or value to reach. The reconciliation treatment model hypothesizes that humans are spiritual beings by nature. And since the stressor types capable of producing posttraumatic stress are as yet undetermined, moral injury and traumatic stress then is first and foremost hypothesized to be a religious/spiritual problem. It is the root of other traumatic stress concerns too. Recently, William Nash's June 26, 2017 blog characterized moral injury as "A Mechanism of Harm."

Moral injury manifests as spiritual shock to the human system. The shock of moral injury injects symptoms such as: social problems, trust issues, spiritual/existential distress, and self-depreciation. These symptoms may be demonstrated through: depression, anxiety, anger, social withdrawal, profound sorrow, anguish, occupational dysfunction, guilt, shame, loss of self-worth, etc. (Drescher *et al.* 2011; Yan 2016). Mitigating moral injury harms thus requires a full range of treatment orientations.

For example, to reduce war-hurts, a cognitive therapist, in contrast to other "schools of therapy," may emphasize "empirical investigation of the patient's automatic thoughts, inferences, conclusions, and assumptions... Control of most intense feelings may be achieved by changing one's ideas" (Beck *et al.* 1979, p.7). Stoics might assert that "human emotions are based on ideas." The philosophical origins of cognitive therapy are entrenched in Stoic philosophical thought (p.8). In league with this orientation are those that believe "the ultimate cause of desire and suffering is a mistaken view of the self...and ignorance of this fact causes suffering [which] results in our taking ourselves far too seriously" (Murguia and Díaz 2015, p.45). While cognitive therapies have demonstrated results (DoD 2010; Kar 2011; Yan 2016), its outcomes may be at odds with moral injury recovery methodologies.

This incongruence may be that moral injury is not routinely addressed in evidence-based treatments. Veterans unable to resolve military trauma with their moral framework are "more likely to have higher scores on the PTSD and depression" (Yan 2016, p.455). Another troublesome issue is when attempts are made to secularize traditional religious practices. This practice may contradict the goal of both secular and religious positions. For instance, Hufford *et al.* (2010, p.76) note that by using

> Zen meditation techniques used by the Samurai to eliminate fear of death and guilt over killing might suggest hypocrisy given combatants' approaches in the war on terrorism. The risk of practicing these techniques in a way that is immoral or antithetical to their roots can be minimized...[W]hen the authors presented this ethical dilemma to respected authorities in Buddhism (the religious and philosophical tradition from which many of these meditative practices are drawn), these experts advised focusing on their potential effectiveness in post-deployment recovery.

Perhaps a companion therapy such as moral injury reconciliation acknowledges a hurt that cannot be reasoned away with stoic indifference. Mitigating war-hurts may be better treated with therapies with internal theoretical consistency (i.e. Scriptures). Recovery without incongruence may further reduce the costs and consequences of war.

MISSED TARGETS

Generally, medical models and evidence-based therapies appear centrally concerned with symptomology. However, undue attention on this aspect may prevent the therapist from getting to the core issues of a soldier's story. Existing treatment paradigms that remain symptom-focused or philosophically inconsistent may accelerate an *iatrogenic effect* (the unintended clinical worsening) (Bryan *et al.* 2016). Conversely, the religious/spiritual framework presented in this book considers not only symptoms, but the story behind the morally injurious event. The story of one's *betrayal* would be an example. And as a servicemember necessarily places "mortal dependency" on the military organization much as "a small child on his or her parents" (Shay 2003, p.5), betrayal may surely have both moral and mortal consequences. This morality also has historical roots.

For a moral people, moral injury is a predictable and *natural consequence* of war. As such, Adams (1776), signer of the U.S. Constitution and the second U.S. President, wrote about the moral fabric of a young country. He states: "[I]t is religion and morality alone which can establish the principles upon which freedom can securely stand. The only foundation of a free constitution is pure virtue." Later, Adams (1798) wrote: "[W]e have no government armed with power capable of contending with human passions unbridled by morality and religion... Our constitution was made only for a moral and religious people. It is wholly inadequate to the government of any other."

Moral injury reconciliation theorizes, then, that the awareness of moral injury or traumatic stress begins the psychic reckoning process. In theory, immediately following a morally injurious event, making sense of the event is a priority. Depression, self-loss (defined below), and self-imposed community disenfranchisement (isolation) is a common price tag. The consequent disequilibrium may cause a veteran or servicemember to lose their sense of meaning at the *global* and *situational* levels (Park 2010; Currier *et al.* 2014).

What follows is the continued discussion of the costs and challenges stemming from how moral injury would affect the individual—the clinical, historical, family-social, financial, and medical dimensions. These issues are of some consequence as they are part of a veteran's or servicemember's generalized resistance resources (Antonovsky 1979). These resources may help caregivers facilitate a client's reconciliation of the associated horizontal (communal) and vertical (existential) aspect of their healing.

MORAL INJURY AS AN EXPENDITURE OF THE SOUL

In 1890, famed playwright and poet Oscar Wilde published the novel *The Picture of Dorian Gray*. Metro-Goldwyn-Mayer's stylish 1945 adaptation of this novel shows a young, debonair Dorian Gray whose life progressively unwinds around each act that separates him from virtue. His toxic persona had the secondary effect of destroying his social support network. And as it was for those of means, Gray, a man of wealth and privilege, commissioned an artist to paint a life-sized picture of himself—a picture that was to capture his likeness in his current state of relative innocence.

In time, however, he continually crossed all moral and ethical boundaries in a single-minded pursuit of personal ruin. And though he pushed relentlessly against his previously circumspect moral codes, outwardly, his countenance revealed no visible display to mar his good looks. But as Dorian descended deeper into an immoral abyss, he notes his life-sized portrait beginning to show a strange blemish, a *soul cancer* of sorts. Initially puzzled, he moves the large portrait upstairs to his childhood classroom, now only a dusty warehouse. Here, he thought, his picture was safe; locked away from curious eyes. Still, as his moral compromise progressed, his portrait so revealed the very transformation of his soul. His *invisible wounds* were now visible.

Barely perceptible, the initially slow downturn of his smile quickened into a full-bodied wretchedness giving way to advanced age and thinning hair. Then, boils, deformity, and an unfamiliar, ghoulish phantom appeared in his picture that startled even Gray. Dorian no longer recognized himself yet knew the true state of his soul was accurately reflected in his now-twisted portrait. With each morally injurious act, stain upon stain, wound upon wound was etched upon his soul, indelible, recorded with precision upon the portrait. And out of desperation, Gray's final act to rid himself of his transformed soul was to stab the picture. But in the process, he actually stabbed himself. There seems to be costs and consequences of moral injury to which Shay and Munroe (1999, p.2) opine: "Of all of these veterans' psychological injuries, their enduring post traumatic personality changes—damage to good character—impose the greatest social, economic, political costs."

Obviously, the above description was a perverse caricature of the transformation process. Such events are far-fetched. Yet there is a real transformation of sorts that impacts one's spiritual nature. These transformations seem to happen to veterans and servicemembers from all eras. An example of one veteran describing his experience during World War II follows below.

This veteran was captured during the infamous Battle of the Bulge as a combat engineer near St. Vith, Belgium. As recorded in *I Once Was…: A World War II Transformation*, he recounts during his prisoner-of-war escape: "I was so angry. I attacked him like an animal. And I didn't just want to subdue him. I actually wanted to kill him. I strangled the guard. Yes, dear God, forgive me. I killed him. I actually felt good, yet frightened because of what I had become" (Dudik 2012, p.75). This veteran has a spiritual struggle, the cost of moral injury. Even today, he would say: "Ashamed is the way I have felt all of these years—about a surrender that angers me to this day… I felt betrayed by the Corps and Division commanders [because of their decision to surrender us]" (p.52). Fortunately for him, he seemed to be actively engaged in the reconciliation process and continues to make progress.

The word transformation occasionally describes a soldier's morally injurious experience. Clinically, moral injury is considered different from posttraumatic stress. However, the moral injury reconciliation model theorizes that both the course and maintenance of moral injury and traumatic stress is primarily a spiritual shock to be found at the root of wartime or military cultural stress. As the transformation into military culture is necessary, the return to civilian life is necessary too.

Going home may appear to be a routine, well-planned-out processing, conducted with joy in anticipation of a happy homecoming. But the moral injury reconciliation model believes that measurable symptoms of moral injury or traumatic stress can foment and produce socially maladaptive behaviors. Unchecked, the moral injury spectrum robs the veteran's vitality and can predispose one to depression and withdrawal. These mounting frustrations eventually impact harmonious family functioning, bringing unwanted environmental dysfunction as well.

It is likely that many who read this book know someone suffering from moral injury or posttraumatic stress. If so, the reconciliation model argues they pay a cost in health decline, failed relationships, or social isolation. Moral injury and posttraumatic stress injuries should not be treated in discrete segments for symptom reduction as the medical model generally does. For there is so much more involved in the trauma recovery process (Smith *et al.* 2016; Yan 2016). Thus, moral injury consequences should be known for their spectrum that includes: shame, guilt, demoralization, self-handicapping behaviors (e.g. self-sabotaging relationships), and self-harm (e.g. parasuicidal behaviors) (Maguen and Litz 2012).

Moral injury undermines the core of one's being and essence of life's meaning. The veteran's or servicemember's values, morals, or religious/spiritual beliefs have been generally rendered incongruent. And while some may argue against one having a soul or spirit, that discussion is best suited for another time (or review Edward Tick's book *War and the Soul* (2005)). Even so, consequences of warfighting are "soul wounds" reported in qualitative research with Vietnam veterans (Yan 2016). Nevertheless, whatever nomenclature used, the *you* aspect that animates the physical frame will pay a price for moral injury, as will those in the immediate family or community network.

MORAL INJURY: A CLINICAL CHALLENGE AND EXPENDITURE

To be sure, not every member leaves military service with moral injury or traumatic stress. However, for the estimated 20 to 30 percent who may have diagnosable posttraumatic stress and/or depression (Currier, Holland, and Malott 2015), some level of moral injury may be present too. Additionally, since moral injury has been declared an "established phenomenon among veterans" (Yan 2016) but not a diagnosed disorder, the number of personnel with moral injury may be higher due to the stigma associated with those seeking mental health treatments (Britt *et al.* 2008; Acosta *et al.* 2014; Hoge *et al.* 2014; Steenkamp, Nash, and Litz 2013; Yan 2016). Also, different sampling methodologies have produced varying results (Yehuda *et al.* 2014) and may account for such levels.

While the above figures are not meant to pathologize military service, it is nonetheless important that spiritual markers for moral injury be discussed. This is to estimate moral injury costs and determine assessment criteria for follow-up treatment. The reconciliation treatment model is the enterprise for anticipated positive outcomes and for increased access to effective spiritual care treatment. To fully appreciate the cost of moral injury, it is helpful to know that a military environment can produce moral injury. Such wounds may be the result of inequities between one's traumatic circumstances and one's ability to fully exploit their generalized resistance resources (Antonovsky 1979).

Moral injury is not PTSD, though they share common symptoms. Moral injury is part of the cost of war—the human response to a wartime military environment. Moral injury reconciliation suggests such an injury demands spiritual interventions. Clinically, several studies listed by Drescher (2011) and colleagues included a number of symptoms or a spectrum reported by combat veterans. While they were not necessarily exclusive features of a posttraumatic stress diagnosis, moral injury, then, is thought to have its own specific symptoms for which this book was constructed.

The military environment is littered with spiritually distressing incidents and the trauma constellation that defines moral injury (Maguen and Litz 2012). For the clinician, a particular difficulty in treating moral injury is in how to grasp military cultural features as well as the phenomenology of war (Gray *et al.* 2012). This is a clear cost and challenge of moral injury. Lacking knowledge of this key dimension adds to the human cost and may thwart attempts to check moral injury and associated trauma.

Constructing a framework with the capacity to both conceptualize and continually produce the necessary instruments to aid healing from spiritual disequilibrium requires a wider clinical scope. It is required to acknowledge the spiritual components of self and combine one's meaning-making system into a unified treatment plan. Attempting to address existential issues with purely secular interventions is apt to prolong distress and could possibly have an iatrogenic effect, producing an unintended clinical worsening. So, until such time as the reconciliation model or other religious/spiritual framework is widely available, moral injury costs may accrue.

Therefore, the clinician's task is to reduce the cost of moral injury through reconciliation of life trauma where moral codes have been purposely or unintentionally violated. Accounting for the spiritual dimension of life is assumed necessary for mitigating one's spiritual distress. This point is of some significance since men and women who value their way of life have risked receiving physical wounds. Thus, they may be at risk for moral injury.

MORAL INJURY AND THE PRICE OF WAR: AN HISTORICAL PERSPECTIVE

Over the many centuries, some religious literature may be shown to have a remarkable grasp of human behaviors and how to recover from spiritual hurt. As untreated moral injury is prone to impact quality of life, the most effective clinicians are those who engineer healing strategies that comport with contextual religious and spiritual doctrines. Such doctrines address moral and existential matters as well as other practical areas of life. Thielman (2011, pp.110–111) suggests that clinicians may possibly reduce the human cost of moral injury if they cede that

> [a] *moral context* of traumatic events must be considered… The moral context of the event, as well as the patient's moral stance during an event, should be taken into consideration when a diagnosis and prognosis are formulated. DSM's indication of the need for clinicians to consider the moral significance of a traumatic event may be vital in a therapeutic direction that may secure healing for the patient, although this is an issue that remains to be fully explored. (emphasis original)

The moral injury reconciliation model is thought to be part of the further clinical exploration. This effort is needed and believes lessons from history, the fields of medicine, and the ancient and select accounts from religious/spiritual literature contain treatment answers. Based on the small, but significant, sample of evidence presented in this book's introduction, we can also estimate costs incurred and other likely outcomes when moral prohibitions are transgressed. Time-tested principles from ancient literature and religious/spiritual foundations are used here to arrest the negative spiritual deficits.

With an historical examination of the relevance of moral codes, an appreciation for existing ethical boundaries may be realized. Such a review may also help establish reference points for understanding the gradual transitions that shape today's rules of engagement. As such, while preparing to mitigate the cost of moral injury, this section attempts to show that, when self-loss is left unchecked, it accounts for various degrees of individual, relational, and societal erosion.

It is assumed that by identifying the factors responsible for moral injury (e.g. acts of commission, omission, killing, violating creeds), the thematic components such as humility, forgiveness, or confession found in ancient religious/spiritual folkways may halt and/or reverse the course of a veteran's or servicemember's spiritual struggle. Besides examining moral codes, two other methods may help our understanding of moral loss. One is having a fundamental knowledge of war history; the other regards the medical model treatment paradigm currently prescribed to interrupt the course of traumatic stress. From an historical perspective, a chief assumption of the reconciliation model is that killing—however well justified—exacts a spiritual toll affecting the perpetrator at various levels.

Specifically, it has been shown that killing "in war is a significant, independent predictor of multiple mental health symptoms. Even after controlling for potent combat experiences such as being injured in war" (Maugen *et al.* 2011, p.25), moral injury is a pervasive spiritual contaminant. It seems capable of wounding the human spirit without regard to the primitive or modern mindset or the sophistication of the instruments of war. This is self-loss and part of the moral injury spectrum.

In this regard, self-loss is a spiritual severing; it is a splintering between one's generally unblemished spiritual nature prior to war and the unknown self. This yet-to-be-known self brings undesirable transactions into the spiritual economy which must be reconciled through one's meaning-making system. And it is believed that for this and other reasons, moral injury may be designated a sub-threshold traumatic stress disorder with a religious/spiritual etiology. Self-loss cannot be repaired; the one affected must be made anew (2 Corinthians 5.17) through various forms of confession and ritual cleansing.

For accuracy, this practitioner's guide seeks to avoid the *category fallacy*. This error is the uncritical attribution of diagnostic features such as posttraumatic stress or the moral injury construct across civilizations (Miller *et al.* 2006). Nevertheless, it is reasonable to suggest the earliest combatants along with today's 21st-century warfighters did and do suffer a degree of self-loss with the taking of life. However, a few points may be worth considering.

The reconciliation model maintains that even sanctioned inter-personal violence by legitimate governments will require a corresponding intrapersonal reconciliation and eventual ritual cleansing as part of self-loss recovery. War is costly, not only in terms of the moral and physical wounds received, but also in terms of infrastructure damage, loss of natural resources, or the partitioning of one's homeland. Affirming the high cost of war is evidenced by the adversary's pre- and post-war activities of conspicuous "winning-hearts-and-minds" initiatives among civilian populations. It is an age-old and well-known tactic of war and has proven to be an effective strategy to reduce the costs of continuous direct combat action (Henriksen 2012).

Scouring historic war documents can be of great value for developing after-service mental healthcare treatments for those with moral injury and posttraumatic stress. Nevertheless, in a proper construction, there are variables to consider and caution to be urged. To draw direct conclusions about the cost of moral injury or traumatic stress from ancient war history is to engage in what Melchior (2011) calls "creep." Creep occurs when one stacks modern research or phenomena on top of war chronicles to bridge gaps where historical records are missing or incomplete. For instance, in early Rome, Melchior suggests that authentic depictions of a veterans' world are uncommon. And for those accounts that are found, some are fictitious. Also relevant are the elements of poetry in describing ancient war. Thus, to preclude this "creep" from becoming "dogma," it may be helpful to contrast the conditions of the Greco-Roman world with the modern age. This may supply a more accurate clinical assessment by examining the progressive transition from a low regard for life to the much higher values and associated moral–ethical standards of today. Today's *war on terror* with its myriad *rules of engagement* is such an example.

Kim (2010) provides some guidance in understanding how to view the "truth-or-fiction" dynamic between the past and present life-world of a soldier. He suggested that accounts relative to the context of the ancient warriors' environment are a form of "destabilization of authority and claims to truth is related to a more general thematization of the interplay between truth and fiction in these texts" (p.219).

Therefore, conceptualizing a proximate spiritual or psychological environment of the ancient warrior encourages caution. Still, the people of old were perhaps far more desensitized to the gruesome realities of their day; the contrasts are striking. This includes their high infant mortality rates, dispensing harsh acts of corporeal punishments by clubbing from fellow soldiers, public executions, and the introduction of gladiator games (Melchior 2011). Such horrors were part and parcel of daily life and may have forestalled a more humane society.

In contrast, many today are familiar with institutions offering a *safe space, helicopter parents*, and protection from *micro-aggressions*. Yet out of this benevolent, safety-conscious generation emerged those who have courageously braved improvised explosive device-strewn roadways, weathered terrorist attacks on U.S. military reservations, and those many unnamed who ran *to* the fight, risking all to save another despite the life-threat. Such sacrifices are endured for higher ideals even at the cost of suffering moral injury. And several of them are women.

Still, throughout the ages and to varying degrees, it is likely that war caused combatants some form of emotional or spiritual distress. Perhaps there is a *universal injury* manifesting as psychic stress responsible for shaping one's respective response to their environment (van Wees 2004). Additionally, fealty, teamwork, honor, courage, and commitment are examples of ethical overlays to an individual's preexisting moral underpinnings. It should be expected, then, that additional moral expectations may cause further distress should such codes be transgressed. For some the trauma of moral injury is immediate and debilitating; for others, long years may pass before a portion of the *lost self* is realized.

The cost of moral injury is borne not only on the shoulders of our veterans and active-duty personnel, but by families as well. For a brief look at how war and military life affects others, the following paragraphs are included. Potential moral injury episodes may be borne by our family and community as they tacitly agree to uphold the same moral–ethical codes as the servicemember. Families appear to undergo the stress of their loved ones facing the threat of danger, the transformation by military culture, and deployments to distant lands.

THE FAMILY AND SOCIETAL COSTS AND CHALLENGES OF MORAL INJURY

"Soldiers have always yearned for home. In 1678, a Swiss doctor coined the term 'nostalgia' to describe a complaint found in young soldiers from country districts who had spent too long away from home" (Shephard 2001, p.242). But while homesickness may be present, the moral injury spectrum is wide. It includes: the self-sabotaging of relationships, social problems, trust, and self-depreciation behavior alterations. Families may experience such symptoms in the veteran's attempt to readjust at home and society. Taking family systems and developmental stages into account, Nash and Litz (2013) hypothesized that families may be susceptible to moral injury through *direct* (primary) and/or *indirect* (secondary) means.

In theory, direct routes of a morally injurious event may be received through news media, the sharing of stories by family or friends, and other community functions. Direct moral injury would also include visual images of war carnage, especially scenes involving women and children. Indirect transmission of a morally injurious experience on moral frameworks of developing families are acts of *betrayal* of trust, actions or failure to act thought to be perpetrated by a member of one's trusted family or social network (Nash and Litz 2013). As an example, a Navy SEAL wife (Kyle *et al.* 2012, p.305) wrote:

> I was coming off months of anxiety for his safety and frustration that he chose to keep going back. *I wanted to trust him,* but I couldn't. His Team could, and total strangers who happened to be in the military could, but the kids and I certainly could not. It wasn't his fault. He would have been in two places at once if he could have been, but he couldn't. But when he had to choose, he didn't choose us. (emphasis added)

Moral injury can impede family growth. Historically, active-duty and veterans' family systems may have sustained unnecessary stress through defective 20th-century military mental healthcare. Neither veterans nor their families received the help they needed. Though "paradoxically, while in Britain the Freudians were the only group not invited to contribute to wartime psychiatry, they provided many of the ideas and the interpretative tools on which it would rest." Thus, "Where Freud led, others followed" (Shephard 2001, p.164). If moral injury affects the family system, it was a cost and challenge of the past and possibly the present.

The cost of moral injury goes further. At the societal level, these costs make evident that although Freud conceptualized novel therapeutic concepts (ego psychology, object-relations theory), some proved destructive. In fact, Freud and others were principal directors in treatment decisions for military mental health including areas of pension limitations (Shephard 2001, pp.165–168). Moreover, in their hopeful expectations to shape how returning warriors were supposed to "act" once discharged, they may have unknowingly suggested a fanciful script that added to the cost and consequences of moral injury—especially for the family. For example, after the British disaster at Dunkirk in 1940, Army advice simply instructed soldiers' wives: "Don't worry if your man screams at night or throws himself down when a plane flies over the back garden" (Collier 1961, p.244). While much has changed since Freud's day, it may be asked "how much?"

Sherman (2015, p.2), for instance, accurately describes veterans' transition as the *afterwar*. In her book *Afterwar: Healing the Moral Wounds of Our Soldiers* she writes: "We have learned that we are supposed to separate the war from the warrior, but we are stuck there, not getting beyond that and haven't really explored why." Freud (below) may have hinted at the reason "why" this is so. Moral injury and the moral injury spectrum have an added cost of causing further negative alternations in family functioning. Some caregivers and family members suppose that their soldiers will "just get over it"; this may have steered many away from what the moral injury reconciliation model believes is our spiritual essence. The challenge is to investigate whether a religious/ spiritual framework can help reduce the cost.

Despite Freud's helpful pioneering research on attachment theory (discussed later), his negative view of religion may have undermined the concept of human spiritual nature. By extension, moral injury and the existential dimension may have been compromised as well. Freud's domineering influence on modern psychology proved more commanding than could have been estimated. Nevertheless, dismissing existential concerns as mere superstitions robs the religious/spiritual therapeutic of its rich and effective complexity. It also unnecessarily curbs academic inquiry and intellectual curiosity.

Freud's theory was that humankind will escape the afterwar Sherman (2015) described above by an inoculation from the hurt of the moral injury spectrum. Origins of this mindset are found in his writings. This may serve to explain the additional cost society pays for moral injury and posttraumatic stress.

Shortly after the outbreak of World War I, Freud's optimistic assessments were penned in his *Reflections on War and Death* (1918). He believed that a civilized man would rule the day by superior thinking impervious to war effects. As psychology birthed a response to the "emotional conflict" that death presented to the "primitive man," he espoused:

Civilized man no longer feels this way in regard to killing enemies. When the fierce struggle of this war will have reached a decision every victorious warrior will joyfully and without delay return home to his wife and children, undisturbed by thoughts of the enemy he has killed either at close quarters of with weapons operating at a distance. It is worthy of note that the primitive races which still inhabit the earth and who are certainly closer to primitive man than we, act differently in this respect, or have so acted as long as they did not yet feel the influence of our civilization. The savage, such as the Australian, the Bushman, or the inhabitant of Tierra del Fuego, is by no means a remorseless murderer; when he returns home as victor from the war path he is not allowed to enter his village or touch his wife until he has expiated his war murders through lengthy and often painful penances. The explanation for this is, of course, related to his superstition; the savage fears the avenging spirit of the slain. But the spirits of the fallen enemy are nothing but the expression of his evil conscience over his blood guilt; behind this superstition there lies concealed a bit of ethical delicacy of feeling which has been lost to us civilized beings. (pp.20–21)

Freud's extended statement may have answered Sherman's (2015, p.2) question of "why" we believe our duty is to separate the war from the warrior as stated above. Military service encodes active-duty personnel with its values, and to a large extent they remain after discharge. It is therefore expected that the family unit endorses and models such values. And to the degree the family subscribes to the military mindset (e.g. supports the military end states, abides in the values of the service, comforts their active duty personnel), it is reasonable to assume that the family system is subject to the moral injury spectrum (Nash and Litz 2013).

Today, however, we know that war not only contributes to moral–ethical crisis, self-loss, and posttraumatic stress, but the reconciliation theory contends the family system is affected as well. A family learning their warfighter has taken a life may be the morally injurious event that infects the individual civilian family member.

Ancient religious documents continue to remain predictive regarding the nature of humanity, war consequences, and the course of world events. All wars continue to confirm the ageless and insightful quality of sacred literature. For example, technological advances and time-saving devices heralding the industrial age and the triumph of human creativity brought death through the flame thrower, tank, aerial bombing, machine guns, chemical warfare, and untold horror and loss for surviving families.

Today, the threat of nuclear devastation is fiercely guarded against and terror ideologies market a grotesque brutality. Insight may be gained about the cost of moral injury to the individual, the family, and society when the tally of American war casualties is considered. And, without a remedy, we can expect more of the same and the costs of war can easily fade into abstraction.

However, Table 1.1 is presented to provide context and to serve to remind healthcare professionals that, for each war-dead listed, there stands a number of surviving veterans, family members, and friends. All may be struggling to make sense of their loss. Perhaps all may learn something from "the savage" Freud described and the collective ritual cleansing needed for the expiration of guilt. Table 1.1 illustrates the highest costs and consequences of war.

Table 1.1 Moral injury costs and consequences

American Revolution (1775–1783)	
Total U.S. servicemembers[1]	217,000
Battle deaths	4435
Non-mortal woundings	6188
War of 1812 (1812–1815)	
Total U.S. servicemembers	286,730
Battle deaths	2260
Non-mortal woundings	4505
Indian Wars (approx 1817–1898)	
Total U.S. servicemembers (VA estimate)	106,000
Battle deaths (VA estimate)	1000
Mexican War (1846–1848)	
Total U.S. servicemembers	78,718
Battle deaths	1733
Other deaths (in theater)	11,500
Non-mortal woundings	4152

Civil War (1861–1865)	
Total U.S. servicemembers (union)	2,213,363
Battle deaths (union)	140,414
Other deaths (in theater; union)	224,097
Non-mortal woundings (union)	281,881
Total U.S. servicemembers (confederate)[2]	1,050,000
Battle deaths (confederate)[3]	74,524
Other deaths (in theater; confederate)[3,4]	59,297
Non-mortal woundings (confederate)	unknown
Spanish–American War (1898–1902)	
Total U.S. servicemembers (worldwide)	306,760
Battle deaths	385
Other deaths in service (non-theater)	2061
Non-mortal woundings	1662
World War I (1917–1918)	
Total U.S. servicemembers (worldwide)	4,734,991
Battle deaths	53,402
Other deaths in service (non-theater)	63,114
Non-mortal woundings	204,002
World War II (1941–1945)	
Total U.S. servicemembers (worldwide)	16,112,556
Battle deaths	291,557
Other deaths in service (non-theater)	113,842
Non-mortal woundings	670,846
Living veterans [5, 10]	1,711,000
Korean War (1950–1953)	
Total U.S. servicemembers (worldwide)	5,720,000
Total serving (in theater)	1,789,000
Battle deaths	33,739
Other deaths (in theater)	2835
Other deaths in service (non-theater)	17,672
Non-mortal woundings	103,284
Living veterans[10]	2,275,000
Vietnam War (1964–1975)	
Total U.S. servicemembers (worldwide)[6]	8,744,000
Deployed to Southeast Asia[7]	3,403,000
Battle deaths[8]	47,434
Other deaths (in theater)[8]	10,786
Other deaths in service (non-theater)[8]	32,000
Non-mortal woundings[9]	153,303
Living veterans [5, 10]	7,391,000

Desert Shield/Desert Storm (1990–1991)	
Total U.S. servicemembers (worldwide)	2,322,000
Deployed to Gulf	694,550
Battle deaths	148
Other deaths (in theater)	235
Other deaths in service (non-theater)	1565
Non-mortal woundings	467
Living veterans [5, 10]	2,244,583
America's Wars: Total (1775–1991)	
U.S. military service during wartime	41,892,128
Battle deaths	651,031
Other deaths (in theater)	308,800
Other deaths in service (non-theater)	230,254
Non-mortal woundings	1,430,290
Living war veterans[11]	16,962,000
Living veterans (periods of war and peace)	23,234,000
Global War on Terror (2001–)	
The Global War on Terror (GWOT), including Operation Enduring Freedom (OEF) and Operation Iraqi Freedom (OIF), are ongoing conflicts. For the most current GWOT statistics visit the following Department of Defense website: https://www.dmdc.osd.mil/dcas/pages/casualties.xhtml	
Living veterans[10]	4,398,000

Source: Department of Defense, except living veterans, which are VA estimates as of September 2016.

Notes

1   Exact number is unknown. Posted figure is the median of estimated range of 184,000–250,000.
2   Exact number is unknown. Posted figure is the median of estimated range of 600,000–1,500,000.
3   Death figures are based on incomplete returns.
4   Does not include 26,000 to 31,000 who died in union prisons.
5   Estimate based upon new population projection methodology (https://www.va.gov/opa/publications/factsheets/fs_americas_wars.pdf).
6   Covers the period 8/5/64–1/27/73 (date of ceasefire).
7   Department of Defense estimate.
8   Covers the period 11/1/55–5/15/75.
9   Excludes 150,341 not requiring hospital care.
10 Veterans can be in more than one wartime period and the total of living war veterans is not the same as the sum of living veterans from each individual war due to double counting.
11 Total will be more than sum of conflicts due to no "end date" established for Persian Gulf War.

THE POTENTIAL FINANCIAL COSTS OF MORAL INJURY

Moral injury may present a spectrum of symptoms similar to posttraumatic stress and may have a common sequel (Drescher *et al.* 2011; Currier *et al.* 2015). The moral injury reconciliation model, therefore, believes moral injury is subsumed within the cost projections of posttraumatic stress disorder's monetary estimates. And in consideration of the new diagnostic criteria for posttraumatic stress disorder, "there is consensus that mental health problems can emerge from a far more diverse set of warzone experiences than traditional fear-based stressors" (Currier *et al.* 2015, p.230). Betrayal or learning of disproportionate violence within one's unit would be examples.

To estimate moral injury costs and consequences, Linda Bilmes from the Harvard Kennedy School found that veteran care studies show increasing costs to be found 30–40 years beyond active service. These years account for the fourth largest category of U.S. government spending. Iraq and Afghanistan veterans, nevertheless, utilize veteran administration medical services and apply for disability benefits at a rate much higher than previous conflicts. If this pace holds, the combined outlays in 40 years are estimated at $600 billion to $1 trillion. Still, this calculation does not include the cost of caregivers leaving a paid job to be unpaid caregivers, loss of income for self-employed veterans, and reduced quality of life (Bilmes 2011).

Examining the costs of moral injury more deeply, varying levels and kinds of hurt may be found within the moral injury construct. These divisions may be seen in the types of moral injury found within the moral injury spectrum. For instance, moral injury of those from the *draft-era* (conscripted service) versus those of the all-volunteer force might be of a higher intensity. Moral injury sustained by means of a draft-era, socially unpopular military service environment may cause a more egregious moral injury so much harder to reconcile. And as moral injury demands a spiritual toll, it exacts a monetary one as well.

An analysis of moral injury costs may be incomplete without another assessment of projected financial outlays. Such expenditures are staggering especially considering where such funds could have otherwise been spent (e.g. cancer and genetic research, childhood disease eradication). In this regard, the Watson Institute on International and Public Affairs at Brown University is of help. They compiled a budgetary cost of war from 2001 to 2016. Such expenditures of resources may also contribute to the moral–ethical costs of war. They find:

As of August 2016, the US has already appropriated, spent, or taken on obligations to spend more than $3.6 trillion in current dollars on the wars in Iraq, Afghanistan, Pakistan and Syria and on Homeland Security (2001 through fiscal year 2016). To this total should be added the approximately $65 billion in dedicated war spending the Department of Defense and State Department have requested for the next fiscal year, 2017, along with an additional nearly $32 billion requested for the Department of Homeland Security in 2017, and estimated spending on veterans in future years. When those are included, *the total US budgetary cost of the wars reaches $4.79 trillion.* (Bilmes 2011, p.1; emphasis original)

Having discussed the human and financial costs of moral injury, a review of the clinical challenges regarding treatment is in order. To make decisions on how best to counter moral injury and traumatic stress, the medical paradigm for treating moral injury and posttraumatic stress is briefly examined.

MORAL INJURY AND MEDICAL TREATMENT CHALLENGES

Treating posttraumatic stress disorder (PTSD) is ever-more challenging. Reports suggest: current PTSD treatments do not sufficiently address the morally injurious features of combat (Litz *et al.* 2009; Nash and Litz 2013; Nash *et al.* 2013; Yan 2016); that PTSD as a classification is "a narrow description [and] reductionistic" (Shay 2016); that "empirical research about moral injury is in its infancy" (Maguen and Litz 2012); and that the moral injury reconciliation model is obligated to challenge the current medical model of care (Steenkamp and Litz 2013; Steenkamp, Nash, and Litz 2013; Smith *et al.* 2016).

As mentioned, the moral injury reconciliation model contends that PTSD and moral injury is believed to be chiefly a religious/spiritual matter. The reconciliation model asserts that there is much more to addressing the moral injury spectrum or PTSD than Miller and his colleagues' (1989) "hospital milieu" of "pharmacotherapy and brief supportive psychotherapy" (Beck and Alford 2009, p.330), as "moral wounds demand moral healing" (Sherman 2015, p.10).

Since moral injury is an emerging construct, it is fair to evaluate the relative *health* of institutional care models expected to treat the morally injured. Questions can be asked such as: "Is the prevailing medical care model focused so that the most effective care is delivered to the morally wounded and traumatically stressed?" Or: "Is the current structure an impediment to those with moral injury or posttraumatic stress?" Also relevant is whether "PTSD" (i.e. the *disease*) is the center of clinical attention or whether attention is rightly focused on the client. And when the current medical delivery system is examined, this writer is inclined to affirm the likelihood that some care delivery shortcomings exist. If this is the case, existing care delivery structures may need adjustments at best or found to be contributing to the costs and negative effects of moral injury at worst.

Acknowledging the steep personal and monetary price of war, the reconciliation model exists to mitigate these costs, starting with the veteran. Moral injury reconciliation makes the case that existing medical paradigms are more challenging for the morally wounded than necessary. Therefore, clinically effective treatments should have the veteran and servicemember at the front and center of any treatment. Out of a belief that the current medical paradigm may need updating, the reconciliation model suggests institutional review of mental health treatment protocols. One unrecognized cost and challenge for the sufferers of moral injury is where the medical operating paradigm has a "disease first" orientation described by Antonovsky (1979) below. Since there is much to learn regarding moral injury as a new construct, the reconciliation model believes that at least two of the healthcare areas warrant intervention.

First, the unexpected medical costs. By continually operating from a *pathogenic orientation* (Antonovsky 1979), the current medical paradigm may be inadvertently missing the treatment focus of the moral injury spectrum. This oversight potentially increases distress and, by extension, healthcare cost. Instead of directing attention upon the patient and hearing their story, the current medical paradigm may be seen managing or focusing more on the cause and cure of a "disease" (e.g. posttraumatic stress disorder). This is at the expense of the client's invisible wounds which impact the family, the community, and society.

Second, the theoretical element remains a cost factor. Since evidence shows positive correlations between faith and wellness, avoiding religious/spiritual interventions may be costly. Additionally, its religious/spiritual architecture may also capture essential features for adaptive learning and corrective behaviors. Features like transitional healing themes, relationship renewal, community building, and confession and forgiveness are examples. All are significant features in the transformation process.

Therefore, by focusing more on story and using available religious/spiritual remedies, transitional themes can contribute to the strength and quality of the spiritual pathways of the human journey. These themes can freely operate within the spiritual economy as clients enter into a necessary therapeutic tension in order to begin the transformation process. As briefly revealed in the introduction, religious/spiritual interventions may be that profound but neglected resource toward a veteran's or active-duty member's resilience and second-order change. It is recommended, then, that a legitimate healthcare industry initiative initially review whether a "disease first" versus a client-centric orientation exists. Second, introduce the reconciliation model for potential reduced costs and increased wellness for all concerned.

Ongoing financial expenditures may lessen veterans' and servicemembers' treatment effectiveness through our well-intentioned but pathogenically oriented medical system. A pathogenic paradigm "seeks to explain why people get sick, [and] why they enter into a given disease category" (Antonovsky 1987, p.xii). Unfortunately, a pathogenic approach "blinds us to the subjective interpretation of the state of affairs of the person who is ill" and "one limits oneself to asking what has caused this specific disease?" (Antonovsky 1979, p.36).

However, a case will be made for *salutogenesis*, an upgrade upon which the moral injury reconciliation model rests. Antonovsky's (1979, 1987, 1996) *salutogenesis* focuses on the origins of health. These subjective factors have allowed many in extremely hazardous environments, tyrannical rule, and genocide to emerge and thrive despite enduring much.

SUMMARY

Combatants and war participants are changed by war and the extremes of military culture. So extreme it may even wrest a portion of one's soul. Some of the invisible wounds of war are anger, guilt, shame, relational and spiritual distress, and other comorbidities. These are almost routinely the costs and consequences of moral injury. Early mental health theories have added undue stress to the combatants and their supporters. Financial and medical model considerations are also associated with the moral injury construct. As challenging as these realities may seem, new options for treatment exist. The next chapter explores the background and foundations supporting the moral injury transdiagnostic therapy so that moral injury costs and consequences are continually reduced.

CHAPTER 2

BACKGROUND AND RELIGIOUS/ SPIRITUAL FOUNDATIONS

The moral injury reconciliation model differs from other moral injury or posttraumatic stress-related treatments as it uses a religious/spiritual framework to make it a *transdiagnostic* (unified) approach to mental healthcare. Its methodology is believed to undermine the root causes of traumatic episodes and may be useful assisting veterans and active-duty personnel in donning their "divine nature" (2 Peter 1.4b, NKJV). As available *evidence* suggests, "it is now known that religion is linked to physical and mental health" (Hill and Pargament 2003, p.72). Thus, the reconciliation model hopes to deliver a treatment which reduces moral injury and trauma symptoms, and increases valued behaviors and overall wellness. The transdiagnostic features of this model will be further explained in the next chapter.

Sacred literature was chosen for its insightful and authoritative voice with respect to the etiology of war; its course, consequence, and remedy relative to the human condition. Though not a medical digest or science catalogue, Scripture does however transcend time, cultures, and technology. And though "the scientific study of spirituality and health is a very new field" (Hufford *et al.* 2010, p.73), what has been demonstrated is that religious/spiritual interventions are both efficacious and evidence-based (Hill and Pargament 2003; Koenig *et al.* 2012; Koenig *et al.* 2014; Miller *et al.* 2014). It must be noted too that such "interventions" are not short-term "fixes." They are—at least for the "devout"—"ways of life to be sought, experienced, fostered, and sustained consistently" (Hill and Pargament 2003, p.68).

At this point, however, it may be important to provide a caveat. That is to say that the *sacred* can never be commercialized. The sacred is the core of this guide's framework and is what separates it from other secular mental health treatments (Hill and Pargament 2003).

To be sure, religion and spirituality are not commodities, but a deep, individual, though not necessarily a private, affair. Attempting to "get-an-angle" on religious/spiritual issues will most certainly confound the profiteer. While some religious/spiritual outcomes may remain measurable (e.g. less anxiety, less depression, positive wellbeing), there is a limit whereby the spiritual domain will forever remain a *mystery*. Worshipping and seeking the divine are practices which divide secular and holy activities. These practices are part of the mystery and that which precludes marketing. Positive outcomes from the religious/spiritual domain cannot be mass-produced (Hufford *et al.* 2010) even in the name of "spiritual fitness." There is contained in such religious and spiritual matters the ineffable elements of profound wonder and awe.

Rudolf Otto (1958) perhaps best describes a sacred experience as an objective, pervading awareness where the Creator–created relationship is affirmed and where a sense of dependence is evidenced. But out of this "rational" encounter with the holy comes an awareness of what Otto called the *mysterium tremendum*. Such an encounter may approximate an esoteric or hidden shudder.

To make the point that religious and spiritual issues are immune from commercialization can be illustrated through a perhaps comical cartoon analogy. In the fictional adventure of Indiana Jones' *Raiders of the Lost Ark*, profiteers sought to obtain the sacred *Ark of the Covenant* and turn it into a "tool" for war. The result was total disaster. However, countless numbers have already found mental and physical healthcare efficacy through humble inquiry and reverence.

The moral injury reconciliation treatment depends upon a religious/spiritual network of doctrines compiled over an estimated 1600 years. This system of instruction is spiritual in nature and is constructed to provide guidance relative to the body (physical properties), the mind (reasoning functions), the heart (emotions and passions), and soul and spirit (self, the will, inner consciousness, drives, and motivations) for authentic healing and subsequent transformation.

A fundamental assumption of this design is the inseparable link between a person's cognitions and their respective religious/spiritual belief systems. As such, the following remedies can be part of a paradigm shift in client care. This includes selected religious/spiritual teachings as a *new wave* or "next step" in a client's mental healthcare. And while current evidence-based therapies are efficacious, the inclusion of a client's values or religious/spiritual resources is of inestimable worth. Western religious/spiritual traditions and the available collection of wisdom literature are often underutilized. However, these crucial elements have already been found to have wide-ranging clinical applications.

This book uses both religious/spiritual prescriptions as well as secular clinical evidence to develop the various transformational themes. These themes are thought to facilitate recovery from the spiritual wounds of moral injury. It should be recognized that this spiritual care treatment methodology should respectfully overlook attempts to reduce sacred literature to a "how-to," self-help compendium or divorce it from its solemn purposes. On the contrary, religious/spiritual beliefs are always to be held in the highest regard. Nevertheless, as research has shown, constructive belief and meaning-making systems contain powerful transformational designs and spiritual self-care disciplines that can lead to *second-order* behavior change initiated by the reasoning mind.

TRANSFORMING THE MIND, BODY, AND SPIRIT

Historically, cognitions have been the subject of the *Stoic philosophers* who are the originators of cognitive therapy. Specifically, this includes Zeno of Citium, the founder of Stoicism (4th century B.C.E.), Chrysippus, Cicero, Seneca, Epictetus, and Marcus Aurelius. Similar discussions about the primacy of our thoughts may be found in the Eastern philosophies such as Taoism and Buddhism (Murguia and Díaz 2015). Concomitantly, the process of regulating strong emotions is also believed to be a function of our cognitions (Beck *et al.* 1979).

Currently, cognitive therapy is a leading clinical method for treating anxiety, anger, depression, and a host of other psychological problems (Beck 2011; Murguia and Díaz 2015; Smith *et al.* 2016; Jordan *et al.* 2017). The 2017 Veterans Administration and Department of Defense clinical guidelines for PTSD suggest that prolonged exposure (PE), cognitive processing therapy (CPT), and Eye Movement Desensitization Reprocessing (EMDR) are "the most effective treatments for PTSD." Thus, "Overall, individual trauma-focused psychotherapies such as PE,

CPT, and EMDR are the most highly recommended treatments for PTSD and have strong evidence bases" (Norman *et al.* 2017).

And since it is believed that perception is the hub of cognitive behavior therapy, Epictetus (125 C.E.) is credited with saying the following: "Men are disturbed not by the things which happen, but by their opinion about the things." Similarly, Adler stressed how people understood their environment:

> We do not suffer from the shock of our experiences—the so-called trauma—but we make out of them just what suits our purposes. We are *self-determined* by the meaning we give to our experiences: and there is probably something of a mistake always involved when we take particular experiences as the basis for our future life. Meanings are not determined by situations, but we determine ourselves by the meanings we give to situations. (Adler 1932 [2010], p.14; emphasis original)

Here is a sharp distinction between the cognitive or behaviorist schools and the religious/spiritual framework of the moral injury reconciliation model. Perhaps Adler and others had not considered veterans' or active-duty members' entrenched religious/spiritual precepts, moral codes, the phenomenology of war, or military culture. However, Adler's clinically sterile statement may have some validity. However, because veterans and servicemembers can and do "suffer from the shock" of their "experiences," a theistic psychotherapy (Richards and Bergin 2005) was chosen as a helpful theoretical guide for the reconciliation of moral injury. This design finds at least one common yet powerful unifying feature in the doctrines of the three major world religions. These faith groups hold theistic worldviews: Judaism, Christianity, and Islam. They equally find transcendence in the command to "love your neighbor as yourself" (Hufford *et al.* 2010).

To increase moral injury reconciliation's viability as an evidence-based therapy, this model will soon be subjected to clinical trials to augment available treatment options. Also, as the reconciliation model hopes to transform those suffering moral injury, it endeavors to be an adjunct and/or complementary model equal to Stoic philosophy's cognitive-behavior therapy conducted by other therapists. Comparing and contrasting theistic psychotherapy with Stoicism, the *Stanford Encyclopedia of Philosophy* expressed:

When considering the doctrines of the Stoics, it is important to remember that they think of philosophy not as an interesting pastime or even a particular body of knowledge, but as a way of life. They define philosophy as a kind of practice or exercise (*askêsis*) in the expertise concerning what is beneficial (Aetius, 26A). Once we come to know what we and the world around us are really like, and especially the nature of value, we will be utterly *transformed*. This therapeutic aspect is common to their main competitors, the Epicureans, and perhaps helps to explain *why both were eventually eclipsed by Christianity*. (*Stanford Encyclopedia of Philosophy* 2017; emphasis applied)

While many have been able to recover from the "shock" of war, military sexual trauma, and grief using cognitive-behavior modalities, the reconciliation model offers a new entry to the field and may be considered as a form of spiritually integrated psychotherapy (Pargament 2011). Moral injury reconciliation's spiritual integration is an acknowledgment of the sacred and believes the spiritual domain is an essential dimension common to humankind as well as its methodological blend of spiritually focused growth interventions.

THE MECHANISM OF RECONCILIATION

Reconciliation is the process of bringing together. It requires synthesizing—the pairing of negative events with positive, spiritually oriented coping skills to achieve a more favorable state of affairs. Reconciliation summons a form of negotiation or reasoning. It is new thinking or the acceptance of past discord in order to produce acceptable, hope-filled future outcomes despite past trauma. However, this acceptance is not accepting the "rightness" of the morally injurious event.

Reconciliation seeks not to fix, change, or repair past hurts as historic events are beyond repair. In fact, the reconciliation process directs the morally wounded to look squarely at the "shock" of past events in order to wrest a new spiritual and mental orientation fully aware of the significant pain it will produce. This is similar to Antonovsky's (1979, 1987) sense of coherence, or being able to make sense of one's experiences. Reconciliation also understands that movement out of the past hurt necessitates lifelong and future work for ongoing transformation.

As a spiritual care framework, the reconciliation model holistically acknowledges the shock and horrors of war summarily dismissed by Freud and others. As warfare affects the human spirit, moral injury reconciliation is thus a meaning-making system. It is a theistic orientation selected as a link for coding standards (norms) using sacred literature of the Bible. This coding is also the meaning-making system for restoration when trauma or the unusual occurrence strikes. The spiritual "shock" of war would be an example. Scripture enjoys a wide level of unifying features and is included because of the volume of veterans and active-duty personnel who would affirm a general knowledge of the existence of the Bible. Many would also assent to belief in deity (e.g. God) whether or not they are active participants at a place of worship (McLaughlin, McLaughlin, and Van Slyke 2010).

Within the marketplace of ideas, the Bible has a longstanding and successful presence in the field of human transformation, as the previously listed research indicates. Furthermore, Gallup Editor-in-Chief Frank Newport notes that while there have been increases in those who state "no formal religious identity"

> America remains a very Christian nation. Nearly 80% of all Americans, according to Gallup data, can be classified within one of two big groups: Catholics and Protestants/other non-Catholics Christians. Given that about 16% of Americans have no religious identity, we can say that 95% of Americans who have a religion are Christians. Let me repeat these two numbers: 80% of all Americans are Christian, and 95% of *all Americans who have a religion are Christian.* (Newport 2012, pp.21–23; emphasis original)

The mechanism of reconciliation, sacred literature, also considered data such as the 2014 Pew Research Center study which found the following: "Nearly nine-in-ten Americans (89%) say they believe in 'God or a universal spirit,' and most of them (63% of all adults) are absolutely certain in this belief." They also found: "Three-quarters of U.S. adults say religion is at least 'somewhat' important in their lives; with more than half (53%) saying it is 'very' important. Approximately one-in-five say religion is 'not too' (11%) or 'not at all' important in their lives (11%)" (see Lipka 2015).

Additional research shows that, when compared to the general U.S. population, the Department of Defense Naval Medical Center, Portsmouth, Virginia, found that a majority of respondents reported a Christian religious affiliation (87%), affirmed their belief in God (91%), and that 53 percent report attending religious services at least a few times a month (McLaughlin *et al.* 2010). Data in the September–October *Military Review* article on religious participation featured a fiscal year 2013 U.S. Army demographic study showing that nearly 75 percent of active-duty soldiers list a definite religious tradition (Koyn 2015). Generally, for Americans, "Majorities of adherents of most Christian traditions say they believe in God with absolute certainty." Even as decline is noted, beliefs remain high: Protestants (down from 73% in 2007 to 66% today), Catholics (from 72% to 64%), and Orthodox Christians (from 71% to 61%) (Pew Research Center 2015a).

Nevertheless, despite decline, America is the home "to more Christians than any other country in the world, and a large majority of Americans—roughly seven-in-ten—continue to identify with some branch of the Christian faith." Approximately 71 percent of the US population endorses Christianity (Pew Research Center 2015b).

The moral injury reconciliation model grounds itself in *theistic psychotherapy* for the aforementioned reasons as well as its credible and practical means for experiencing wellness and *rational hopefulness*. With the abundance of available transitional themes (e.g. forgiveness, hope), theistic psychotherapy aids in directing a veteran's or warfighter's recovery and makes religious/spiritual therapies an ideally suited foil against spiritual despair. As a mechanism of reconciliation, a theistically based psychotherapeutic approach was selected for its familiarity, near-universal availability, historical and cultural considerations, and the now-blossoming research momentum.

While several faith traditions are not included as part of this model's methodology, no slight is intended. Nevertheless, attempting to include various other faith groups is ill-advised. Attempts to accommodate all faith traditions would clearly undermine the potency of moral injury reconciliation's spiritual care framework. To be sure, some religious/spiritual traditions may at points be clinically, theologically, and philosophically untenable with the intended purposes of this book. While ongoing discussion between the various faith traditions is both important and encouraged, all viewpoints cannot be represented.

In other words, it would not be expected of, say, a behaviorist to include psychoanalytic orientations or techniques just so "clinical inclusive-ism" might exist. Unanimous belief is not the goal of moral injury reconciliation's approach to healing. However, reconciliation surely is. Even so, the reconciliation model should not prove objectionable to any person, culture, or institution since its outcomes seek individual transformation and to cultivate such character traits as: love, forgiveness, anger resolution, self-acceptance, trust, altruism, and family and societal stability.

Theistic psychotherapy's pragmatic quality is that it can be the starting point which provides a basis for understanding life's meaning. This includes: origins, defining good and evil, pain and suffering, death and dying, hope, forgiveness, and life-purpose. Here, religious teachings instruct and supply the ground for transitional themes that furnish a roadmap for new thinking, symptom reduction, and stress relief. Religious/spiritual literature helps reshape cognitions and hoped-for behavior change. This complex transaction is performed in the spiritual economy of the self where the medium of exchange is *meaning-making*—the tie integrating theology and psychology.

The following well-known and oft-repeated *prayer* is an example of a religious/spiritual intervention. The spiritual discipline (habitualization) of prayer transforms the mind and may start the spiritual transformation process. It includes features that affirm one's meaning-making system (i.e. theology), teaches the limits of human control, and encourages help-seeking behaviors (e.g. prayer) and the use of reason, insight, agency, acceptance, and behavior change. This combination of actions *codes* the new pathways for thinking and prepares the body for alternatives to dysfunctional behaviors. In its abbreviated form, it acknowledges helpful ways to prepare oneself for transformation. Simply stated:

> *God, grant me the serenity*
> *To accept the things I cannot change;*
> *Courage to change the things I can;*
> *And wisdom to know the difference.*

(Attributed to Reinhold Niebuhr, 1892–1971)

Change happens as the spiritually wounded client engages in the *spiritual awareness* exercises designed to "introduce" self to how one tends to respond to internal excitations to its outside environment. The vocalization of one's moral injury or traumatic stressors is an early-stage spiritual care goal. Spiritual awareness is viewed as the dual and progressive process of *sensitization* (alertness, attention, perceptions) and *habit-training* (or *habitualization* into new routines resulting in behavior and lifestyle transformation). As this scenario plays out within a client's spiritual economy, subsequent change may be realized through their ongoing execution of spiritual disciplines. These disciplines include: prayer, spiritual self-care (e.g. sleep hygiene, activity/recreation, nutrition), and active pursuit of characterological transformation. Other helpful transitional themes may be found as part of the "fruits of the Spirit" (Galatians 5.22–23). This counterintuitive methodology is illustrated in Figure 2.1.

Moral injury reconciliation: Change process

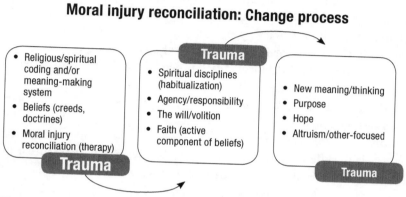

Figure 2.1 Moral injury reconciliation's change process

RELIGION AND SPIRITUALITY

Key articles thought capable of supplying meaning to life's traumatic events may be found in sacred writings. Despite opinions and definitions about *religion* and *spirituality*, faith issues hold resilience potential for reconciling morally injurious episodes—even under traumatic circumstances. Understanding that the religious/spiritual domain has been historically minimized in mental health literature (Koenig *et al.* 2012), faith practices have been shown to be effective in mediating spiritually injurious events or the psychic pain of spiritual disequilibrium. Being that religious/spiritual issues are complex, Zinnbauer *et al.* (1997), to bring clarity, sought to measure: how individuals define the terms religiousness and spirituality; gauge how they define their own religiousness and spirituality; and determine if definitions are associated with specific variables. This project was titled "Religion and spirituality:

Unfuzzying the fuzzy" (1997). This study suggests that the inherent phenomenology of spirituality needs to be contained within the broad-band of religion and that spiritual elements are central features of religion altogether.

For the purposes of this practitioner's guide, religion is defined more by the Western traditions and includes the corporate activities around specific beliefs, practices, and rituals related to the transcendent God. Explicit dimensions would include: affiliation, chosen membership, orthodoxy, attitudes, experiences, giving, knowledge, love, service attendance, or the giving of money/time. These dimensions should be considered conceptually unique from one another and from any other psychological or social construct. An important aspect of religion is that it is associated with quantitative measures that are capable of assessing the degree of individual applicability (Koenig *et al.* 2014).

On the other hand, spirituality has been defined as "the experience of conscious involvement in the project of life-integration through self-transcendence toward the ultimate value one perceives" and may or may not include religious tenets (Schneiders 2003, p.166). Spirituality involves the transcendent. This is the search to find and employ that which is outside yet inside one's self. To further define the issues, this book describes spirituality as the intentional awareness and pursuit of the sacred to effect relationships with the divine, self, and others far above normal states of consciousness. Therefore, in order to advance research, build effective treatments, or foster a community language, religion and spirituality are found to be inseparable.

For ease of understanding, this writer likens religious and spiritual definitions to more familiar issues in life. For instance, religion may be akin to a classic cake recipe in a cookbook or a musical composition found on sheet music. Cookbooks or sheet music are freely available commodities. Exposure to either is optional; almost everyone has access and may join a musical guild or a cooking club. *Objective* instructions for baking the cake or playing the music are on the printed pages; it is the purposeful and descriptive intent of the enterprise. The pages contain the "what" and the "how-to" of the activity. The documents define the terms of the endeavor. *Subjectively*, however, just how well the cake is baked or the music is played is an experiential activity. Its end state is in the hands of the aspirant who hopes to produce a masterpiece.

That the moral injury reconciliation model does not rely solely on vague spirituality may extend opportunities for greater recovery.

A stand-alone, personally directed spirituality is thought not capable of such a recovery. In effect, because the reconciliation model subscribes to historic ancient religious/spiritual traditions and holds the *past*, *present*, and *future* in an ordered methodological tension, it is an experiential activity that may be counterintuitive to a "here-and-now," cognitive-behavior treatment (Beck *et al.* 1979, p.7) strategy.

Once the initial reconciliation process begins, the corresponding *adaptive work* (Heifetz 1994) of habitualization into the reconciliation methodology begins. To further the religious/spiritual vocabulary, this model assumes the inseparability of religion and spirituality. It also adopts the functional (doctrinal) and substantive (individual meaning) perspectives of Zinnbauer and colleagues (1997) in its treatment of moral injury. And to complement the functional and substantive perspectives, moral injury reconciliation seeks to actualize an *operational* or measurable component for determining how well veterans or servicemembers adapt to new life situations and family growth. Since a large segment of society affirms some level of religious/spiritual affiliation, therapies of the future may consider including canons from religious/spiritual precepts that infuse meaning and purpose in clients' lives.

In the meantime, however, clients continue at an elevated suicide risk. Therefore, it is suggested that a wider venue for healing interventions be considered, particularly those noted for their religious/spiritual transformational themes. Well-developed religious/spiritual healing strategies may be in order as current and future U.S. military engagements will continue to demand much from its fighting forces. To make the point, researchers surprisingly find that deployments alone to either Iraq or Afghanistan are not sufficient to explain the elevated suicide threat (Kang *et al.* 2015). It would appear, then, that something is yet unseen and yet to be addressed. And to get to the heart of this multifaceted issue, morally injurious scenarios are explored and those remedies offered in resistance to the soul malady known today as *moral injury*, defined below.

MORAL INJURY DEFINED

Spiritual distress is hypothesized to be the core feature of moral injury and traumatic stress. As cited earlier, moral injury has been tagged as an *instrument of harm* (Nash 2017). At the micro level, moral injury may be understood as the secular term for spiritual distress. Moral injury is thought to be a schism in the spiritual economy where trauma is present without the corresponding religious/spiritual transitional themes to affect recovery. Moral injury may be identified as a wound received when one's belief system or expectations about right or wrong have been violated within a military context.

Conceptually, moral and ethical behaviors are generally coded from religious/spiritual precepts or values and integrated into daily living or military life. With the taking-of-life, for example, moral injury may result. Clinically, moral injury may stem from exposure to war's effects. It can present as the direct result of killing or the indirect violation (witnessing) of rules or from acts of commission or omission—on and/or off the battlefield. A morally injurious episode challenges one's meaning-making system and resilience resources. As coded norms filter life experiences, myriad expressions may register as spiritual states of tranquility, stasis (equilibrium), distress, or despair.

The moral injury reconciliation model views moral injury as sub-threshold posttraumatic stress, and varying levels of distress can be present at any given time. Innovative techniques designed to treat moral injury are indicated, since moral injury is not a formally diagnosed disorder and no available marker signifies its presence (Litz et al. 2009; Maguen and Litz 2012).

Before further outlining why the reconciliation methodology emerged and what it is, it may be helpful to understand what it is not. First, while moral injury reconciliation is part of a new paradigm in client care, it is not social advocacy. Moral injury reconciliation has responded to the noticeable conscious or unconscious marginalization of religious/spiritual research and the dearth of spiritually oriented healthcare interventions.

Second, the reconciliation method is not necessarily in competition with the other effective mental health treatments currently in use. However, it seeks to be a therapeutic adjunct to be duly considered in the overall spiritual care of clients. Properly understood, spiritual care should remain a distinct and separate discipline yet simultaneously complement what the other fields of caregiving have contributed.

Third, moral injury reconciliation is not moral repair or soul repair, as "repair" may be misunderstood as a "fix-and-forget" curative. Also "repair" may otherwise convey a false sense that "all's well" if initial positive change is noted. By using "repair" as a treatment descriptor, it may also confer an inanimate or wooden quality to those in moral anguish. Instead, moral injury reconciliation would choose to replace the concept of "repair" and champion the spiritual nature of one's being and the lifelong growth and spiritual formation emphasis to life. Therefore, the term reconciliation is the operative word. Together, war and the military culture change things in ways that will require a continued transformational mindset throughout the lifespan.

MORAL INJURY RECONCILIATION: A RATIONALE FOR HEALTHCARE CHANGE

As physical war-wounds kill and maim, so too can moral injury. Moral injury is a severe wound that costs spiritual and material capital. It is an invisible injury occurring within the unique military cultural experience. Moral injury is hypothesized to be of a religious/spiritual origin. Still, a helpful secular descriptor finds that "moral injury is an essential part of any combat trauma that leads to lifelong psychological injury. Veterans can usually recover from horror, fear, and grief once they return to civilian life, as long as 'what's right' has not also been violated" (Shay 2003, p.20).

Moral injury corrupts the "what's right" in a person's moral code. And for those with moral injury, a rigid compliance to exposure or cognitive-behavior therapies "may not be optimal." This situation stems from veterans' or active-duty personnel's knowledge that their issues have nothing to do with "distorted cognitions or arousal symptoms," but with clear existential issues (Litz *et al.* 2009; Yan 2016). As religious doctrines and faith practices continue to define many moral constructs, they also form the basis of how our core beliefs shape our understanding of how life is "supposed to work." And since it is believed moral injury damages the spirit and disrupts one's spiritual economy, an appropriate religious and spiritually centered response is recommended.

Moral injury reconciliation is submitted as that response. It evolved from gaps that may exist in conventional posttraumatic stress treatments. Such gaps may be responsible for so-called treatment failures or origins of the moral injury construct (Drescher *et al.* 2011). Owing to urgent necessity and the distress caused by moral injury, this treatment strategy was developed to utilize the heft of the spiritual disciplines (e.g. prayer, spiritual self-care, meditation) and to bring order and symmetry out of life's chaos.

As an additional rationale for healthcare change, religious/ spiritual traditions are rich with wisdom from specific, time-tested correctives. Various religious/spiritual teachings affirm and allow many to come to grips concerning the limits of human *control* (Pargament 2011, p.11). Such teachings may free some from the want to exercise tight rein over thoughts, emotions, or the unpredictable issues of life. These issues invariably lead to failed coping strategies, inviting frustrations and lowered self-worth. Religious/spiritual transitional themes can address one's limitations and moral injury through the exploration of such virtues as patience, joy, love, grace, forgiveness, and altruism for better spiritual health resonance.

Moral injury reconciliation is indispensable to the extent moral injury wounds the spirit and is recognized as a debilitating emerging construct. Suicides, healthcare costs, and higher rates of psychiatric comorbidities in veterans with a mental health diagnosis (Currier *et al.* 2014) further necessitate corrective procedures. Moral injury reconciliation's framework may not only help clients accept the limits of control, but utilizes *spirituality* as a potentially less stigmatizing type of undertaking. Since it is argued that humans are spiritual by nature, it may be reasonable to suggest that almost everyone may benefit from an exercise which is a natural part of one's makeup. Accepting the idea that one is pursuing "spiritual stigma" growth rather than "mental health treatment" may be more palatable. Changing the face of mental healthcare may start with efforts to de-stigmatize. Many avoid needed treatment to prevent the hurt of both "public stigma" and "self-stigma" (Greene-Shortridge, Britt, and Castro 2007). Additionally, moral injury reconciliation was envisioned to reduce perceived stigma for those seeking mental healthcare (Greene-Shortridge *et al.* 2007; Miggantz 2013; Acosta *et al.* 2014; Hoge *et al.* 2014).

The religious/spiritual core of moral injury reconciliation may also be needed to improve veterans' and servicemembers' mental healthcare as an instrument to answer the "important" call. This call is for "specific techniques that chaplains can use for moral injury that interface with existing empirically supported treatments for PTSD" in a "VA [Veterans Administration] context" (Foy, Drescher, and Smith 2013, p.574). Thus, any agenda for such "techniques" would be part of this spiritual care framework's new model for outcome-oriented chaplaincy (OOC). It could also possibly commission OOC as the "operant paradigm for professional chaplaincy for the twenty-first century" (Peery 2012, p.346). The spiritual care framework on which moral injury reconciliation is based aims to inject new life into each veteran, servicemember, or family as they realize they are real people undergoing surreal life-changing experiences.

Positively, religious/spiritual tenets are the backbone of the reconciliation model. Another rationale for an updated mental healthcare perspective is to provide stress relief and a proven coping resource. As a relatively large percentage of Americans have some form of a religious/spiritual orientation (see the introduction), it is believed that international threats, asymmetrical warfare, and terrorism both here and abroad will linger even as those ideologies opposed to our way of life proliferate and the world's oceans are no longer the security buffers they once were.

While most can identify with a "war-weary" public, a religious/spiritual framework is recommended to proactively reinforce those who will bear the future burdens for our safety and strengthen those who have already done the heavy lifting of war-fighting in our defense. And while America owes a debt to the American military, this practitioner's guide strives to address the special pre-service considerations of both men and women veterans that so often go neglected.

These pre-service issues involve reports of the "higher prevalence" of men with adverse childhood experiences (ACEs) such as living with someone who: 1) was depressed or mentally ill, 2) used illicit drugs, 3) had parents divorced or separated, 4) was at least five years older than them and forced them into sex, or 5) physically abused them. It was shown that men with a military history "had twice the odds of reporting sex abuse before the age of 18 years...compared with men without military service" (Blosnich et al. 2014, p.1041). Studies also found that, of the 520 women receiving Veterans Administration care, more than 50 percent affirmed physical or sexual assault prior to military service and that 86 percent entered service to escape their stress-filled civilian circumstances (Sadler et al. 2004). Prompt veteran care is highly relevant as ACEs have been known as "extremely potent correlates of adulthood suicide risks" (Blosnich et al. 2014, p.1042; Bruffaerts et al. 2010; Fergusson, McLeod, and Horwood 2013). These concerns matter. Likewise, such issues are prone to surface if one remains on active duty or in transitioning out of the military service into the new challenges of civilian life.

MEETING THE MORAL INJURY CHALLENGES

To the degree there is pre- and post-service moral injury or other trauma, this model has anticipated some of the challenges of perspective clients. Such difficulties include the necessity of a secure *identity*; an identity apart from military service no matter the level of achievement or military decorations received. Discharged veterans will need to connect with new roles, rules, and responsibilities so that transition into civilian life is more complete.

However, as moral injury may have already scarred the client's moral constitution, it appears that it is also capable of depriving one of their identity. Reforming one's identity will require new thinking as well as *humility*. Discovery of a new identity requires connection with the transitional theme of humility. Humility is thought to be indicative of one's level of spiritual awareness and receptivity to spiritual care. Other key factors such as the need for community are essential.

Since moral injury reconciliation treatment is a religious/spiritual care model, it may be helpful to examine it with other treatments that are more secular in nature. One such companion model is one designed by Litz and colleagues called adaptive disclosure (Litz *et al.* 2016). This program seems to have innovative research behind it and may provide needed relief for trauma sufferers. It is discussed briefly below and contrasted with the moral injury reconciliation model in Table 2.1.

Adaptive disclosure interventions exist to help satisfy clients' mental healthcare needs. Primarily, adaptive disclosure seems geared toward active-duty personnel and seeks to maintain the warrior ethos and to not undermine the missions of war (Litz *et al.* 2016, p.8). It was also developed to support veterans and servicemembers to provide the means to "experientially and emotionally process" the "three war-related principal harms" which are: life threat, loss, and moral injury (Litz *et al.* 2016, p.3). And, as adaptive disclosure provides needed assistance to address the three principal harms, the scope of moral injury reconciliation aims at a slightly more ambitious goal of second-order change (Fraser and Solovey 2007). This goal seeks the full life transformation for veterans now outside military service. By using each veteran's religious/spiritual foundations or *values*, moral injury reconciliation also desires to help unearth and/or recover one's "self" through using other generalized resistance resources (GRRs) (Antonovsky 1979; discussed in Chapter 3).

Moral injury reconciliation differs from adaptive disclosure mainly because it believes it is now necessary to go much deeper and further with its assumption that the toxicology of moral injury and *all* trauma is of a spiritual origin. Distinct religious/spiritual foundations are believed to provide remedies using spiritually oriented experiential activities.

The reconciliation methodology incorporates a three-fold approach to spiritual wellness. It has a religious/spiritual grounding and uses transitionally themed goals for progressive healing. It also targets veterans first, active-duty personnel second, and then the family unit. Table 2.1 offers a brief contrast between the moral injury reconciliation and adaptive disclosure models.

Table 2.1 Moral injury reconciliation versus adaptive disclosure

Moral injury reconciliation	Adaptive disclosure
Modality: group or individual	Modality: individual
Principal focus: veterans	Principal focus: active-duty personnel
Full-life trauma processing	Discrete trauma processing
Holistic, biopsychosocial-spiritual	Medical model
Chaplain as moral authority	Search for imaginal moral authority
Chaplain bridges mental health (MH) divide	MH staff is lead
Moral injury reconciliation	Moral repair
2nd-order change, transformation	1st-order change, stability
Warrior to Soul Mate	Maintains "warrior ethos"
Theistic psychotherapy	Hybrid CBT/other strategies
A "whole self" orientation (past, present, and future)	"Present" orientation

Multiple other causes give rise to the formulation of the reconciliation model; they should become evident later within this work. War trauma is complex. However, this proposal hopes to advance the appropriate arresting, healing, and hope-generating methods beyond what is currently available. Though there may be notable differences between the adaptive disclosure and moral injury reconciliation models, a unifying belief seems to be the recognition that a religious/spiritual framework is required for the healing of moral injury.

MORAL INJURY RECONCILIATION: A RELIGIOUS/SPIRITUAL INTERVENTION

Chiefly, moral injury reconciliation is a nine-week, three-pronged spiritual care treatment methodology. It is designed to transform morally or traumatically wounded veterans and active-duty personnel. Its secondary purpose is to interrupt other disorders such as depression and anxiety through its religious/spiritual healing framework. Cognitive restructuring and spiritual awareness are features of this treatment. New thinking targets one's schema (beliefs) after having reflected and operationalized religiously oriented transitional themes—themes worked out within one's spiritual economy. The reconciliation model explains how to reconcile *past* trauma, facilitate a "here-and-now" focused *present*, and increase hope-filled *future* expectations.

In part, a client's lifestyle and their generalized resistance resources (Antonovsky 1979) are utilized. Moral injury reconciliation's effectiveness is believed to be found in its merging of religious doctrines (e.g. forgiveness) relative to moral–ethical trauma and one's generalized resistance resources. These are part of the reconciliation process. As this model's spiritual awareness activities (for sensitization and habitualization) are activated, transactions are completed within the spiritual economy. Subsequent coding is progressively shaped into new behaviors.

To this end, moral injury reconciliation also places a high priority on veterans' and active-duty members' families. It considers family systems in its construction. Family health is a fundamental spiritual wellness keystone. As a treatment framework, the reconciliation model is designed to heal and fortify families as moral injury may mimic depression and posttraumatic stress symptoms (Haskell *et al.* 2010; Litz 2016). This dynamic likely causes added family strain. And since there is "compelling evidence of mental health problems in military spouses and children including posttraumatic stress disorder" (Nash and Litz 2013, p.366), the reconciliation model posits that its methodology intervenes to reorder family functioning for strengthening the family unit.

As a religious/spiritual intervention, that supports families and those that have served, it actively blends *substantive* and *functional* (Zinnbauer, Pargament, and Scott 1999) aspects in its reconciliation processing. The functional and substantive features appear to prevent polarization of either a sterilized religious treatment plan or a privatized spiritual muddle which is difficult to comprehend or incapable of being tracked for clinical evaluation. The moral injury reconciliation model adds an *operational* dimension to measure the anticipated actions of how the substantive and functional elements combine for client transformation.

The substantive aspect considers those faith structures such as beliefs and practices of a person with respect to what one considers the divine. The core of the *substantive* method of inquiry is the sacred which characterizes religiousness. Second, the *functional* component considers the utility that religiousness serves within one's life. Beliefs, emotions, practices, and experiences are observed with attention reserved for such strategies that impact the "how-to" of daily life that contains a host of life problems such as death, suffering, disappointments, or injustice (Pargament 1997). Third, the operational dimension helps identify which transitional themes are most responsible for objective movement toward the healthy end of the healthcare continuum (Antonovsky 1979).

THE INSEPARABILITY OF RELIGIOUSNESS AND SPIRITUALITY: THE CONTINUITY OF WELLNESS

The reconciliation model does not dissect the existential domain into religious or spiritual camps as some attempt today (Schneiders 2003). Rather, it embraces the historical perspective that binds religion and spirituality. Therefore, the reconciliation model endorses a "broad-band" (Zinnbauer *et al.* 1999) approach. In this way, the broad-band construct maintains the necessary, time-tested, and measurable remedies for the psychic wounds of war and other military traumas. And as the historic utility of the broad-band model has been to ground spirituality with a structure capable of transmitting values over time, the broad-band concept protects both religion and spirituality. These entities are deemed an inseparable combined therapeutic. It also may protect against the pitfalls of eccentric personalities or potentially harmful privatized spirituality.

The broad-band perspective can shield against the unaffiliated private practices of spirituality that may cater to one's felt needs. It may also help dispel the idea that one can single-handedly construct the boundaries of who God is, and what God asks, as well as learn to accept character critiques of personal deficits (Schneiders 2003).

COGNITIVE-BEHAVIOR THERAPY, A SENSE OF COHERENCE, AND MORAL INJURY RECONCILIATION

As a holistic approach, the reconciliation methodology advances a part of researcher Aaron Beck's work on dysfunctional beliefs (schema) or "thoughtless thinking" (Beck *et al.* 1979, p.5). It also offers prospective clients an opportunity for new thoughts—a way to *make sense* of life or their world and discover a part of self not previously attended to.

The moral injury reconciliation framework also expands upon the *negative cognitive triad* (Beck *et al.* 1979, p.11; Beck and Alford 2009, p.xix). Its theory for transformation employs three movements for arresting moral injury through experiential exercises. Whole-life reframing of *self* in Phase 1, the *world* in Phase 2, and the *future* in Phase 3 are its goals. It also describes how moral injury reconciliation understands a client or family member in relation to the healing process using the iconic *fire triangle* as a metaphor (to be explicated in Chapter 3).

If "all advances are made by exploiting the past" as Antonovsky (1979, p.viii) asserts, then the moral injury reconciliation model builds from and out of ancient religious/spiritual teachings. This model goes on to expand Beck and colleagues' (1979) three-point model of depression and synthesizes a spiritual care framework with Antonovsky's (1979) generalized resistance resources from which his "sense of coherence" (p.10) emerges. A sense of coherence is the framework that makes it possible to organize life's ever-present stressors. And out of this coherence bloom three core components associated with people who have a well-developed life congruence or the ability to make sense of their present health difficulties.

Associated with those with a strong sense of coherence, who successfully cope, are the three pillars: comprehensibility, manageability, and a life that is meaningful. *Comprehensibility* refers to a life that makes "cognitive sense." It is a life that is in at least some ways "predictable" even though "death, war, and failure can occur, but such a person can make sense of them" (Antonovsky 1987, p.17). Next, *manageability* is the degree one believes their available resources are sufficient to meet the demands of the varied stressors. Such a "one will not feel victimized by events or feel that life treats one unfairly" (Antonovsky 1987, p.17). Finally, a *meaningful life* refers to the "motivational element" in *life* of things that matter (Antonovsky 1987, p.18). A meaningful life is a life that makes sense not only in the cognitive but in the emotional sense.

Meaningfulness invests effort and commitment to the worthy aspect of one's existence. These facets are part of moral injury reconciliation's plan for transformation.

Thus, these questions remain: "How are clients and their families best helped in arresting and recovering from moral injury and other trauma?"; "How do we see beyond current medical models of care to integrate a religious/spiritual framework care model?"; and "How do caregivers address the horror and carnage of war?" These questions may further suggest that new treatment designs are needed. The immediacy of these have prompted the reconciliation model to include treatments that have considered the phenomenology of war and the spiritual shock that often attends military conflict.

New and healing pathways are critical for successfully serving the distinct veteran and active-duty populations. Accordingly, moral injury reconciliation seeks to treat the emotional-cognitive (guilt/ shame, anger), behavioral (isolation), and spiritual responses (lament) that threaten spiritual wellness and overall mental health. A key goal, therefore, is second-order change (Fraser and Solovey 2007) or simply whole-life transformation. For those who desire relief from the spiritual distress, it is believed that there is ample evidence (Hill and Pargament 2003; Koenig *et al.* 2012) for religious and spiritually oriented treatments.

WHAT MAKES THE MORAL INJURY RECONCILIATION MODEL A RELIGIOUS/SPIRITUAL FRAMEWORK OF CARE? ARE THERE SAFEGUARDS?

As I write this section, the 1974 series *The World at War: Remember* (Season 1, Episode 26) plays in the background with the voice of Sir Lawrence Olivier narrating. This episode "remembers the dead" and the other great costs of war. But what distinguishes the moral injury reconciliation model as being a different model? The reconciliation model assumes *deity* ascribed to God and is designed around these assumptions. It actively encourages its client to *remember*, too. It is further believed that the reconciliation model includes the *six domains of religious experience* (Grame *et al.* 1999) in its treatment design. These tenets are thought to be part of the rich and transformative quality of this reconciliation model.

The six dimensions of religious experience as outlined by Grame and colleagues (1999) are: 1) the *ideological* dimension (helping clients find meaning in their life particularly in the context of suffering or trauma); 2) the *intellectual* dimension (religious doctrines, narratives, information, images); 3) the *ritualistic* dimension (prayer, worship services, religious music); 4) the *experiential* dimension (spiritual awareness of God's presence and immensity, union with the divine, the feeling-state, and connection with deity); 5) the *consequential* dimension (one's spiritual qualities and its secular presentation, the resultant transformation as witnessed by others, changed behaviors such as: self-care, altruism, sobriety, reduced suicidal ideation, improving relationship quality); and 6) the *supportive* dimension (religious community, sense of belonging, support, and associated wellbeing).

Some of the differences making moral injury reconciliation a religious/spiritual framework may be found in its points of departure from what information the sciences can provide. Regarding the human condition and the evidence found in the religious/spiritual literature, Scripture speaks with clarity regarding world events. Other differences are that the reconciliation model takes into account the real life (and death) issues found in "story." For example, these issues are clearly illustrated by the riveting personal testimonies and the reading of soldiers' letters, official correspondence, photos, and the combat photography contained in such real-life drama as *The World at War* series documentary.

In humankind's search for relief of stress, this model has considered Antonovsky's (1987) reasoning for evaluation and applying a religious/spiritual framework to moral injury and other posttraumatic stressors. He writes:

> When one searches for cures for particular diseases, one tends to stay within the confines of pathophysiology. When one searches for effective adaptation of the organism, one can move beyond post-Cartesian dualism and look to imagination, love, play, meaning, will, and the social structures that foster them. Or, as I would prefer to put it, to theories of successful coping. (Antonovsky 1987, p.9)

Still, there seems to be much more beyond mere "theories." The following assumptions serve to advance a novel approach to healing that supplements existing remedies of care. First, out of consideration of the Divine as listed above, the reconciliation model assumes *creation* by the Creator and an inherent spiritual nature to life. That there is something more than material in life seems evident. This may be observed in the unseen striving or a pulling toward life called *spiritual surging*.

Spiritual surging is always seeking life; a life that burns in the hearts of men, women, and children which endeavors to find meaning. Spiritual surging assumes that the human heart is forever restless and will only find peace when it reconnects with the Divine (Augustine 397 C.E./1997, p.39). This is especially true when there has been the taking of life or when one experiences trauma. Second, moral injury reconciliation asserts that humankind is finite and will surely die. However, humankind may find the best description of the state of the world and the expression of human experience bound in the pages of sacred literature.

Out of the abundant good that a religious/spiritual orientation can do, like any other noble offering, abuse is possible. However, having a professionally credentialed Chaplain Corps monitoring the administration of the reconciliation process, such abuses should be greatly minimized. Still, the aforementioned six dimensions of religious experience (Grame *et al.* 1999) are potential safeguards from an individual provider's deviations.

SUMMARY

The reconciliation model presented in this book is structured upon the wisdom of the historic documents of Scripture. Its aim is to relieve the symptoms of moral injury and posttraumatic stress and realize behavior change for good and productive living. This process of transformation is the donning of one's divine nature. That religion and spirituality are the core of the reconciliation model may cause some to marginalize this methodology out of a want to limit that which may be found mysterious. Embracing the doctrines of ancient literature has been shown to be an effective lifestyle choice toward wellness nonetheless.

Transforming the mind, body, and spirit has historic roots and finds a common thread between Judaism, Christianity, and Islam. Thus, theistic psychotherapy is thought capable of uniting through the transcendent command to "love" one's neighbor. And by using a theistic psychotherapeutic orientation when treating moral injury or trauma, the key word is reconciliation. Reconciliation allows the client to respond to the past, present, and future. All finding meaning at each stage. When utilizing components of religion and spirituality, it is imperative that providers have knowledge of the fundamental definitions of this field.

With this foundation, moral injury may be more fully defined and treated as there are limited treatment options that specifically address moral injury. However, in order to consistently have a theistic approach to therapy available, religion and spirituality are to be held together in what is known as a "broad-band" construct. This may be done as the structure of the reconciliation process follows the six dimensions of religious experience, helping the provider to bring maximum clinical effectiveness to each client or family member.

CHAPTER 3

ASSESSMENT AND METHODOLOGY

Story is a provider's powerful assessment tool. Witness the following monologue: "They were kind of young and they were scared, but I was in charge; I had the training. I was picked to go to school. I was in charge and had been there before. So, I told them what they needed to hear. I told them that 'everything was going to be okay…they'd be alright. Everything was going to be okay.' We had a job to do… (sobbing)… They didn't make it."

The effects of moral injury can be far-reaching, though moral injury is not a diagnosed mental disorder. And despite the fact that research on moral injury is relatively new (Maguen and Litz 2012), we need answers to fundamental questions such as: How pervasive is moral injury? What are some of the spiritual–clinical challenges when assessing moral injury or posttraumatic stress? How is *morality* defined? How does case conceptualization influence the diagnostic impressions of the assessment process? And, what character-behavioral alterations might indicate second-order change? By using language that may bridge gaps between various helping-professions, it is hoped that such questions will be answered. And while the scope of change is broad, sections of this book may be demanding. However, since a new treatment model is presented, some fine detail is included.

As mentioned, the moral injury reconciliation model assumes that the spiritual shock of a traumatic experience is first and foremost a spiritual wound, demographics and philosophical orientations notwithstanding. Because moral injury disrupts one's spiritual equilibrium due to the inability to make sense of trauma, a unified or transdiagnostic approach is recommended due to the course and prognosis of unchecked spiritual distress.

The opening quotation was a possible example of a veteran retelling his *story* during the assessment process. Issues of guilt/shame and betrayal of another's trust would appear evident. In addition to clinically diagnosed posttraumatic stress disorder, one's degree of global assessment of self (*shame*) is of particular significance (Lewis 1971; Tangney and Dearing 2002). These are some of the inherent *costs* and *consequences* of war (Drescher *et al.* 2011). Nevertheless, spiritual caregivers are required to do much during the assessment process. This includes making clinical decisions in light of the knowledge that *disorder-specific* treatments may lack the efficacy to fully treat various disorders (Mansell *et al.* 2009; Clark and Taylor 2009; Craske 2012; Gutner *et al.* 2016). Surprisingly, even recommended, *evidence-based* treatments for posttraumatic stress may be insufficient to address the unique nature of moral injury and the phenomenology of war (Litz *et al.* 2009; Litz *et al.* 2016, p.7; Yan 2016; Jordan *et al.* 2017).

A SPIRITUAL CARE TREATMENT: A NEW WAVE

Since disorder-specific treatments (e.g. cognitive processing, prolonged exposure) (U.S. Department of Veterans Affairs 2017) are recommended for the unique veteran and active-duty populations, a new diagnostic and treatment paradigm may be worth considering. For if evidence-based therapies are insufficient to treat posttraumatic stress, the moral injury reconciliation model presents a new treatment prototype. This model is thought to bring relief from not only moral injury, but also a host of various spiritual struggles and other mental health challenges. Its basic structure is deemed compatible in a military or civilian context. If positive outcomes for this unique population are sought, caregivers treating veterans and active-duty personnel may do well to be vigilant for symptoms of moral injury and familiar with the phenomenology of war. As the dimensional nature of moral injury varies in intensity and may or may not be present at any given time (Maguen and Litz 2012), this book hopes to remedy the challenge presented when confronted with the variability of presentations of moral injury and other trauma-related disorders.

In theory, when receiving a morally injurious wound, the person's spiritual economy reacts to search for resources to help bring consequent spiritual disequilibrium back to stasis. During this state of spiritual shock, a reference point is needed to help reduce and return a person's life-orienting framework back to set-point. This set-point aligns with previously coded messages defining what makes sense. However, if a familiar set-point is not found, a re-mapping is necessary where corrective encounters, spiritual awareness, and new learning are required to accommodate the new realities of the psychic wound.

Essential to the spiritual care assessment process is the client's story. Story can often reveal critical inner aspects of spiritual distress the *Diagnostic and Statistical Manual of Mental Disorders, Fifth Edition* (DSM-5) is not equipped nor commissioned to discuss. Thus, the reconciliation model endorses a spiritual care "new wave" where a *salutogenic* (or health-promoting) orientation exists (Antonovsky 1987, p.6). This is in contrast to a *pathogenic* or a *disease-first* perspective. The pathogenic model focuses on *why* people get sick and puts great effort into eradicating the problem (Antonovsky 1987). However, the salutogenic model seeks to understand "the story of the person—note, not the patient, for salutogenesis constrains us to look at people on a continuum—rather than the germ or germs that caused a particular disease, [to] arrive at a more adequate diagnosis" (Antonovsky 1987, p.9).

It is suggested, then, that *listening* to the lament is the beginning. This act, therefore, helps to assess, diagnose, and treat what areas of spiritual, psychological, emotional, physical, and functional expressions have been affected. This serves to guide care plan construction for improved outcomes. Such a construction can be part of a *unified* method of care which aids in the efficient and effective treatment of moral injury and introduces a new *methodology* (i.e. treatment philosophy and techniques) for 21st-century care.

In addition to answering foundational questions regarding the moral injury construct and the appropriate treatments, this chapter hopes to provide guidelines for understanding the *moral injury reconciliation methodology*. It also hopes to develop an appreciation of the value of story and its ability to find *coherency* in spite of moral injury. And for the sake of treatment efficiency, this model has adopted a transdiagnostic approach for viewing the moral injury syndrome and making clinical judgments about a client's treatment through *case conceptualization.*

THE DILEMMA OF ASSESSMENT AND DIAGNOSIS

To mitigate the effects of moral injury, the reconciliation model contends that, at the point of a morally injurious experience, a variety of psychic and behavioral alterations are present (Litz *et al.* 2009; Drescher *et al.* 2011; Nash and Litz 2013; Currier *et al.* 2015). And further complicating this already difficult situation is the following knowledge: "There is no simple method of assessment... No formula can fully capture the uniqueness of an individual... This point holds particularly true for new approaches to treatment, such as spiritually integrated psychotherapy" (Pargament 2011, pp.239–240). This view would certainly include the moral injury reconciliation model presented herein. However, through story and the religious and spiritual composition of this model, its theory hopes to expand the lens through which spiritual distress is understood.

Clearly, the *Diagnostic and Statistical Manual of Mental Disorders, Fifth Edition* (DSM-5) is of great worth to the helping professions. Vast resources and great effort have gone towards its construction to render "reliable diagnosis" (American Psychiatric Association (APA) 2013, p.5). And in diagnosing trauma and stressor-related disorders, the DSM-5 declares:

> Psychological distress following exposure to a traumatic or stressful event is quite variable... Because of these variable expressions of clinical distress following exposure to catastrophic or aversive events, the aforementioned disorders have been grouped under a separate category: *trauma- and stressor-related disorders*. (APA 2013, p.265; emphasis original)

Given that the DSM-5 is used to make "reliable diagnosis," it is also instructive to note that post-exposure "psychological distress" is "quite variable" (p.265) as well.

While reconciliation's method for assessment, diagnosing, and treatment is borne out of a spiritual–clinical concern and practicality, it seeks to increase the reliability of diagnosis (especially amongst the special veteran and active-duty populations). This model is believed to comport with other issues Craske (2012) offers for adopting a *transdiagnostic* approach to therapy. Craske infers: "Recent interest in transdiagnostic therapies that transcend DSM diagnostic boundaries represents an important paradigmatic shift in evidence-based treatments." Also of concern is the numerous volumes of "treatment manuals for different disorders"; they are "a *major barrier* to the implementation of evidence-based practice in service settings" (Craske 2012, p.749; emphasis applied).

Moral injury presents with symptoms such as: 1) a downward direction of ethical–behavioral attitudes (Mental Health Advisory Team 2006); 2) guilt, shame, and forgiveness difficulties (Kubany *et al.* 1997); 3) alterations in or the loss of spirituality (Drescher and Foy 1995; Fontana and Rosenheck 2004); 4) anhedonia and dysphoria (Kashdan, Uswatte, and Julian 2006); 5) aggressive behavior (Begić, and Jokić-Begić 2001); 6) poor self-care (Schnurr and Spiro 1999); and 7) self-harm (Pitman 1990; Lyons 1991; Braš *et al.* 2007; Sher 2009). Confusingly, such symptoms may also present in other disorders as well. Therefore, the treatment of moral injury may need to be viewed wholly differently. And for this reason, moral injury is believed to be better treated transdiagnostically.

In other words, the reconciliation model hypothesizes that since moral injury presents asymmetrically and is a dimensional problem (Maguen and Litz 2012), the consuming nature of a morally injurious event (or spiritual wound) may be a *causal factor* in other disorders. Further, moral injury is thought to perhaps even *maintain symptoms* across classes of disorders such as: 1) trauma- and stressor-related disorders; 2) anxiety disorders; 3) sleep–wake disorders; 4) depressive disorders; 5) dissociative disorders; 6) sexual dysfunctions; 7) substance-related and addictive disorders; and 8) personality disorders (APA 2013).

Similarly, Sauer-Zavala and colleagues (2017) note that, "for many years, panic attacks were thought to be specific to panic disorder (APA 1994; Barlow *et al.* 1986)…panic attacks are now described as ubiquitous and potentially occurring in the context of any disorder (APA 2013)" (p.129). Therefore, the moral injury reconciliation model suggests a similar sequela (or consequence of another condition or event) may be operating as part of the moral injury syndrome.

The assessment dilemma proliferates when one surmises that even though the DSM-5 remains a trusted tool, and "despite three decades of research and multiple revisions of the diagnostic criteria for PTSD, it remains unclear which stressor types are capable of inducing post-traumatic stress symptoms" (Nash *et al.* 2013, p.646). Thus, based on these realities, another theory may suffice. The moral injury reconciliation model respectfully suggests, then, that *spiritual distress* is the primary stressor type that induces moral injury and posttraumatic stressors. Spiritual distress is hypothesized to be the ignition source of the moral injury spectrum, the posttraumatic stress sequela, or perhaps bound in the etiology of many other mental health disorders as well.

To provide assessment and diagnosis clarity, sacred literature is a suggested companion to other existing instruments. Scripture is also commissioned to account for the wide and individual variances when veterans or soldiers receive moral injury or traumatic stressors. Sacred literature may supply the reference points and diagnostic categories of spiritual pain experienced during moral injury. This new yet ancient reference may enrich and expand the evaluation process and make assessments increasingly more reliable. Our veterans' and servicemembers' stories contain such clues leading to appropriate treatment modalities. And though the client's story contains strategic contextual information, it should not necessarily replace any other diagnostic instrument currently in use, but rather serve as an adjacent clinical tool.

As behavior maladjustments impact wellbeing and functioning, *causal agents* of individual variances may be found inside each veteran's or warfighter's story. However, spiritual–clinical assessments are so much more than that. For within the story lies data as to what resources the veteran or soldier has used (or not used) to keep them functioning. It must be reiterated that the moral injury reconciliation model is not simply a disease- and trauma-focused model whose goal is to identify and treat *symptoms*. Rather, moral injury reconciliation's goal (in part) is the spiritual awareness and reconciliation between the *horizontal* (intrapersonal and interpersonal connectedness) and the *vertical* (spiritual, existential, and sacred) aspects of life. These goals advocate for the specific identification of morally injurious experiences and the consequent reconciliation of moral injury and other trauma. This is thought to produce whole-life spiritual and behavioral transformation using a religious/spiritual framework.

The reconciliation model relies on assessing the veteran's or active-duty member's story through *themes* such as: personal transgression, guilt/shame, grief, identity issues, and so forth. This model is composed of three Movements and sub-divided further into three thematic intervention phases. Each *movement* constitutes a shift in emphasis from "self," the "world," or the "future," while each *phase* is the progressive development and engagement of specific spiritual disciplines in the form of corrective themes.

For example, Movement I (self) might encourage a client's sense of *daring* to engage in aspects of reconciliation processing such as *forgiveness* or to make lifestyle changes so that the *spiritual self-care disciplines* are now actionable. And through a clinician's assessment of a *past* trauma, clients may be inclined to examine their "here-and-now" *present*-day levels of functioning and evaluate their expectations for the *future*. In this, it is believed that specific care plans may be developed to accentuate a *flourishing* of sorts through new thinking and corrective behavior changes.

Considering the challenges of the assessment and diagnostic process, Figure 3.1 was constructed to illustrate the assessment domains explored under moral injury reconciliation's transdiagnostic approach. Its technique is to listen. The veteran's or servicemember's story determines coherency. So, the goal is to ask how and where their story may break down so that their areas of coping deficiency become apparent.

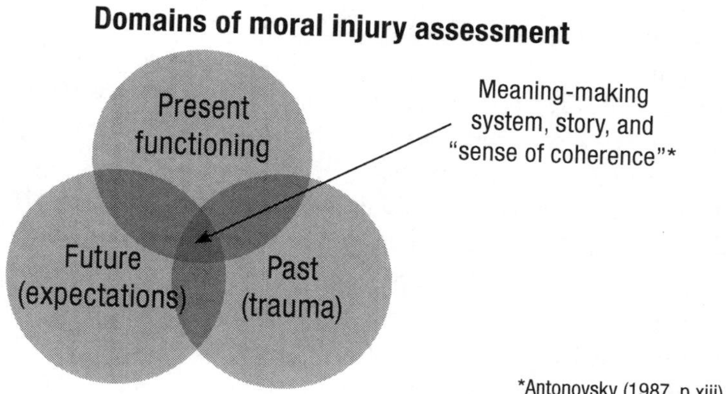

Domains of moral injury assessment

Present functioning

Meaning-making system, story, and "sense of coherence"*

Future (expectations)

Past (trauma)

*Antonovsky (1987, p.xiii)

Figure 3.1 Moral injury reconciliation's domains of moral injury assessment

RENDERING A MORE RELIABLE DIAGNOSIS

In the preceding paragraphs, the distinct challenges within the assessment and diagnosis process were discussed. While many clinicians diagnose patients relying on DSM-5's diagnostic insights (minus sacred literature), the moral injury reconciliation model, however, uses *both* the DSM-5 and Scripture for assessment and treatment guidance in *all* instances. This is to emphasize a transdiagnostic perspective to mental healthcare. Such a method sees sacred literature as the primary reference used for *contextualizing* every case as a treatment plan is constructed. This contextualization views the mutual ills of humanity from a religious/spiritual standpoint, whereas Antonovsky (1979, p.5) would perhaps see common "facets" woven throughout "all diseases" encountered by humankind. These "diseases"—as he calls them—would include the parallels in trauma-related disorders and other problems such as mood, anxiety, substance-related problems, and addictive disorders.

The DSM-5, in turn, is perhaps the tool that can sharpen the clinical attention for further understanding a disorder at a deeper physiological, chemical, or analytical level. Conversely, sacred literature supplies the broader perspective and likely remedy when providers suspect veterans or soldiers have moral injury or notice a co-occurrence of several mental health symptoms (spectrum). Sacred literature may then assist in case formulation as it presents a diagnosis founded on plausible theory and worldview. And based on the prevalence of "bugs" that range from various spiritual, biological, emotional, and environmental challenges (Antonovsky 1979, p.14), Scripture may feature a much larger window to contextualize, under which a disorder may be understood.

For instance, some *basics* of life may serve as general guidance for the provider. With respect to spiritual distress, many clients are thought able to reconcile their distress by accepting the following instructions: "Be angry, and do not sin. Meditate within your heart on your bed, and be still" (Psalm 4.4); and: "Judge not, and you shall not be judged. Condemn not, and you shall not be condemned. Forgive, and you will be forgiven" (Luke 6.37). Basic direction is found for treating stress with the following knowledge: "Anxiety in the heart of a man causes depression, but a good word makes it glad" (Proverbs 12.25). Or, understanding that "tribulation produces perseverance; and perseverance, character, and character, hope" (Romans 5.3b–4). And other instances provide guidance, where the morally wounded are encouraged to "confess your trespasses to one another, and pray for one another, that you may be healed. The effective, fervent prayer of a righteous man avails much" (James 5.16). Finally, humankind's *knowledge* to appropriate the divine nature calls for one's diligence to add to their meaning-making system (i.e. faith): virtue (*moral excellence*), knowledge, self-control, perseverance (patience or endurance), godliness, brotherly kindness, and—most of all—love (2 Peter 1.5–7).

While these are but only samples of how sacred literature instructs highly competent spiritual care providers, sacred literature contains a literal warehouse of instructions for the healing of moral injury. This framework is utilized based on a present-day review of research outcomes (see the introduction), objective data from history, reliable ancient manuscripts, archeology, statistical probabilities, and eye-witness accounts.

It is assumed moral injury reconciliation's methodology holds a tenable worldview and subscribes to a universal similarity of human experiences. Such scenarios are linked by common struggles that span human history. However, this universal order also has a *particularism* (Shay and Munroe 1999) built in whereby the full account of a veteran's or warfighter's story may be an illuminating feature. War, misery, and grief are all a "normal" albeit unfortunate part of life's continual fight to maintain *spiritual equilibrium*.

In other words, the moral injury reconciliation model insists that moral injury and traumatic stress are distinct and indivisible features of military culture and, by extension, life in general. This model is neither surprised by *suffering* nor shocked by the unpredictable nature of life. Even so, it provides a counterintuitive response for meaning-making (coherency), comfort, recovery, and enduring hope. By adopting a life-stance that assumes discomforts will arise, our foreknowledge and readiness to respond may shorten the time of such spiritual distress. This is a *basic* of life discussed earlier.

In making a more reliable diagnosis, sacred literature is believed to set forth a complete account of conditions affecting past, present, and one's future. It also lists the prevailing tensions that give rise to spiritual struggles. The reconciliation model does not view problem resolution through *symptom alleviation*, but seeks second-order change of the veteran or warfighter. While rendering transdiagnostic assessments and diagnostic decision-making may not be a new process, however, assessing the veteran or servicemember through a religious/spiritual lens for follow-on case conceptualization may be.

Alternatively, the DSM-5 catalogues specific features of disorders and has been shown to be a generally effective utility with benchmarks for making mental health diagnoses. Coupled with the reconciliation model, a transdiagnostic paradigm emerges as a means for diagnosing and treating the mental health concerns of clients. Transformation is thought possible when the assessment and treatment calculus expands, and such an expansion contains perhaps evidence-based components like cognitive processing and/or other corrective behavior strategies.

Still, even as the Bible must maintain its sacred significance and lines of separation from secular science, its universal and "top-down" application is believed capable of delivering effective "therapeutic techniques to multiple disorders without explicit consideration for whether all disorders treated with that technique are maintained by similar processes" (Sauer-Zavala et al. 2017, p.130). As a result, this model's use of its religious/spiritual framework necessarily makes the universally applied therapeutic principles actionable in much the same way as any other classic "school"—psychodynamic, humanistic, psychodynamic, or cognitive or behavioral—would. Additionally, the reconciliation model's use of its therapeutic triad (discussed below) would be a *modular* feature of the reconciliation strategy. Here, a provider may utilize the religious/spiritual themes of a client's specific problem area, such as guilt and shame, believed to contribute both to the development and maintenance of moral injury. Such an intervention targeting a *shared mechanism* (e.g. guilt or shame) may influence a host of other disorders and may be of healthy significance. And since the moral injury construct is not believed to be simply "descriptively transdiagnostic" (i.e. assuming a construct is present without considering how or why it may be true) (Sauer-Zavala et al. 2017), the moral injury reconciliation model's interventions are therefore considered transdiagnostic for its qualities previously mentioned. Using Scripture to augment a clinical picture is explained next.

THE MORAL INJURY TRANSDIAGNOSTIC PARADIGM

Figure 3.2 is the assessment model used during intake and throughout the entire treatment process. The *moral injury transdiagnostic paradigm* may also serve as an assessment tool to understand a veteran's or warfighter's past, their current level of functioning, and expectations for making prognosis relative to *hope*.

Here is how it works. As a diagnostic tool, the moral injury transdiagnostic paradigm provides a model with the ability to expand and contract as needed in order to respond to the *dimensional* nature of moral injury presentations (Maguen and Litz 2012). For example, as a veteran or active-duty member exhibits features of the moral injury syndrome (e.g. guilt/shame, anger, depression, isolation) during the course of the disorder, sacred literature may provide structure to continue with the spiritual healing pathways and a thematic approach to various treatments. As the "psychological distress following exposure is quite variable" (APA 2013, p.265), Scripture is believed able to capture spiritual distress categories and recovery themes to correct relationship alienation or identity problems. Even spiritual distress resulting from the fear of death/dying or other anxieties are able to be contextualized and treated using the model in Figure 3.2. With sacred literature serving as the foundation for later case conceptualization, a process may be in place that directs treatment interventions for a more precise holistic clinical diagnosis.

The moral injury transdiagnostic paradigm

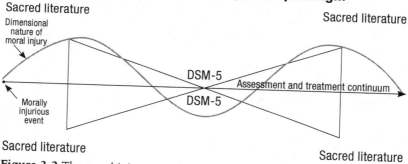

Figure 3.2 The moral injury transdiagnostic paradigm

However, should the veteran or active-duty member present with more clearly defined clinical symptoms as catalogued in the DSM-5, the DSM-5 is put to good use in assessing and further classifying the specific disorder as sacred literature continues providing the wider context for case conceptualization and later treatment. Simply said, the DSM-5 may be used to "fine tune" a diagnosis and treatment plan. And as the dimensional nature of moral injury waxes and wanes through the life of the injury, sacred literature offers ongoing reflexive guidance as additional evidence regarding a client's story is gathered. Clinical differentiation between the various diagnoses will depend on the *deep listening* skill of the provider.

Pastoral care specialists may be aided by a religious/spiritual framework that informs pastoral caregivers' treatment decisions. Clinicians with a religious/spiritual orientation would seem to have a greater diagnostic competence. Spiritual literacy should help bridge gaps so that stories are interpreted within a religious/spiritual context for a more comprehensive approach to treatment. And since it is hypothesized that humankind is essentially spiritual by nature, assessment and diagnosis *without* the aid of sacred literature may be equated to a well-meaning veterinarian treating a bird, fish, or reptile without knowing such creatures were ultimately meant to exist in different environments. Inattention to the spiritual domain may result in continually less-than-adequate therapeutic outcomes at best, or at worst, an *iatrogenic effect* (i.e. unintended clinical worsening caused by the clinician).

Therefore, relative to trauma and stress-related disorders, the reconciliation model would encourage all professionals to use *both* sacred literature and the DSM-5 to better comprehend the complexity of a client's humanity through greater knowledge of: the *mind* (or the full nature of self, reasoning ability, and what *self* is capable of in art, science, activity, etc.), the *heart* (center of emotion, desire, feelings, and passions), *strength* (physical properties), and the *soul* (volition, will, desires, imagination). Viewed existentially, a transdiagnostic approach may provide the clinical cohesion that increases the diagnostic accuracy and treatment outcomes due to the *variable expressions* of trauma and stress disorders (Clark and Taylor 2009; Craske 2012; APA 2013; Nash *et al.* 2013).

DEFINING MORALITY

The concept of *morality* is central to this book, and a brief treatment of the term is provided for clarity. As a construct, moral injury is the invisible psychic wound caused by a violation to one's moral code. Codes are a fundamental aspect of military culture and training (Drescher *et al.* 2011). Morality assumes standards, edicts, and ordinances—the *right* and *wrong* or the acceptable behavioral expectations within a society or group. The *Code of Conduct for Members of the United States Armed Forces* would be a prime example. "The Code" (as it is called) lists behavioral standards regulating the conduct of servicemembers during war or in the event one is captured by the enemy.

Morality and ethics provide direction for a group through its orthodoxy (beliefs) and orthopraxy (practice). It may be said that religious traditions have had some influence on the study and application in the construction of various secular moral and ethical codes. As morality may be defined in at least two ways (normatively and descriptively), this adds to the sophistication needed to accurately appraise moral and ethical transgressions (see below).

The reconciliation design characterizes trauma as an infraction of *norms* of "what should be." These norms provide a degree of predictability to life and are part of what provides a "sense of coherence" (Antonovsky 1979, p.8). Morality and ethics are the bricks and mortar for "how things are supposed to work." The study of morality and ethics can be very complex and philosophical, as discussed below.

> More particularly, the term "morality" can be used either *descriptively* to refer to certain codes of conduct put forward by a society or a group (such as a religion), or accepted by an individual for her own behavior, or *normatively* to refer to a code of conduct that, given specified conditions, would be put forward by all rational persons. When used with its descriptive sense, "morality" can refer to codes of conduct with widely differing content, and still be used unambiguously. This parallels the way in which "law" is used unambiguously even though different societies have laws with widely differing content. However, when "morality" is used in its descriptive sense, it sometimes does not refer to the code of a society, but to the code of a group or an individual. Those who use "morality" normatively hold that morality is (or would be) the code that meets the following condition: all rational persons, under certain specified conditions, would endorse it. Indeed, this is a plausible basic schema for definitions of "morality" in the normative sense. (Definition of morality, *The Stanford Encyclopedia of Philosophy*, 2017)[1]

Though religion has colored the complexion of various moral codes, the above definition goes on to say that "morality and religion are not the same thing... Morality is only a guide to conduct, whereas religion is always more than this."

And though the experienced chaplain or pastoral caregiver maintains a firm grasp of psychology fundamentals and human behavior, the nuance of story may further extract a more precise assessment of a veteran's or active-duty member's spiritual struggle.

---

1   www.plato.stanford.edu/entries/morality-definition

MORAL INJURY RECONCILIATION METHODOLOGY

Pastoral caregivers concern themselves with veterans' or service-members' spiritual distress of traumatic events. Moral injury and posttraumatic stress degrades the liveliness of a client's *spiritual signature*. This signature is the *tell*; the tell is observed as the climate generated by the veteran and impacts the veteran's family system and their social networks. Anhedonia (the inability to experience pleasure), depression, anger, or trust issues are part of the constellation of symptoms that may manifest within the moral injury syndrome (Nash and Litz 2013; Drescher *et al.* 2011; Currier *et al.* 2014). Assessing the impact of moral injury stressors is important, and several tools exist to aid in the assessment process. Moral injury reconciliation's *clinical goals* are to discover how the trauma affects the client, the degree to which they are affected, and what transitional themes are best suited to restore spiritual equilibrium.

Since moral injury is a new construct and not a diagnosed mental disorder, currently few interventions exist that target the source of moral transgressions (Maguen and Litz 2012). To this end, moral injury reconciliation's means for symptom and behavior alterations is manifold. It is believed this treatment model has assembled both a foundation for understanding moral injury and the necessary treatment strategy that provides the mechanisms thought to provide healing through spiritual care pathways.

Key assessment instruments are available to gauge morally injurious intensity and range of exposure such as: the Moral Injury Event Scale (MIES; Nash *et al.* 2013), the measure for combat experiences (Combat Experiences Scale (CES); Keane *et al.* 1989), moral injury exposure (Moral Injury Questionnaire—Military Version (MIQ-M); Currier *et al.* 2014; 2015), and the forming of meaning of stressors (Integration of Stressful Life Events Scale (ISLES); Holland *et al.* 2010). All may be put to good use in forming a clinical picture of spiritual disequilibrium. However, as useful as these tools are, the reconciliation model concentrates more on: the spiritual history, the level of spiritual awareness, the availability and utilization of resources, and the caregiver–client's spiritual alliance. The deep listening exchange between the veteran and the caregiver who concentrates on the story is indispensable here.

The *methodology* of this practitioner's guide enlists sacred literature as the template for understanding human trauma. This orientation may also help providers to remain mindful of the wide variations in clinical presentations of trauma and stress-related disorders (APA 2013; Nash *et al.* 2013) as well as the high rates of comorbidity associated with posttraumatic stress disorder (Kessler *et al.* 1995; Brown *et al.* 2001). Thus, the reconciliation model has adopted the iconic fire triangle as a metaphor for conceptualizing moral injury and treating it. This icon sets in motion the three Movements and treatment techniques for the progressive and hoped-for extinguishing of moral injury and/or other stressors as represented by the fire triangle. It may also provide a more substantive representation of how spiritual disequilibrium develops and how it may be the source of the spiritual signature found in each individual's story. As used here, methodology refers to the theories, philosophy, and techniques to effect transformation.

As a treatment modality, moral injury reconciliation may be considered a new entry to the field of specialized therapy groups. Yalom with Leszcz (2005) list over 50 different specialized therapy groups offering distinctive treatments for unique cases. This book seeks to be a quantum change from traditional mental health therapies. It is a unified or transdiagnostic approach that rests on the inherent spirituality of personhood as the nexus for change. The spiritual domain is seen as the linchpin for operationalizing a unified treatment approach and therefore kindly recommends that experienced pastoral caregivers or mental health providers study and utilize this methodology. Components of this approach include: moral injury reconciliation's religious/spiritual framework, its transdiagnostic paradigm, and intervention techniques that add to the clinician's available treatment strategy inventory. Moving forward, it is hoped that the reconciliation model will be a transdiagnostic treatment paradigm recognized as an effective therapeutic.

On its face, this model's methodology is simplistic in its approach, yet believed effective in its transformative potency. Because experienced providers are utilized, detailed client assessment procedures will not be included here. Trainees are encouraged to remain under instruction or refer out. The sequence for moral injury transformation follows the general pattern and is illustrated in Figure 3.3.

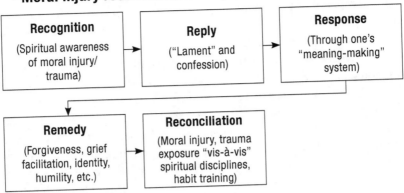

Figure 3.3 Moral injury reconciliations transformation sequence

As the moral injury reconciliation model of care assumes a direct relation between one's wellbeing and one's level of spiritual distress, a spiritual assessment is to be conducted. Although detailed assessment procedures will not be provided, Pargament (2011) lists at least 26 spiritual assessment instruments available to gather useful data. And as much as the DSM is helpful with its classifications for rendering medical diagnosis, however sophisticated, spiritual assessment measures have their limitations too. And to be sure, a comprehensive clinical picture can never be achieved through instruments alone (APA 2013, p.19). With this understanding, assessment and diagnosis may proceed.

Although the APA "recommended the GAF be dropped from DSM-5" (APA 2013, p.16), the moral injury reconciliation model's scope of assessment utilizes a type of *global assessment* to further develop the spiritual–clinical case. For guidance, providers may review the Global Assessment of Functioning (GAF) scale found in the DSM-IV-TR (APA 2000) or the self-administrated *World Health Organization Disability Assessment Schedule 2.0* (WHODAS 2.0) found in the DSM-5 (APA 2013, pp.747–748) to consider relevant categories.

While the reconciliation assessment structure is ambitious, it is considered a necessary component of the overall reconciliation process. As this model seeks whole-life transformation, an understanding of a veteran's or active-duty member's life is significant. And since the essence of moral injury is framed within the religious/spiritual dimensions, one's whole life should be assessed for the extent to which moral injury or traumatic stress exists. Simultaneously, a viable care plan to address moral injury can be manufactured.

The moral injury reconciliation therapeutic triad

Figure 3.4 is the engine of the moral injury reconciliation methodology. As the prime mover of the transformation process, it guides both the therapist and client through a progressive, three-phased approach to pastoral care treatment. In theory, each Movement and related phase affords the veteran or servicemember opportunity to resolve issues with self, the world, and/or the future to achieve desired change. Finding meaning and engaging methods towards reconciliation operationalizes reconciliation between a client's faith or value system and their specific transgression. This is done through: 1) religious/spiritual existential processing; and 2) exposure to corrective thinking and subsequent behavioral changes.

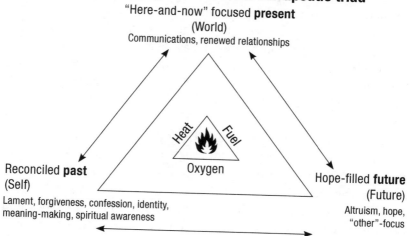

Figure 3.4 The moral injury reconciliation therapeutic triad. Adapted from Beck *et al.* (1979) *Cognitive Therapy of Depression.* Copyright Guilford Press. Adapted with permission of Guilford Press.

This model recognizes that while reconciliation is not necessarily a linear process, it nevertheless begins with examination of the past since there is much truth in Jean-Paul Sartre's adage that "introspection is always retrospection." Therefore, the iconic fire triangle is used as a metaphor for treating moral injury by arresting moral injury at one of the three potential healing lands (past, present, future), but ideally starting with the past.

Based in part on Beck and colleagues' (1979) cognitive model of depression and their "cognitive triad" (p.16), moral injury reconciliation's tripartite methodology was formed. It differs from Beck's model, however, in that it is set within the unique context of military culture, considers the phenomenology of warfare, and is grounded upon a religious/spiritual framework. This construction may be defined as a transdiagnostic intervention as such symptoms as anxiety or depression may appear alongside moral injury. Additionally, they may be simultaneously treated alongside moral injury and/or posttraumatic stress. The constellation of features associated with the moral injury syndrome is designed to be treated with this three-stage approach as part of this transdiagnostic (unified) intervention. This is the moral injury reconciliation model's strategy for second-order change. Spiritual awareness interventions, experiential exercises, and counter intuitive change strategies (Fraser and Solovey 2007; Isaiah 55.1–13) are programmed components of the reconciliation model.

As change may be very challenging, it should be noted that initiating the reconciliation process may temporarily increase distress. For instance, the challenge of entering into the forgiveness process, confession, or expressing laments may spark spiritual distress during this nine-week treatment. Nevertheless, while the veteran or soldier encounters the spiritual crucible, it is recognized that all clients are in a non-linear holding environment. During this period, it is assumed that a spiritual awareness breakthrough may emerge at any one of three Movements of treatment. Even still, such a breakthrough at any point in this transdiagnostic process will always need to revert back to examination of one's past which must be reconciled. Reconciling one's past begins through spiritual awareness, meaning-making, and correcting of maladaptive coping strategies.

The theory and technique (methodology) for change and healing may be explained using the fire triangle as metaphor. The fire tetrahedron asserts that it takes the three elements of heat, oxygen, and fuel (or an ignition source) to start and sustain a fire. Removal of any one element denies the sufficient conditions required to maintain the fire. If any one element is removed, the fire is extinguished. Similarly, the moral injury reconciliation therapeutic triad simply believes that at whatever point the veteran or active-duty member responds therapeutically, in theory, corrective change and healing begins. For example, should a client find a new appreciation for a loved one in the "here-and-now" of Movement II or find "hope" in the altruistic activities of Movement III, second-order change (or transformation) may be said to have begun.

However, the experienced caregiver will stay alert to ensure that any new focus for a client's activity is not an avoidance strategy, but that the reconciliation process is truly in motion. Avoidance strategies are used to escape the spiritual crucible where the tension of accommodation, new learning, and meaning-making takes place. And though moral injury can never be fully repaired or extinguished, new meaning may emerge despite the invisible war-wounds. In this way, the reconciliation methodology may continue and transformation may ensue.

In simple terms, Movement I of the therapeutic process (Figure 3.4) begins with a focus on self and encourages spiritual awareness through experiential exercises. These skills are designed to help veterans and servicemembers become more accustomed to noticing self with all its feelings and sensations—no matter their intensity. This is the encounter with the spiritual crucible whereby the morally injurious event is confronted. Movement I goes on to use such Phase 1 transitional themes as the lament, confession, forgiveness processing, or humility for the exposure feature. Training to become more self-conscious of bodily stimuli in response to the past or the current spiritual distress of moral injury is emphasized to increase stress tolerance.

Movement II (*world*) and Phase 2 themes reinforce the absolute necessity of relationships (Tick 2005; Litz *et al.* 2009; Hoge 2010; Nash and Litz 2013; Sherman 2015; Litz *et al.* 2016). While reintegration back into civilian life may prove difficult, consolidation of social support networks is prized. Once a spiritual awareness of self is established, a key competency leading back into community is communication skills training. Communication stress styles (Satir, Stachowiak, and Taschman 1994) and emotional intelligence (Goleman 2006) proficiencies are part of this methodology.

The third and final movement (with its third-stage transitional themes) involves the future and encourages altruism. It is hypothesized that as veterans or servicemembers increase in spiritual awareness and self-confidence, their new-found identity better accommodates stress and tends to avoid isolation. Thus, internalizing and responding to the needs of others generates a form of selflessness often expressed as meaning and life-purpose. This may promote an other-focused awareness that may allow clients the opportunity to step outside "self" to accomplish virtuous acts. Such behaviors are believed to be at least one marker signifying healing and spiritual transformation. This milestone is considered to be second-order change and may be achieved through a combination of spiritual awareness skills and the intentionality of the repeated spiritual disciplines (habitualization) for corrective behavior modification.

Ritual healing and reintegration

Although war is never to be glorified, unfortunately there are times when it becomes all too necessary and right. Brinkmanship or passivity are only political devices rooted in a specific worldview. Exclusive use of either is seldom effective or wise. Therefore, since war may be inevitable, two rituals are recommended so that veterans and warfighters regain their spiritual equilibrium. One is a community reintegration event to acknowledge the warriors' contribution to their society, and the other is a form of ritual cleansing to designate a clear endpoint of warfighting and military status and a beginning of a new identity and reconciled self.

Demarcation is needed for adjustments of one's spiritual economy once discharged from active duty. Knowledge of this landmark is a necessary transaction in order to reorient life themes and meaning-making systems. While on active duty, military bearing is what makes a successful servicemember. Nevertheless, a military mindset generally needs to be deconstructed as certain unneeded skills are no longer compatible and may be destructive within a civilian context. For example, hypervigilance, continued practice of peak shooting or driving skills, or maintaining an exaggerated mistrust of others.

However, the convertible qualities such as selflessness or courage are to be cultivated. The reconciliation process would surprisingly discourage attempts to forget military service. In fact, as part of the spiritual crucible, clients are highly encouraged to remember morally injurious events and trauma—even the most traumatic ones. Recovery is about making sense of one's new civilian status while establishing one's own new identity. Such points of demarcation may be satisfied through ritual cleansing, purification, and reintegration strategies.

While there are several strategies to enact reintegration and ritual cleansings, one of the most important features of any reintegration process is to address the spiritual component of a veteran or servicemember. It should be echoed that because active-duty personnel can again be deployed, they can never actually experience community reintegration or the necessary spiritual cleansing until discharged. Any effort to approximate real transformation would seem to only frustrate reconciliation processing.

For ritual cleansing and community reintegrating strategies, the following references may be of support: Tick's *War and the Soul* (2005), Sloan and Friedman's *After the War Zone* (2009), Hoge's *Once a Warrior—Always a Warrior* (2010), Sherman's *Afterwar* (2015), and Schiraldi's *The Post-Traumatic Stress Disorder Sourcebook* (2016).

Assessment guidance

The assessment process can be said to begin upon first knowledge of a morally wounded client (see Figure 3.2 earlier). There is much to consider, even our own bias and cultural factors. Nevertheless, while no therapist can completely remove such predispositions, the veteran's or servicemember's care must be given primary consideration. This step is also taken so that a more complete clinical picture develops using the client's available assessment data and story.

Still, the medical and scientific communities generally appear to default to quantitative measures and symptom reduction treatment protocols. This may be a responsible process. However, a rigid adherence to this practice may tend to dismiss a wealth of knowledge from case studies, story, qualitative research, and personal observations (Litz *et al.* 2009; Yan 2016). For this reason, the following assessment principles of this methodology are provided to expand the assessment structure in order to understand the invisible wounds and "hear" a greater story playing out in the lives of clients.

Assessment Principle 1

We may know, but perhaps soon forget, that the provider is being assessed too. As a spiritual caregiver or therapist, the moment the 1:1 or group encounter begins, the spider web of evaluation takes shape.

The back-and-forth assessments commence, and continue throughout the therapeutic process. Clients may muse: "How old is he?" Or: "What's her life experience?" Other questions may be: "What does he know about the military?" Or: "Has she ever served?" It is likely, too, that veterans and servicemembers would even assess and make judgments about the provider's physique, eating habits, family background, hair, lifestyle, neatness of appearance, manner of speech, etc. This assertion suggests that a caregiver's persona should not detract from the spiritual alliance. Our non-verbal communications and physical presentation should reflect that we understand this dynamic and we intend to bring credibility and hope to the therapeutic process.

Assessment Principle 2

While a veteran or servicemember may first demonstrate corrective behaviors at Phase 2 or Phase 3, reconciliation of moral injury must clinically start with the past. Traumatic episodes are to be systematically exposed and processed from awareness to extinction. Finding a vehicle upon which to accommodate past trauma is a gateway to a "here-and-now" focused present and an expectant, hope-filled future. Such a vehicle may be found in one's faith, value system, or a relationship. Discovering and articulating one's meaning-making system is an objective of the reconciliation model.

Assessment Principle 3

Assessment Principle 3 understands that many diagnosed disorders have root in a person's limited spiritual formation and their view of self. Spiritual formation is the operationalization of specific disciplines. It is thought that formation exercises achieve second-order change which is a major transformation mechanism of this treatment methodology. Formation involves habit training as well as systematic patterning for reaching emotional, spiritual, physical, and whole-life transformation. Habitualizations into cognitive and behavioral adjustments are also thought necessary. Limited spiritual formation is believed to be partially responsible for a general and chronic disappointment with life and low measures on *hope* assessment scales. Spiritual growth should be considered an iterative, enduring process of new behaviors thought to hasten symptom reduction and correct dysfunctional cognitive alterations.

In language perhaps familiar to mental health professionals, these changes may be brought about by first helping to *shape* transformation through "successive approximations" (Olson and Hergenhahn 2013, p.80) of both new thinking and systematically applied behavioral applications. Combined, reformulated beliefs and incremental behavior patterns *re-code* one's system. This is accomplished by: reading, prayer, worship, reflecting on personal or family goals, lifestyle changes (especially sleep hygiene, activity/recreation, and nutrition), values development, or service to others.

Basic guidance in the spiritual formation process is two-fold. The following example may provide a shaping illustration. First, the provider might include gently directing/instructing a client in forgiveness processing. Second, the physical components of the formation process are stressed, which are habit training and encouraging lifestyle change (e.g. sleep hygiene). Then, by their completing one-third of the reflection homework assignments (for instance), getting five hours' sleep (out of eight), or eating, say, ten semi-nutritious meals throughout the week out of a possible 21, a pattern for change may be established. And by repeated chaining or "secondary reinforcements," it is thought that ongoing change occurs (Olson and Hergenhahn 2013, pp.84–85).

The facilitator who verbally rewards a client for her continual completion of all assignments would be a likely example of one using the chaining process as part of the spiritual growth and learning continuum. Successful habitualization during reconciliation activities is a fundamental aspect of this treatment methodology. It anticipates a demonstration of the capital virtues of love, joy, peace, patience (or longsuffering), kindness, goodness, faithfulness, gentleness, and self-control (self-mastery) (Galatians 5.20–21).

The ancient philosopher Aristotle (384–322 B.C.E.) provides helpful insights into character transformation. He is credited with saying: "We are what we repeatedly do. Excellence, therefore, is not an act, but a habit." Lifelong spiritual formation must use sacred literature to provide the roadmap and context for synthesizing life issues unto reconciliation themes. And through the formation of one's developing existential perspectives, second-order transformation may be achieved through the habits that are behavior-altering.

Assessment Principle 4

Effective transformation is believed possible through viewing one's life from a 35-thousand-foot vantage point. Somewhere around 35-thousand feet, it is said that one can see the curvature of the earth. When applied to life, it is thought to be important to see where life begins to bend and significant events arise. But it is not just identifying the curves of life that matter, but rather the ability to identify and utilize one's resources that assist in making sense of the distortions and corresponding correctives. These are most advantageous.

This principle may also be applied where one's life may have changed through trauma; particularly before one entered military service or after being discharged. These transitional landmarks are deemed to be sentinel events. Such experiences may often announce monumental transitions from one state to another. Moving from a state of spiritual calm into one of spiritual disequilibrium (e.g. moral injury) would be an example. Though often defined in the negative, morally injurious events can transition into opportunities for personal growth, religious/spiritual conservation, or a return to one's religious roots (Pargament 2011).

Assessment Principle 5

Finally, finding the *lament* (or prime complaint) is the key to Assessment Principle 5. Often, there are myriad complaints that are part of the moral injury syndrome. However, the clinician's task is to help facilitate articulation of the primary issue. During assessment, deep listening skills will be essential in drawing out the spiritual (existential) and psychic (emotional, intrapersonal) pain found in the veteran's or servicemember's story.

SPIRITUAL DISTRESS, MORAL INJURY, AND CASE CONCEPTUALIZATION

It starts with pain. Understanding this basic human response to spiritual distress provides the clinical roadmap for alleviating veterans' or servicemembers' moral injury. Such a process guides follow-on assessment and treatment considerations. It is also a theoretical heading. A heading likely to spot developmental and behavioral patterns, spotlighting a client's culture, beliefs, experiences, thinking processes, and subsequent responses to moral transgressions.

Case conceptualization is also how the pastoral care professional broadly envisions the specific applications of therapeutics that will be brought to bear during the reconciliation process's two-step formulation.

First, this practitioner's guide believes that case conceptualization includes the simultaneous tasks of: 1) conducting the theory-informed assessment of individual demographics (e.g. the veteran's or warfighter's lament, background information, family systemic assessment, cultural features, and the client's perspective and worldview); and 2) making the diagnostic clinical assessment (e.g. the monitoring of the client's safety, relevant medical/psychiatric features, the mental status exam, or social support issues outside the scope of practice) a part of the follow-up treatment implementation (Gehart 2010). From this dual-track data collection stream, the clinician makes a hypothesis on how best to "use the available contextual and diagnostic information in developing a comprehensive treatment plan that is informed by the individual's cultural and social context" (APA 2013, p.19).

Knowledge that many veterans and service members have a spiritual history is of note and may be a potential source of healing. This is the hoped-for unifying mechanism in moral injury reconciliation's transdiagnostic approach. Such a belief is a guiding feature for case conceptualization. Thus, case conceptualization regards moral injury and the phenomenology of war. These two aspects add to the complexity of each clinician's case. Awareness of a client's spiritual struggle informs those decisions that help construct individual and/or group care plans and the specific spiritual pathways that lead to transformation.

However, because the moral injury reconciliation process is a holistic and not a medical model or a *symptom-focused approach*, by necessity and for the purpose of conceptualization, the moral injury diagnostic begins with *origins*. Basic case conceptualization for the moral injury reconciliation process begins with the origins of a client's spiritual distress, be it childhood, teenage, military, or post-military trauma.

Since veterans and active-duty personnel are a unique population, unique "chaplaincy care pathways" are required (Roberts 2012, p.354). Further, the clinician's embedded theme of *hopeful* expectations may add to the dynamic of patient–client interactions during the client's story-telling. Thus, despite the fact some have no formal affiliation to a denomination or religious orthodoxy, some willingly subordinate themselves to oaths or the religious codes of sacred literature and its existential realities that are at least marginally derived from religious doctrines. Military service is a case in point. Figure 3.5 is moral injury reconciliation's case conceptualization model that may be useful in case construction.

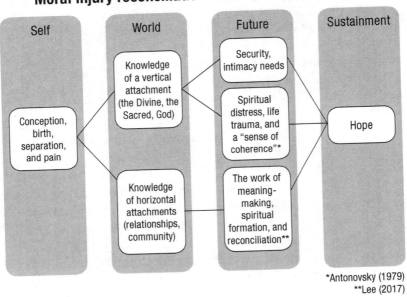

Moral injury reconciliation: Case conceptualization

*Antonovsky (1979)
**Lee (2017)

Figure 3.5 Moral injury reconciliation's case conceptualization

The moral injury reconciliation model views life beginning at conception. And from this point, a certain undeniable reality of pain and difficulty in life should be affirmed. Self-awareness is thought to highlight one's security requirements, meaning-making necessities, and specific attachment needs. Such becomes increasingly evident as the life-resources required to negotiate life's challenges.

For the purpose of case conceptualization, the reconciliation model has an affiliation with aspects of Bowlby's and Ainsworth's attachment theory (Bretherton 1992). While the reconciliation model would diverge at various points with Bowlby and Ainsworth, moral injury reconciliation's theory-informed case conceptualization holds the belief that humankind is inherently restless until we have re-attached (reconciled) with the supreme point of comfort and security (Augustine 397 C.E./1997, p.39).

In theory, humans desire a sense of coherence. The reconciliation model would posit that the quest to *detach* from the comprehensive idea of human self-sufficiency or independence is never fully achieved (nor ever actually desired). In fact, there is a propensity to *bond* to that which will soothe the deepest longing of the soul. As used in this book, "Attachment is limited to behavior normally directed towards someone conceived as better able to cope with the current situation" (Bowlby 1982, p.377).

Therefore, subsequent spiritual distress in the form of moral injury or traumatic stress duplicates pain and separation. This separation gives rise to the profound truth of our security needs and a want for the more comfortable and predictable. Failure to make sense of events creates spiritual disequilibrium, out of which functional impairments may occur. And hundreds of years after Augustine's 4th-century writings, others seem to acknowledge an inherent spiritual connection to the Divine. Granqvist, Mikulincer, and Shaver (2010), for example, suggest that "attachment theory and research provide a plausible framework for studying and understanding core aspects of many religions, particularly believers' perceptions of God or other supernatural beings and their own private relationships with these divine figures" (p.49).

MEANING-MAKING AND A SENSE OF COHERENCE

Finding meaning after a morally injurious event or trauma is critical. Global meaning and its beliefs, goals, and feelings (Pargament 1997) needs congruence with situational meaning (Park 2010). This seems to maintain spiritual equilibrium. Situational meaning is meaning in context relative to an event. An elaborate model has been developed to illustrate the complex sequence of meaning-making (Park 2010). The moral injury reconciliation model provides additional insight into an intricate structuring of human connecting of experiences as well as a concept for trauma relief.

As it seems apparent, recovery from moral injury or other trauma requires that the world make sense; there must be cogency. The reconciliation model values caregivers as agents in the meaning-making process. Therefore, trauma recovery efforts would find the *therapeutic alliance* of great value and to be developed upon first contact. Some have proposed the therapeutic alliance to be the greatest determinant of patient outcomes (Krupnick *et al.* 1996). However, others suggest that the veteran's or active-duty member's family and peer support groups (Lambert and Barley 2001) are the most influential predictor of outcomes. Whatever the case, a trusted family and social support network supporting the meaning-making efforts of a morally wounded client can prove to be of high value.

The reconciliation care model addresses the moral injury syndrome containing the variable expressions of physiological distress. As a moral injury and trauma recovery model, it accounts for the necessary meaning-making process and furnishes a means for the continued outworking of meaning in this treatment model. Simply put, it helps veterans or servicemembers *make sense* of their world using the client's inherent religious doctrines or values.

Therefore, Antonovsky's (1979) sense of coherence is adopted since there are many life examples of those who faced extreme personal (e.g. trauma, ill-health) and environmental (e.g. slavery, concentration camps) stressors yet somehow managed to endure and, in turn, thrive. Connected to how one views their world (coherence), specific components were found to augment resilience. Such constellations of factors were termed generalized resistance resources (Antonovsky 1979). Together, one's sense of coherence and their generalized resistance resources pushed individuals and/or groups toward the healthy end of the continuum of wellness. Such a structure may be shown to build stability and predictable order in life, considering the steep challenges they may have faced. A common thread of these resources was found to be that they collectively facilitate meaning-making in our world where stressors are pervasive, unending, and inherent.

From intake to termination, the reconciliation model casts a wide net for information-gathering and is constantly assessing the global features of a client's environment. It also assumes that what may be a critical element of change for one veteran or servicemember may not necessarily be the mechanism for change in another. To this end, this model looks at the structure of an assortment of potential resource helps. It considers the utility and availability of the client's tangible or intangible supports.

Generalized resistance resources support, sustain, and provide resilience factors identified by Antonovsky (1979). The moral injury reconciliation model considers a client's collective level and variety of resources which are part of their orientation to health or what are part of the *salutogenic* model of health (Antonovsky 1987). The salutogenic model is counterintuitive to what seems to be the prevailing *pathogenic*, stress-avoidance, or disease-focused approach to healthcare. The pathogenic model would appear to dominate healthcare even though stress and disease are ubiquitous to humankind and generally unavoidable. In other words, since dis-ease and germs are not likely to vanish, it might be asked whether the healthcare focus should be so dedicated to dis-ease eradication. Or, is it prudent to investigate what mechanisms keep people well despite the all-encompassing presence of disease?

The reconciliation model suggests that instead of chasing and attempting to conquer every ailment, increased attention should be given to the features that maintain health even though dis-ease and pain will be with us. And those with the ability to make use of one's life resources (or generalized resistance resources) and assemble a life orientation (or sense of coherence) will generally demonstrate high levels of resilience (Antonovsky 1979). This collective helps us to make sense of life trauma and suggests methods for living in spite of a stress-filled world. This is a basic life tenet sacred literature reiterates.

Our general resistance resources in some ways appear to create a sense of coherence. As a concept, a sense of coherence is defined as "a generalized orientation toward the world which perceives it, on a continuum, as comprehensible, manageable, and meaningful" (Antonovsky 1996, p.15). Those found with a strong sense of coherence (i.e. "a generalized, pervasive orientation") were found to be high in these three components. These unified facets which "facilitate effective tension management" (Antonovsky 1979, p.99) are, first, a life that has a reasonable degree of predictability despite its surprises; it is a world that is comprehensible. Essentially, life is said to have comprehensibility when in its cognitive judgment it may consent that "things will work out as well as can reasonably be expected." It does not imply one is in "control" (Antonovsky 1979, p.123), but has a "solid capacity to judge reality" (p.127).

Next, manageability is where adequate resources are available and capable of meeting the demands of life. Such resources may be in one's possessions or in the possession of "one's spouse, friends... God...physician—whom one feels one can count on, whom one trusts" (Antonovsky 1987, p.18). Here, Bowlby's attachment theory (1973, 1982) is most relevant. And those who believe life is manageable are also less inclined to see themselves as a victim when treated unfairly.

Finally, even though quantitative, measurable features are part of the comprehensible aspects of life, a more emotionally grounded and motivational element is characteristic of a life found to have elements of life's meaningfulness. Meaningfulness speaks of feeling that life "makes sense emotionally…and [that the] demands posed by living are worth investing energy in" (Antonovsky 1979, p.18).

THE MORAL INJURY RECONCILIATION THERAPEUTIC STRUCTURE

A final core feature of the moral injury reconciliation model is a structure for viewing and enacting the entire reconciliation process. Veterans and active-duty personnel may begin reconciliation and the meaning-making process of whatever moral injury or posttraumatic stress they face. Figure 3.6 is the full representation of the active components for change—starting with spiritual distress.

The core change components include the domains of moral injury assessment (Figure 3.1; see earlier), moral injury reconciliation's transdiagnostic paradigm (Figure 3.2; see earlier), the therapeutic triad (Figure 3.4; see earlier), and the case conceptualization model (Figure 3.5; see earlier) contained in the therapeutic structure of Figure 3.6. In effect, a moral and trauma treatment model is available for a pastoral care provider's assessment, diagnosis, and treatment of a client's sense of coherence—all part of the assessment, case conceptualization, and treatment process.

Moral injury reconciliation (MIR): Therapeutic structure

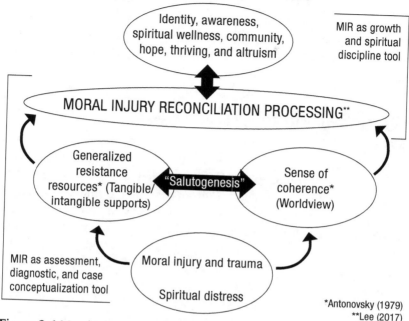

Figure 3.6 Moral injury reconciliation's therapeutic structure

In simple terms, the moral injury reconciliation model is used as a transdiagnostic or unified utility to treat the full range of clinical problems and the management of such problems from start to finish.

ASSESSMENT AND OBSERVATIONS

It seems reasonable that manifestations of moral injury be recognized when one has served beyond their initial boot camp experience and has had a morally injurious episode sometime thereafter. Figure 3.6 above is designed to help the clinician deliver an effective treatment to reconcile moral injury and other trauma occurrences. This author's training, education, and experience has enabled new thinking to view moral injury and traumatic stress from different levels. This treatment is activated upon knowledge of the lament.

The lament is the essence of the spiritual harm behind the hurt. Lamentations (or "loud cries") are the expressions of anguish that indicate a spiritual struggle. This state is generally accompanied by a change of *mood* or the "pervasive and sustained emotion that colors the perception of the world" (APA 2013, p.824). This mood change often disrupts one's ability to effectively function in other areas of life. As a result, this author is satisfied that the intentional engagement with the interventions outlined will aid in the mitigation of moral injury and traumatic stress. The next step is clinical trials for this treatment methodology.

MORAL INJURY RECONCILIATION GOALS

Although there are themes and dimensions associated with the moral injury construct (Maguen and Litz 2012), correspondingly spiritual care remedies may be found within sacred literature to augment treatment options. The end result of the moral injury process is designed to produce second-order transformation through spiritual awareness and behavioral changes. This transformation is especially important since a loss of identity is often a critical undertaking as the veteran returns to civilian life.

From years of treating veterans and families experiencing moral injury or posttraumatic stress, it is evident that loss of identity emerges as a prominent challenge. For veterans who once held key leadership positions and have taken men and women in battle, moving back into civilian status may prove to show their sense of worth and function diminished. Part of this erosion of confidence may be borne along by a slower pace causing restlessness. To this end, pathways to healing include the spiritual disciplines.

What this model targets for reconciliation (synthesis) is first a rejoining of one's past to their meaning-making system (orthodoxy). Next, it uses the standards dictated in their meaning-making system to transform their lives through new thinking and behavior modifications (orthopraxy). Prepared with the aforementioned information, the larger work of moral injury reconciliation may commence. However, since mere symptom reduction is not the focus of this model, how will the spiritual care provider proceed? This is the subject of the following chapters.

SUMMARY

This chapter supplied the methodology (philosophy and methods) of the moral injury reconciliation model. As the challenges of caregiving are vast and multidimensional, a transdiagnostic paradigm is offered to reduce the burden on mental healthcare while addressing the moral injury spectrum. A transdiagnostic or unified approach hopes to shrink the surplus of disorder-specific treatments and treatment manuals. And since moral injury and other traumas may present common symptoms, the moral injury reconciliation treatment model is provided to combine assessment methods, diagnostic insights, and case conceptualization processes.

Although there is wide clinical variability in stress and trauma-related presentations, the moral injury reconciliation model is a multi-faceted tool believed capable of delivering sound treatment protocols. Additionally, it may also serve as a transformation, sustainment, and hope-generating framework. Toward this goal, the moral injury assessment domains were constructed so that a transdiagnostic paradigm and therapeutic triad emerges. Treating military stress-related problems and other spiritual and mental health concerns is further explored in Part II. Chapter 4 is where the moral injury reconciliation process begins.

COURSE OF TREATMENT

PREPARING THE HOLDING ENVIRONMENT
BEGINNING THE MORAL INJURY RECONCILIATION PROCESS

SESSION 1

Now that the reconciliation methodology has been provided, treatment may begin. Establishing a quality spiritual alliance may contribute to a client's overall wellness. Whether this first session is part of a group, family, or individual modality, the initial face-to-face contact will say much about subsequent treatment success. The moral injury reconciliation approach emphasizes the value of the alliance and encourages the provider to build a strong healing environment. So long as the core structure of this model's three Movements and the integrity of the religious/spiritual framework remains in place, the provider has liberty to create that which secures intended outcomes. Beginning a treatment program requires trust.

To achieve these outcomes, the provider must work to meet treatment goals for second-order change. That is to say, an intentional focus on credibility and the development of trust are essential caregiver objectives in the overall treatment design. Taken together, a trusted holding environment (i.e. the religious/spiritual care community) is more apt to restore that which is likely at the core of moral injury—broken trust.

What distinguishes a religious/spiritual care community from a traditional mental health setting is client transformation through spiritual formation. Through habit training, a client's spiritual growth equips them to heal themselves for symptom reduction and behavior alterations. Habit training also further promotes an orientation towards lifelong spiritual growth. Since this framework recognizes moral injury and trauma as a primary result of spiritual distress, developing one's spiritual nature to combat such distress is part of the therapeutic goal. For this reason, moral injury reconciliation's framework subscribes to theistic psychotherapy.

If reconciliation is to begin, the starting point is found where the client and therapist meet. Movement I opens the trust-building. Trust deficits can destroy attempts to mitigate the invisible wounds of war, thus undermining the entire reconciliation process. In relation to the client's goals, the caregiver's goals are considerable. For where there is moral injury, mistrust and suspicion are generally present within the veteran or servicemember. Compounding this challenge may be an encounter whereby betrayal is the central theme for the veteran or warfighter. Betrayal by a superior or unit organization would make developing the holding environment more challenging as the phenomenology of war and the military culture are descriptive features of this unique population.

Disregarding the holding environment equates to failed therapy and a clinical worsening caused by the clinician (i.e. *iatrogenic effect*). Note that, for the veteran, betrayal is equated to a moral danger which is processed as a physical danger. Thus, the moral syndrome of isolation or failed relationships breeds mistrust of others (Shay and Munroe 1999). On the other hand, as the veteran provider dynamic is a powerful interchange that leaves little room for error, supporters who recognize this delicate balance share that

> the clinician has *ideals* of professional conduct, [and] feels justifiably proud of having fulfilled ambitions to attain a responsible job title... [but] the normal mental health professional takes offense at being treated as a question mark rather than as an established certainty... The predictable result is a counter-transference narcissistic rage... [that] makes it easy to apply derogatory labels, such as "borderline," "character disordered," "anti-social," "...and hopelessly untreatable." (Shay and Munroe 1999, p.9; emphasis original)

Since the reconciliation model is based on a religious/spiritual framework, this practitioner's guide interrupts its direct launch into its therapeutic techniques so that the religious/spiritual domain has time to be appreciated. Appropriate considerations would be the caregiver's therapeutic or pastoral presence. With this scenario in mind, this chapter was written to reinforce the importance of the spiritual alliance which is the essence of a well-formed holding environment. This development sets the stage for all that follows. Extra care, then, is needed when forming such a critical interpersonal bond.

THE NATURE OF THE HOLDING ENVIRONMENT: A SPIRITUAL CONSTRUCTION

The spiritual alliance is that conscious and active connection between the provider and client that advances the development of a client's spiritual nature. The quality of the holding environment allows socialization into the reconciliation process. Building a holding environment where credibility and trust are present requires at least two features: a spiritual alliance and a sense of connectedness with diverse, unique populations.

First, it is hoped that the caregiver not only pays attention to their own spiritual health—the vertical and existential planes—but also uses their understanding of spiritual connectedness to cultivate the spiritual care community. Considering that only qualified spiritual care providers (or clinicians) are to administer reconciliation therapy, techniques for achieving spiritual care competencies is beyond the scope of this book. Nevertheless, the spiritual disciplines should be familiar interventions so that spiritual development and behavioral adjustments ensue.

Since the holding environment is a spiritual construction, the caregiver therefore molds the environment in which moral injury reconciliation takes place. This model views the development of the spiritual alliance not so much an overt act, but rather the intentional care given to the construction of such connections. For instance, it would seem difficult to "tell" clients that "a spiritual alliance exists." Rather, developing the spiritual alliance requires a certain persona of spiritual maturity, and for these reasons clinicians without firm credentials may perhaps be uncomfortable facilitators. Nevertheless, over time, this maturity, can evolve into an enlightened state where a deeper level of credibility and trust can develop. Such spiritual growth may become an almost automatic response to routine person-to-person contacts.

To develop this higher level of spiritual awareness, the providers are encouraged to first have a keen knowledge of self and a widespread exposure to others—particularly individuals and groups of other cultures. This exposure is part of a wealth of experience in self-expression—one-being-to-another. And for those who grew up in a multicultural environment or have military service, a distinct advantage is likely.

Second, developing this alliance with diverse populations may be achieved by the client's "buy-in" to the spiritual merger. Often, this buy-in is no more than a "gut feeling" and may usually be understood as a sensing or feeling-state demonstrated through non-verbal communications (e.g. good eye contact) or cooperation during group activities. It is the provider's persona and how others may be affected by our presence that matters. And, regarding diversity issues, some cultures are more highly sensitive to this phenomenon. Cultural insensitivity often triggers a spiritual alarm and resistance (McGoldrick, Giordano, and Garcia-Preto 2005; Boyd-Franklin 2006; Lessem and Schieffer 2008). Positive traits for the provider in building the spiritual alliance include: love of self and love for others, humility, self-knowledge, patience (longsuffering), hopefulness, passion, and self-confidence.

PRESENTING THE MORAL INJURY
RECONCILIATION MODEL: PRELIMINARIES

The first meeting is the introduction and orientation session. It also includes the course overview and the facilitator's motivational statement. This session is part of Movement I, Phase 1, and the provider's first opportunity to construct the religious/spiritual community. And as the initial session begins, the group leader is not only fabricating the holding environment, but is working to build the group culture with its "unwritten code of behavioral rules and norms" as well (Yalom with Leszcz 2005, pp.120–121).

Movement I's focus is self. Self is the context of the movement, while the phase refers to the collection of those specific themes (e.g. forgiveness, humility) serving as the transitional vehicles used in the experiential process. Such themes are the necessary features of each movement and are designed to set the spiritual economy of each client in motion. Once the theme is introduced, the provider turns the theme into an experiential encounter (exposure) to elicit change. The starting point of the reconciliation process is marked in Figure 4.1. This mark is where the actionable processes start and it starts, in the building of the religious/spiritual community.

The moral injury reconciliation therapeutic triad

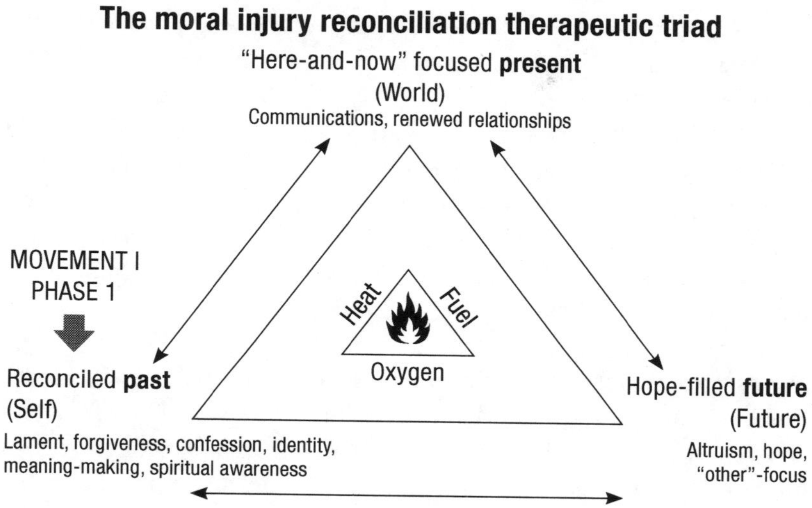

Figure 4.1 The moral injury reconciliation therapeutic triad. Adapted from Beck *et al.* (1979) *Cognitive Therapy of Depression*. Copyright Guilford Press. Adapted with permission of Guilford Press.

The holding environment is a psychoanalytic concept and term coined by Winnicott (1960), yet such a concept is ancient in practice. Those from a religious/spiritual community may be more familiar with other language such as "flock" or other nurturing configurations (Genesis 12.1–3, 45.3–11, 50.19–21; Exodus 3.10–12; Judges 2.16; Matthew 26.31; Acts 20.28–29; 1 Peter 5.2–3). According to Winnicott, this environment refers to one of the three "overlapping stages" of "satisfactory" parental care, which are: "a) holding, b) mother and infant living together...the father's function (of dealing with the environment for the mother) is not known to the infant, and c) father, mother, and infant all...living together" (Winnicott 1960, p.588).

On the other hand, a holding environment may also be said to be *"any relationship in which one party has the power to hold the attention of another party and facilitate adaptive work. The holding environment can generate adaptive work because it contains and regulates the stresses that work generates"* (Heifetz 1994, pp.104–105; italics original). During the initial session, the provider and the veteran or servicemember come to reconcile the trauma of moral injury. The point at which the "trauma" occurs is what may also be called the adaptive challenge (Fraser and Solovey 2007).

The initial dynamic of the therapist–client encounter is a critical religious/spiritual one. This orientation places high value on the relationship and community dynamic for its ability to create a change-oriented atmosphere.

Therefore, the moral injury reconciliation therapy model would generally recommend against 1:1 therapy as the first treatment option. The group is thought to offer veterans or servicemembers greater opportunity to re-establish identity and an immediate place inside a safe community. Here, isolative behaviors and attendance requirements may reinforce social learning opportunities.

Additionally, research shows that "human-generated traumatic events carry a higher risk of developing Posttraumatic Stress Disorder (PTSD) than those exposed to other kinds of events" (Charuvastra and Cloitre 2008, p.301). Further, Charuvastra and Cloitre (2008) built a "social ecology" which integrated advances in the fields of developmental psychopathology, attachment theory, and social neuroscience. This resulted in a conceptual framework suggesting that "both PTSD risk and recovery are highly dependent on social phenomena" (p.301). And since morally injurious episodes almost always involve others (Litz *et al.* 2009, p.699), reestablishing social bonds is of significance.

A strong community and social support network would also seem to serve as a protective factor against suicide or other self-destructive behaviors. Additionally, those clients daring to come to Group are perhaps more highly motivated. In fact, they may exhibit the urgency required to do the necessary adaptive work (Heifetz 1994) for the most complete transformation. Moral injury reconciliation also believes that should a veteran or active-duty member elect to attend Group, they are likely to be at a different place on the "health–disease continuum" (Antonovsky 1979, p.16) if their condition were assessed. They may also tend toward readjustment progression and possibly ready to make those corrective behavior and core belief transactions sooner. This degree of enthusiasm may augment their sense of identity and serve to develop their sense of belonging to the developing religious/spiritual community.

As mentioned, in establishing the holding environment, clinicians are encouraged to remember there are perhaps two aspects to keep in mind during the preparatory steps of therapy. One is to hold and further develop credibility. The other is to create an atmosphere of trust. Taken together, these issues orient the group, individual, or family and may establish favorable conditions for a positive therapeutic holding climate. And for overall "group cohesiveness" (Yalom with Leszcz 2005, pp.54–55), it is trust and credibility that are indispensable in forming the culture of the holding environment.

MORAL INJURY RECONCILIATION: THE TRANSDIAGNOSTIC ADVANTAGE

The reconciliation model was constructed to be an effective therapy across a class of disorders. The etiology of several categories of mental health issues are believed to be of a spiritual nature and may develop into a spiritual struggle. Such distress is thought to cause disequilibrium between a morally injurious event and the failure to reconcile one's self to the traumatic episode. At the point where one's spiritual economy is unable to accommodate a spiritual wound, moral injury or posttraumatic stress may occur. And since "there is increasing evidence that some *DSM* disorders do not represent unique constructs and instead reflect relatively trivial variations in a common underlying syndrome" (Sauer-Zavala *et al.* 2017, p.128), moral injury reconciliation offers what is believed to be an appropriate and effective transdiagnostic treatment option.

This reconciliation model is changing the direction to make a necessary departure from the traditional medical models. A unified treatment protocol seems necessary. This new strategy is based on the following criteria. First, its foundation is a theistic psychotherapeutic orientation (Richards and Bergin 2005) and may be universally applied to several disorders irrespective of the religious/spiritual background or life-view of the client. Second, it is modular or able to be uniquely tailored to a specific person, group, or family. Lastly, the reconciliation model's religious/spiritual foundation believes that spiritual distress is the shared mechanism "implicated in the development and maintenance of certain classes of psychopathology" (Sauer-Zavala *et al.* 2017, p.129).

What this means is that the pastoral caregiver or therapist may direct treatment and tailor every treatment modality (e.g. individual, family, or Group) to the needs at the moment. No two individual or Group treatments need be the same so long as the reconciliation model's methodology is honored. This is part of the dynamic quality of this brand of therapy. What steers the Group treatment is the spiritual caregiver's reading and assessment of client problems and applying modular interventions to address the need(s). In large measure *story* guides the process, and for this reason seasoned spiritual care providers should conduct treatment.

Treatments are conducted by selecting the most accurate transitional theme (e.g. forgiveness, acquiring spiritual identity, hope) as the therapeutic vehicle for transformation. One client recently had such a problem issue that the transitional theme of "forgiveness" was selected to explore latent pain as a spot treatment while the Group benefitted concurrently. This can be an example of the modular feature of this design.

Therefore, the following presentation provides the template on how the reconciliation process should be conducted. It is not a specific step-by-step script. This allows the provider room to flex with the complex nature of individuals and the variability of comorbid presentations found across a range of disorders. However, since this is a holistic design and not a symptom-focused treatment, it will in some ways differ from a perhaps more familiar medical model of care.

PRESENTING THE MORAL INJURY RECONCILIATION MODEL

In the previous chapter, a methodology for securing second-order change was introduced. This methodology is a counterintuitive approach designed to reconcile morally injurious events. Such events are mitigated through spiritual awareness, exposure, and the religious/ spiritual discipline processing thought to establish new "meaning" (definition, valuation, or significance) and "purpose" (place, direction, reason, or function) in life.

Veterans' and servicemembers' milestones of this therapy include: 1) the identification and expressions of their lament; 2) acquiring "daring" (willingness) to expose their moral injury (or trauma) to transitional themes and the therapeutic process of reconciliation (accommodate, synthesize, or blend moral injury/trauma into "new thinking"). Other milestones are encouraged in order to make sense of past experiences, such as: 3) developing the capacity for "intentional" giving of one's attention to spiritual awareness; and 4) humility to acknowledge an inability to move forward.

There are still more objectives such as: 5) a client's affirmation that forgiveness, self-forgiveness, and anger (resolution) are often part of their spiritual struggle as well as potential spiritual healing pathways to recovery; 6) support for their reintegration through birthing their appropriate civilian identity and "new name" in view of their military service and transition back into civilian society; 7) active development and restoring trust, forming relationships, and community as an indispensable facet of spiritual transformation; 8) gaining knowledge and practice that resilience may be found in lifestyle change, particularly contained in the "Big 3" (sleep hygiene, activity/recreation, and nutrition); and 9) acknowledging that an active altruism or being other-focused is a key part of moral injury reconciliation's recovery technique. How these key pieces interlock will be subsequently explained. And as the physical self-care disciplines align with the spiritual–mental health components, change may occur. Figure 4.2 should help provide the therapist's direction for treatment.

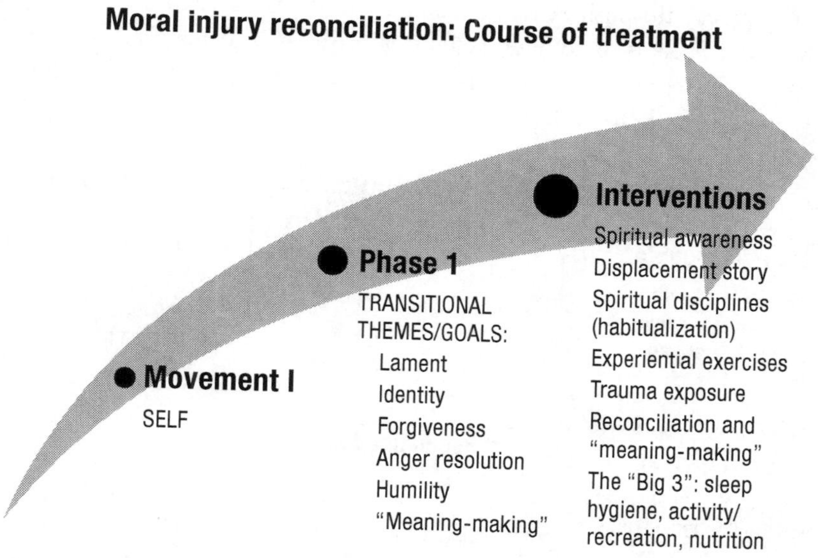

Moral injury reconciliation: Course of treatment

Interventions
Spiritual awareness
Displacement story
Spiritual disciplines
(habitualization)
Experiential exercises
Trauma exposure
Reconciliation and
"meaning-making"
The "Big 3": sleep
hygiene, activity/
recreation, nutrition

Phase 1
TRANSITIONAL
THEMES/GOALS:
Lament
Identity
Forgiveness
Anger resolution
Humility
"Meaning-making"

Movement I
SELF

Figure 4.2 Moral injury reconciliation's course of treatment—Movement I

Socialization into the moral injury reconciliation process

Contributing to spiritual wellness are the component resources of what have been called general resistance resources. These resources "facilitate effective tension management" (Antonovsky 1979, p.99) and are a companion resource to the integrating concept known as a sense of coherence (Antonovsky 1979, p.123). A sense of coherence is that "long-lasting way of seeing the world and one's life in it." A sense of coherence is determined to be a "crucial element" found in one's accumulated character qualities, their historical context, and their cultural influences (p.124). As the spiritual care provider's goals are to develop a client's spiritual nature, the clients involve themselves in the socialization of the new "self." This new state is equipping the client to manage tension and engage in lifestyle changes.

In the first session where trust and credibility are being assembled, it is helpful to inform Group members that they already have key components that contribute to their own healing (i.e. generalized resources and their sense of coherence) or those religious or secular values to help reconcile moral injury. As the socialization process progresses through the reconciliation model's Movements, the provider's task is to now help clients appropriate the necessary spiritual resources to sequence toward recovery. The sequence of transformation is shown in Figure 4.3.

Moral injury reconciliation: Sequence of transformation

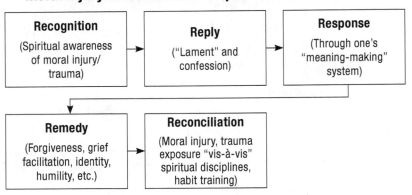

Figure 4.3 Moral injury reconciliation's transformation sequence

Hence, sequencing towards the healthy end of the healthcare continuum, one may find that the origins of health are bound in a sense of coherence (Antonovsky 1979). This is where belief affects one's view of the situation and attitude towards moral injury or trauma. For instance, believing that life is "manageable" may equate to one feeling less like a victim (Antonovsky 1987) when wronged. Antonovsky's *salutogenesis* attempts to ask and answer the question: "How do people manage to stay reasonably well despite the prevalence of 'disease' and trauma?" The response is the *salutogenesis* model of health (Antonovsky 1979). By incorporating these foundational elements into this model's introduction, veterans and military personnel may be found to be more hopeful in the knowledge that change is possible. With such hopefulness, clients may entertain the reconciliation model sooner, since the root issues of recovery and the furtherance of one's spiritual nature are addressed.

As the spiritual alliance develops through credibility and trust, the provider's pastoral care expertise is put to practice. Relying on spiritual and clinical experience, a caregiver may anticipate a likely first encounter described below. No matter the treatment modality, the dialogue might sound something like the featured exchange. However, since the Group configuration is recommended, the rest of moral injury reconciliation will address a Group scenario.

During a Group presentation, each member would have a moral injury reconciliation Group information folder and be guided through an accompanying PowerPoint presentation developed by the provider. As the Group process begins, the Group's generalized resistance resources and sense of coherence will be pointed out to the Group by the provider. This is done to bring about a sense of agency connected with hopefulness into a spiritual frame of mind.

Opening dialogue and connections

In this sample dialogue kick-off, the spiritual alliance-building process includes fashioning the holding environment and shaping the Group culture. It also includes helping the Group to sequence through the reconciliation structure for change (see Figure 4.2), which is: recognition (spiritual awareness of the distress), reply (expressing the lament or confessing one's pain as an act of humility), response (engaging one's meaning-making system), remedy (select a transitional theme such as forgiveness for exposure and assimilation), and reconciliation (the habitual training in new thinking and behaviors through spiritual discipline correctives).

Pre-course preparation will be addressed in more detail in Chapter 5 and will include: therapists' objectives, veterans' and service-members' objectives, environmental preparations, and completing the PCL-5.[1] The PCL-5 (Monthly) will be completed during Session 1 and the PCL-5 Weekly thereafter. The spiritual awareness/watchfulness (SA/W) exercises, moral injury reconciliation didactic, experiential activity, and the provision of homework assignments will complete the major tasks.

The introduction and orientation case examples are now presented as Session Number 1. You should expect a likely scenario at this session. (Note: All names are fictitious and the *sequence of transformation* is highlighted.)

Pastoral caregiver/therapist (bringing credibility and developing trust): Hi, thanks for coming. First off, I'd like to say it takes a great deal of strength to come in and be part of a Group. While I may not know every detail of what you've been through or the exact nature of your challenge, I think I do have an appreciation for being in the military, building resilience, and doing hard work. We're here to deal with moral injury and posttraumatic stress issues. We're also here to better understand how the unique culture of military life changes things and makes recovery so much more difficult. This difficulty may be your "identity" now that you're a civilian. I know many people have heard of PTSD or posttraumatic stress disorder, but let me ask, have any of you ever heard of moral injury?

First veteran: No, not really. My provider told me about it when I last saw her. She said that it might be good to talk to you.

Second veteran: I think it has something to do with right and wrong... morals or ethics stuff.

---

1   The PCL-5 (Posttraumatic Stress Disorder Checklist) is a self-report instrument found to reliably measure PTSD symptoms (Blevins *et al.* 2015). As previously discussed, moral injury may mimic symptoms similar to PTSD, and a morally injurious event may be present in conjunction with life-threat. The PCL-5 is used instead of the Moral Injury Event Scale (MIES) due to MIES measuring the *potentiality* and *perceptions* (Nash *et al.* 2013) of a moral injury occurrence, the dimensional nature of moral injury, and the clinician's general familiarity with the PCL-5.

Pastoral caregiver/therapist (bringing credibility and developing trust): Okay, thanks. That's why we're here: to discover more about who we are in light of our experiences and military background; our culture. *Moral injury* is a syndrome of guilt and shame. It can include anger, self-handicapping behaviors, and relational and religious/spiritual problems often encountered in the military. It's part of those actions that violate your sense of right and wrong. You don't necessarily have to be in combat either. For instance, *betrayal* by leadership or disproportionate violence may cause moral injury. The moral injury reconciliation model sees the root of moral injury as an assault against our spiritual nature. We'll be talking a great deal more about it, but I'd like to introduce myself by way of a little background.

Briefly, I'm a retired Navy SEAL. I served almost 26 years in the Navy, about 23 as a Naval Special Warfare operator. I've been in San Diego since 1979 when I started Basic Underwater Demolition/ SEAL Training in Coronado. I spent all my time here on the West Coast. My first assignment was with Underwater Demolition Team ELEVEN (UDT-11), which was later commissioned as SEAL Team FIVE. Later, I spent time and deployed as an SDV Team ONE (or SEAL Delivery Vehicle Team) operator of wet submersible mini-submarines and trained as a pilot and navigator. I then went on to serve at SEAL Team THREE, Special Boat Unit TWELVE, Special Boat Squadron ONE, and with the Naval Special Warfare Center. My training as a Chaplain didn't come out of a tragic combat experience or battlefield conversion. I was called to ministry at about ten years of age, and it was and is religious doctrine and spiritual strength that continues to sustain and help me make sense of a lot of the crazy things that go on day-by-day. This *resilience* factor and lifestyle change is also part of what we'll discuss during our time together.

Before we get into your introductions, I'd like to highlight at least *three goals of this course*. First, being able to clearly express what chaplains call your *lament* (or chief complaint). Being able to specifically say what's really troubling you is a good first start. Next, developing a sense of *daring* or a controlled yet ruthless effort to acknowledge what's wrong and doing that which will transform you and your community life. For instance, making intentional and lasting effort to develop your sense of "spiritual awareness" can pave the way for healing and getting some of the better things you want out of life. Third, making lifestyle changes that can start to pay resilience dividends *today* through what I call the "Big 3"; that is: sleep hygiene, activity and recreation, and proper nutrition.

Now, I'd like to hear about you; your *story*. What brings you here? Please talk about your *lament* or what's really troubling you, your branch of service, specific challenge, expectations of this Group (if any), and what you've done to try to cope with your challenges (such as kinds of groups, your willpower, trying to control your thoughts, drugs (legal and illegal), etc.).

First veteran (Jimmy): My name is Jimmy. I was in the Marines for six years. My memories tear me up; they just eat me up. It's about the lives I took. I can never forget. I've tried just about everything to forget... All I want is something different. (*RECOGNITION*)

Second veteran (Robert): I'm Robert; Army for eight years. I want peace... I still can't deal with my issues from the Army... I want to explode. I don't know where to go... I don't give a f--k. Life sucks... None of this stuff works. (*REPLY*)

Pastoral caregiver/therapist (aware that the veterans have completed the *recognition* and *reply* sequences (the other sequences follow later), so may say the following): I hear you... Thanks for your responses; again, I say it takes "daring" to come into a Group of strangers to talk. But we're not entirely strangers, because we have the military culture out of which we came. All of you have expressed various elements of moral injury and/or other trauma. In simple terms, moral injury occurs when one's moral and ethical codes have been violated. Things you may have done or the things you failed to do can set in motion a syndrome of emotional and behavioral symptoms. The key word in the title of this therapy is *reconciliation*. This Group may help you accommodate your morally injurious experiences so that you're able to "make sense" of them using *resources* you already have. Reconciling morally injurious episodes may also help us to make better choices too.

Using *generalized resistance resources* (explained), this system may help you further develop what's called a *sense of coherence* (worldview). Within moral injury there are themes. The themes are betrayal, disproportionate violence, incidents involving civilians, and within-rank violence (e.g. MST, friendly fire), which all contribute to the moral injury syndrome. And without treatment, things don't often get better...

The reconciliation process is broken down into three parts or *Movements*. Movement (or the point of focus) through each segment should increase your *spiritual awareness* across the three domains. These divisions are *self, world,* and the *future,* in the hopes of breaking the downward trajectory of maladjusted behaviors. We start with Movement I—*self* (therapist refers to moral injury reconciliation's therapeutic triad graphic of the PowerPoint presentation). I say "spiritual awareness" and not simply "understanding" or "knowledge" because this process is about your being, your essence; your spiritual nature. It's about you consciously giving your attention to the inside of who you are. It's about feeling and sensing any discomfort or anxiety, yet *not* running from uncomfortable thoughts, but confronting and acknowledging them. By doing this you simply agree that your mind is capable of such thoughts, but also saying I can tolerate "bad thoughts." And, it might even surprise you to learn that this process isn't a *passive* activity. You can grow stronger in so many different ways as you harness those resilience resources you already have and maybe even used during military service. Yes! Question?

Third veteran (Joseph): Will we talk about *religion*?

Pastoral caregiver/therapist: Well, yes and no. What I mean is that when I speak of *your* "meaning-making" system, this may be equivalent to one's religious beliefs, life philosophy, or simply how you *make sense* of the world. You may hear me use the term "sense of coherence." It's roughly equivalent to whatever system we use to "connect" pieces of various events in life or how you organize and code our world to determine good or bad; right or wrong. In fact, you're probably here because your life is currently to some degree "incoherent." It's interesting that sometimes our life philosophy may even be derived from say "the golden rule"; a song or movie, but these constructions can often be traced back to a specific philosophy, worldview, or religious belief. And even if someone were to say, "I don't have one," then we might discuss how others have found great healing to their lives once they've decided to stand on certain beliefs and principles. This can give their world a particular structure or "coherence." Selecting a meaning-making system is necessary so that symptom relief is experienced as the reconciliation process completes its three Movements. It is helpful to further explore and develop more elaborate articles of faith to move successfully through life.

Finally, before we close, I'd like to show you what's called a *displacement story*. We'll use these to help more clearly demonstrate and actually practice concepts like *spiritual awareness*. Talking about spiritual issues can be difficult because of the many ideas about what it is, but these short video clips should give clues. These clips aren't for entertainment, but shown so that you can personalize, find, or go deeper into "self." They can help provide space to reflect upon a situation perhaps close to your own, but at a distance so that you can "see" options or reflect on how you might respond. It is part of social learning. They also help you practice how you might feel about a situation, or "see" yourself making choices without being too caught up in the *content* of the issue. After we watch the clip, we'll discuss your reactions, then talk briefly about homework. (Show video clip.)

The moral injury reconciliation model allows each provider the freedom to select video clips most appropriate for their particular Group or situation. This is the *modular feature* of its transdiagnostic design. At the end of the showing, the care provider might ask the Group something like: "What is going on in that scene?" Or: "What feelings or raw emotions do you think is going on inside each person involved?" "How do you or don't you relate?" Take some time to get reactions to the video. It is common for an awkward silence or some discomfort to prevail; that is to be expected.

It is useful to allow this "silence" to continue for several moments as the Group wrestles internally with their own mild tension. Stop and process it. What were you feeling? This is all part of helping them to feel, sense, or *notice* how they react in various situations. This is part of the *spiritual discipline* of cultivating spiritual awareness while processing feelings and emotions in the moment and making corresponding choices. This questioning process may be followed after the showing of other clips throughout the program. All responses should be in the form of "I-statement." It is common to hear the following reactions:

First veteran: Well, it seems like even if you're in a bad place, no matter where you are, you can do something about it. It's how you react on the inside. I have "say-so" about how I respond.

Second veteran: Yeh, that guy was trying to show them that they don't need to think like they want them to think; to control them and keep them down. I've had a similar thing happen and I felt like crap, but I think differently; if you have "hope," things change. Things can be different even if you're in a prison.

After taking a few comments, summarize and return to a brief closing statement about the purpose and goals of the reconciliation process. As the pastoral care provider, the object of this position is to consistently infuse a sense of realistic hope for change and improvement. Such change may even start immediately through the veterans' or servicemembers' lifestyle choices and their level of "daring" to think differently and respond in counterintuitive ways. Their new-found choices are part of this therapeutic response. The remaining sequence milestones (i.e. *reply*, *response*, *remedy*, and *reconciliation*) should be reached in subsequent sessions and will be the focus of the following chapters.

Finally, homework will be assigned at the close of each session and is an essential part of the reconciliation model through *shaping*. In the pastoral care world, the *exposure* or the uncovering of one's transgression in the form of *confession* is a corrective and necessary component for recovery. For example, "Confess your trespasses to one another, and pray for one another that you may be healed. The effective, fervent prayer of a righteous man avails much" (James 5.16). Similarly:

When I kept silent, my bones grew old through my groaning all the day long. For day and night Your hand was heavy upon me; my vitality was turned into the drought of summer. I acknowledged my sin to You, and my iniquity I have not hidden. I said, "I will confess my transgressions to the LORD," and you forgave the iniquity of my sin. (Psalm 32.3–5)

Conscious sensitivity and expressions of distress are a major task of the reconciliation model. For through the articulation of moral anguish, relief may be found. Thus, it is the responsibility of each of the clients to become spiritually aware through the intentional exposure of self to the moral injury or traumatic events. And each weekly homework assignment should help clients to view themselves in context. They learn to view themselves in context and apart from the content. They learn to view themselves "spiritually." Hope, therefore, is the objective believed capable of sustaining the morally injured so that individual and family thriving will result.

So, each veteran or servicemember will write in detail about their moral injury or trauma. The first rendering need not be long, but the goal is for each Group member to submit at least five sentences. Each paper will be processed in Group each session.

THE MOVEMENTS AND PHASES OF MORAL INJURY RECONCILIATION

The moral injury reconciliation model proceeds through each Movement and phase progressively. Each Movement is designed to increase spiritual awareness. This helps to develop *insight* so as to consolidate the challenges and make morally injurious and family life experiences more *understandable*. As a result, it is hoped that a state of being "other-focused" emerges. Consolidation of traumatic issues may first bring distress, but later, a degree of peace and orderliness may characterize one's life. Awareness or insight is foundational for the reconciliation process to succeed and the holding environment to endure.

The following chapters are the continued roll-out of the moral injury reconciliation process. To prevent confidential disclosure of veterans' or servicemembers' information, fictitious names and situations are used in all case examples that illustrate the process. The subsequent procedures will assume that case conceptualization, assessment, diagnosis, and the initial contact for establishing credibility and trust (above) have been completed.

SUMMARY

The importance of securing the spiritual alliance cannot be overstated. The care with which this is done will directly affect the spiritual–clinical outcomes. Most people, whether active military, veteran, or civilian, have a "gut feeling" about whether a caregiver is attentive and genuine or cold and out-of-touch. And for the spiritual care provider, trust and credibility are the gateways unto which healing may occur.

The veteran's or servicemember's task at this stage is to receive the initial socialization lead-ins by the provider. A client's connection with and preparations to respond to the upcoming interventions prepare the transformation sequence. The goals of this movement include: 1) expressions of the *lament*; 2) "daring" (willingness) to expose the content of their moral injury; 3) the capacity for the "intentional" giving of one's attention to *spiritual awareness*; 4) *humility*; 5) a client's acknowledgment that *forgiveness, self-forgiveness*, and *anger* (resolution) are necessary; 6) that reintegration through birthing their appropriate *civilian identity* and "new name" builds self-confidence; 7) actively developing and restoring *trust*; 8) knowing that *resilience* may be found in lifestyle change (or the "Big 3"); and 9) acknowledging that altruism or being *other-focused* is an important part of moral injury or trauma healing. These goals may be reached within the moral injury reconciliation sequence (i.e. *recognition, reply, response, remedy*, and *reconciliation*).

In closing Session 1, it is important to be reminded of the provider's ongoing role as trust and credibility-builder. As such, this may facilitate a conscious goal focus for the therapist. Nevertheless, even though the veteran or servicemember receives the provider as "trustworthy" and "credible," there is more. The next chapter will discuss helping clients "see" their challenge through their spiritual eyes, loosen their grip on their failed attempts at change, and make the initial efforts toward counterintuitive changes actionable. For this is the heart of spiritual transformation.

CHAPTER 5

EARLY-STAGE TREATMENT

SESSIONS 2–4

Treating moral injury may be especially difficult, for it may be that "humans experience traumatic events differently from all other animals because we ascribe *meaning* to events that befall us" (Charuvastra and Cloitre 2008, p.302; emphasis added). Since meaning is central to the reconciliation process, a transdiagnostic technique (or what Fraser and Solovey (2007) call a *transtheoretical* method) is utilized. The moral injury reconciliation model applies treatments designed to extract meaning from morally injurious episodes or traumatic events. This is achieved through one's meaning-making system. Thus, the meaning a client assigns to an event should have both a universal (global) and a particular (individual and personal) relevance.

The thrust of some biblical texts is counterintuitive, as can be seen for example in a text like the following:

> Let love be without hypocrisy…abhor what is evil. Cling to what is good…rejoicing in hope, patient in tribulation, continuing steadfastly in prayer… Bless those who persecute you; bless and do not curse… Rejoice with those who rejoice, and weep with those who weep… associate with the humble. Do not be wise in your own opinion. Repay no one evil for evil… If it is possible, as much as depends on you, live peaceably with all men…do not avenge yourselves, but *rather* give place to wrath; for it is written, "Vengeance *is* Mine, I will repay," says the Lord. Therefore "If your enemy is hungry, feed him; If he is thirsty, give him a drink; For in so doing you will heap coals of fire on his head." Do not be overcome by evil, but overcome evil with good. (Romans 12.9–21)

Techniques for achieving such counterintuitive outcomes in other contemporary therapies are known as: restraining change, normalizing, framing, reframing, predicting or prescribing difficulties or relapses, positioning, prescribing the symptoms, and adopting a goal-oriented future position (Fraser and Solovey 2007). This strategic amalgam may help address a wide category of mental health disorders.

Early-stage treatment consists of *Movement I* (self) composed of Sessions 1 (see Chapter 4) through 4. As continued attention is given to the maintenance of the religious/spiritual community, Sessions 2–4 will be discussed according to the sequence of transformation found in Figure 5.1.

Moral injury reconciliation: Sequence of transformation

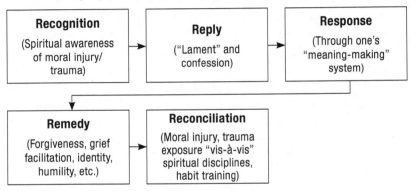

Figure 5.1 Moral injury reconciliation's transformation sequence

The goals of Sessions 2–4 is the recovery of spiritual equilibrium. In other words, it is the *spiritual differentiation* and *spiritual growth* through the *reconciliation sequence* that is needed. Progression through the reconciliation process should help clients distinguish (or differentiate) between self and a morally injurious event or trauma. Spiritual differentiation is the ability to connect with one's divine nature or essence. This is thought to loosen the grip of the guilt/shame complex that brings hope and the agency described in one's meaning-making system. Thus, correctives like humility, forgiveness and self-forgiveness, hope, and love can now be part of the veteran's or servicemember's life-orientation through re-coding (i.e. new meaning).

At this point, the therapist is prepared with a working knowledge of the moral injury reconciliation methodology and ready to conduct therapy. A walk-thru of common group equipment and other items will be listed as part of the pre-Group preparation.

EQUIPMENT, TOOLS, AND EARLY-STAGE GOALS

Prior to conducting treatment, select instructional aids are necessary. First, pens or pencils will be used to complete forms such as the PCL-5 Weekly and/or the PCL-5 Monthly checklists (posttraumatic stress checklist weekly and monthly) (Weathers *et al.* 2013) checklists prior to each session. The monthly (PCL-5 Monthly) checklist is to be filled out at the first session and the weekly PCL-5s thereafter. These and other activities are vital assessment instruments for progress monitoring. However, they only serve the larger purpose to increase the client's *spiritual awareness*.

Spiritual awareness is similar to *insight*, but more expansive. Spiritual awareness involves intentionality in the process of connecting with one's spiritual essence in relation to the sacred. The reconciliation model sees *insight* more as the secular and base biological stream of cognition, facts, or knowledge. Spiritual awareness, on the other hand, is the process of actively *perceiving* our *spiritual nature* for conscious betterment of self or circumstances. It is "functioning" in life according to one's divine nature and helps one to affirm: "I have a spirit, a 'self,' operating inside my flesh."

All course accessories serve to actualize clients' spiritual nature. This act is the *intentional* and conscious human sensing, noticing, paying attention to, and the intuit quality of being. From a religious/ spiritual context, spiritual awareness is required for the reasoning and thinking that invites corrective cognitive restructuring and behavior change.

Program tools highlight the targeted area for change yet capture the core substance of personhood and existential realities such as life, death, relationships, faith, or the *functional* and *substantive* aspects previously mentioned (see Chapter 2). Reflection activities (e.g. PCL-5s) or *displacement stories*, for instance, can start the change process by identifying at least one's state of being and the immediate challenge that frustrates spiritual wellness. Moral injury reconciliation therapy assumes it is possible to suffer from moral injury or posttraumatic stress and be wholly unaware due to the *dimensional* nature of moral injury

(Maguen and Litz 2012) and the variable presentations of traumatic stress (APA 2013).

As the veteran's or servicemember's story can reveal much during assessment and diagnosis, the spiritual care provider can create opportunities for spiritual disequilibrium relief. *Seeing* a story may invite hope. Guerin (1976a) used *displacement stories* as part of Bowenian family therapy. This technique can create distance enough for families to see themselves in the context of their presenting problems while viewing others in similar circumstances. Similarly, this method encourages the use of selected films and other media. Properly used, "people can become emotionally involved with a movie so that it has an impact but at the same time remain sufficiently removed to be objective" (Nichols and Schwartz 2001, p.157). And as the holding environment is being constructed, trust may develop during viewing a displacement story and may provide sufficient space to think and limit a veteran's or servicemember's "defensiveness" (p.169). Using this technique requires basic classroom IT equipment for DVD/CD playback, monitoring, and listening.

The reconciliation model makes extensive use of displacement stories to highlight transition themes for corrective thinking. And because this model relies much on the reasoning mind in the spiritual transformation process, *differentiation of self* is a key objective. This goal is deemed necessary as moral injury involves self and others. Differentiation of self is one's "ability to separate feelings from thinking," thus avoiding the entanglements of "getting caught up in reactive polarities" (Nichols and Schwartz 2001, p.140). Moral injury and traumatic stress can potentially excite high levels of emotional reactivity.

Therefore, the kind of media most instructive for creating this healing distance represents a context a veteran or active-duty member can relate to. This temporary visual context may allow the veteran to put themselves in another's "shoes," perhaps providing a brief moment for examining their issues and choosing a new healing pathway. A wide variety of media is available and may be applied so long as it follows the framework and illustrates the appropriate transitional theme(s) presented in this model (e.g. forgiveness, humility, acceptance).

Many titles are available, and the selection will depend upon the skilled therapist selecting content based on problem themes found within the Group. Media that provides spiritual awareness, exposure, healing encounters, and hope is encouraged. Displacement story segments should be of high visual quality and audio fidelity. Clips should generally not last longer than eight to ten minutes. A caution is warranted that careless selections depicting random chaos, war footage, gratuitous violence, and movies generally involving children may have no redeeming qualities relative to the reconciliation model. But by keeping the treatment focus in mind, missteps can be avoided.

Following are case examples for providers to become familiar with actual treatment procedures. Included are individual case profiles for case conceptualization rehearsals. The remaining transformation sequences are also highlighted.

CASE EXAMPLES

Each case is a fictional construction containing features the provider may encounter. These fictional representatives depict the actual elements of the moral injury syndrome a caregiver may face in treating veterans and active-duty personnel. While each scenario is fictitious, these case constructions should help conceptualize the moral injury construct and integrate the moral injury reconciliation model of care. Each case will be used to illustrate various treatment aspects.

ROBERT

This 70-year-old veteran has been receiving ongoing spiritual and mental healthcare since his transition to civilian life. As a U.S. Marine, he completed two tours in Vietnam as an infantryman. Experiencing a constellation of symptoms such as depression, sleep disturbances, and panic attacks, he has repeated episodes of increasing confusion and anger, and increased drinking episodes. He gets regular medical check-ups and, outside modest weight-gain, he appears to be in reasonably good health. Family disruption continues to increase, and his "flare ups" are increasing in both frequency and duration. He often ruminates often on "why" he lived and others didn't and *laments* how failed leadership got people killed. This seems to be the focus of his waking thoughts and disturbances of his nighttime dreams. He has progressively developed a vague sense of his spirituality which used to be vibrant, and he no longer attends church with his wife.

THOMAS

Thomas is a 29-year-old Army veteran whose career was marked with hazing events and "initiations." Those events, he believes, cost him opportunities for select job assignments and advancement. Since his discharge, he has tried to work at various jobs, but seems unable to resolve the anger and frustration with others and himself. Social relationships are tenuous and frequently end in heated arguments. His closer family contacts are strained, and the household climate has been described as "chaotic." He comments that his "anxiety" and "restlessness" are escalating. He perseverates on how he wishes he had taken action and told others that his repeated "initiations" were taking their toll. He now considers those occurrences as "hazing" and wonders if these rituals were part of the military which made him one of the team. He just wanted to be one of the "guys," so he kept his mouth shut. He thought the "blanket parties" would eventually let up, but they didn't.

JOSEPH

Joseph is a 94-year-old U.S. Army Air Corps veteran. As a B-24 navigator, his plane was shot down over Europe flying bombing missions. At the height of World War II, he had reservations about various bombing targets assigned in the European theater. He often spoke of the "innocents" and the devastation on the ground. He was 25 years old when he was captured by a civilian militia and later handed over to the German regular army. Having sustained several injuries during his shoot-down and subsequent parachute bailout, he has chronic pain and stiffness. As a POW for 16 months, he made two escape attempts, but was recaptured and severely beaten. He was liberated by British forces in early 1945 and spent one year in and out of hospitals for treatment and physical rehabilitation. Joseph's wife died three years ago, and he has now become virtually isolated. He ruminates over his capture and becomes tearful that he was caught by the enemy and failed in his escape attempts. When he does attend church, he prays, but continues in a state of despair and regret. He regrets his capture and failed escape attempts. He's also convinced that his failure to escape may have gotten others hurt or even killed. He is increasingly angry and frustrated and shared that he cannot live with himself because he was unable to avoid re-capture.

JIMMY

Jimmy is a 30-year-old U.S. Marine Corps veteran. He feels his combat experience was particularly distressing and that "we killed a lot of people." Although highly decorated and awarded two *Purple Hearts*, he emphasizes that "I'm not a monster." A growing dislike of crowds or family gatherings is noted, and frustration and anger have led to drug and alcohol problems. He was recently encouraged to attend inpatient drug and alcohol treatment. He finds himself more isolated and distrustful of others. Jimmy's transition into the civilian community has been difficult with feelings that he "doesn't belong," and admits to struggling with "identity" issues. He complains that "nothing makes sense anymore."

TRANSFORMATION TOOLS

The *reconciliation model* uses thematic intervention techniques to initiate change through spiritual formation strategies. However, using "spirituality" as a mechanism for change is likely to invite confusion and misunderstanding. Thus, an instrument to focus Group attention is needed so that clear *thematic focus* is brought to each session. To achieve this objective, the *displacement story* (Guerin 1976b) was chosen to link the client's challenge (e.g. anger) with a clear pathway to a solution (e.g. forgiveness) through a brief audio-visual presentation.

As a key tool of the reconciliation model, the displacement story is used as part of moral injury reconciliation's belief that visuals are a powerful experiential medium. Attempts to make use of the visual, abstract, and concrete learning styles are the spiritual care provider's optimal strategic treatment tools to maximize reconciliation's potential during this dynamic treatment. Simply put, if the provider's experience and case conceptualization determines that the needed transitional theme for Movement I (self) is "identity," a corresponding displacement story is selected to advance the processing of how one's identity affects one's current quality of life and what corrective actions may be taken towards arresting and recovering from symptoms. When the displacement story is viewed by the Group, ambiguity should be greatly reduced and the therapist's point of focus may be enhanced through additional clarifications as needed.

Herein is an opportunity for the exposure element (e.g. confession) to be exploited with corrective interventions. Such encounters can begin the meaning-making process towards *reconciliation*. This seems to be the case especially since it is generally found that the Group's use of their *generalized resistance resources* (particularly religious/spiritual supports) has been underutilized.

The displacement story provides the medium from which Group members get in touch with their spiritual selves. It is assumed that displacement stories help steer the veteran or servicemember into *exposing* their moral injury or trauma to new thinking. Once exposed, their goal will be to clearly understand the event (minus distortions), experience their deep feelings, express the lament, and subject their lament (e.g. grief) to the spiritual crucible and transitional theme (e.g. grief resolution) of spiritually healing pathways. Other spiritual pathways include: forgiveness processing, anger resolution, forming a new identity, or tension management through lifestyle changes (e.g. sleep hygiene, activity/recreation, and nutrition).

SESSION 2

Each session will be conducted along the lines of the template presented below. While it is left up to the provider to tailor each session according to their best clinical judgment, the reconciliation model's design, and Group and individual needs, should not waver much. The techniques found in Movement I (Sessions 2–4) are directed toward *self* and the *past*. The safe holding environment created by the Group leader should be the predicate for each Group member to slowly allow exposure and the eventual correctives of the reconciliation process.

Therapist's objective

Every session has goals for the provider. For Sessions 2–4 the provider's goals are to: maintain the spiritual alliance, fortify Group cohesion (build the Group healing culture), communicate clearly, engender hope, and define and promote spiritual awareness throughout the reconciliation process. Other goals for the therapist are to continually assess all Group members for *socialization* into the reconciliation process and evaluate spiritual transformation progress.

Veteran's or servicemember's objective

Sessions of the reconciliation model are designed to have a theme that leads to transitions from spiritual disequilibrium and into a reconciled state of spiritual equilibrium. Transitional themes are those religious/spiritual pathways thought to bring healing and spiritual formation upgrading. For Session 2, a transitional theme is often *anger resolution* through *forgiveness* processing. Forgiveness is a major transitional theme encountered throughout this program. It is the veteran's or active-duty member's goal during *Movement I*, Phase 1, to also: 1) notice, sense, pay attention to, perceive, and detect feelings or sensations of *self*; 2) identify and express *lament* or *confession*; 3) appropriate the initial steps in the *forgiveness process*; and 4) synthesize forgiveness elements into one's *sense of coherence* (Antonovsky 1979). Such goals are thought to mediate anger and promote the quickening of spiritual awareness (*differentiation*).

Environmental preparations and completing the PCL-5 (weekly)

Sessions begin at the appointed time as the Group facilitator pre-stages the room with pens/pencils; posttraumatic stress checklist (PCL-5) weekly (Weathers *et al.* 2013) sheets are to be scored at the end of session. Pretested and cued media presentation (displacement story video) should also be readied. The Group leader will also check the room for the quality and quantity of the chairs, room temperature, restroom facilities, and lighting. The Group room lighting should not be too bright or dim. Some veterans may be light sensitive due to migraines, traumatic brain injuries, or other medical conditions. However, a room too dimly lit may present the appearance of gloom and depression.

Begin the session with having each veteran or servicemember complete the PCL-5. The PCL-5 (weekly) checklist is completed to provide the pastoral care professional or therapist a snapshot of each member's prevailing level of distress and/or functioning. It is also to help the veteran begin the key discipline of *reflection* leading to spiritual awareness. The systematic reflecting on the previous week's mood and state-of-mind leads to *habitualization* (repetitive behaviors of learning, re-coding, and training that instill new, corrective behaviors). This is part of the *spiritual discipline* procedure for transformation and a move into new, wanted behavior change.

Completion of the weekly PCL-5 checklist leads to the next event in spiritual awareness training: the *spiritual awareness and watchfulness* (SA/W) exercise. This experiential activity is meant to further develop the initial *recognition* sequence of moral injury reconciliation therapy found in Figure 5.1 earlier.

Spiritual awareness and watchfulness (SA/W) exercises

Getting veterans or active-duty members to participate in this exercise may depend in large part on the spiritual alliance and level of trust and credibility developed. The SA/W exercises are for the building of an inner awareness and spiritual differentiation. For a veteran or active-duty member to be asked to "close" their eyes during this activity often invites defensiveness and anxiety; even a sense of helplessness or vulnerability. Nevertheless, closing one's eyes may increase awareness simply because when the eyes are closed it seems to heighten sensitivity and eliminate visual distractions. If closing the eyes is too stressful, the participants may fix their stare on the floor or wall.

The SA/W exercises hope to pre-condition veterans to the exposure component activities. Opening each Group session with a SA/W exercise may facilitate the reconciliation sequence stages, which are: *recognition* (spiritual awareness of the distress), *reply* (expressing the lament or confessing one's pain as an act of humility), *response* (engaging one's meaning-making system), *remedy* (select a transitional theme such as forgiveness for exposure and assimilation), and *reconciliation* (the habitual training of *new thinking* and behaviors through spiritual discipline correctives).

The SA/W exercises may be taken from an array of commercially available mind–body exercise manuals or they may be individually constructed based on experience. The goals of the spiritual awareness exercises are to habit-train for intentional insight (spiritual differentiation) and reflection unto new behaviors through actualizing the spiritual disciplines.

Moral injury reconciliation didactic

The *didactic* or teaching portion of this session is designed to more fully explain moral injury, posttraumatic stress, and the moral injury reconciliation process. Additionally, the issues responsible for potentially morally injurious events, spiritual pathways, and remedies for *change* are presented. Also, lifestyle modifications, particularly *sleep hygiene* as a topic, are accentuated due to the prevalence of, for example, obstructed sleep apnea in veterans and active-duty personnel (Ross *et al.* 1989; Colvonen *et al.* 2015; Gehrman, Harb, and Ross 2016). Other lifestyle modifications suggested are: activity and recreation and nutrition for mind–body transformation. Nevertheless, for the pastoral caregiver it is their responsibility to inject a sense of confidence in the recovery process which may foster enduring hopefulness.

Since this is a spiritual transformation therapy that seeks whole-life transformation, veterans and servicemembers are intimately involved. Recovery takes hard work. However, this population is not unfamiliar with tough situations. Nevertheless, by using a religious/spiritual framework (a generalized resistance resource of sorts), transformation is thought possible. And it is also here and throughout this program that the spiritual care provider makes clear that through their completion of homework and their continued intentional use of their new habits (spiritual disciplines), extinction or a reduction in intrusive thoughts, nightmares, anger levels, grief and fear mitigation, etc. may be realized. This point should be stressed throughout each Movement of the program.

During this didactic portion, the Group facilitator may use this time to continue to build trust and credibility. It will also be important to instruct on the strong cultural influences of military life and how making the transaction back to the civilian world will surely challenge them. Thus, building a veteran's *identity* may help create the confidence needed for second-order change. This sense of identity will be important. Veterans who so often have held responsible positions may now find themselves abruptly required to make sense of the now strange world of the civilian culture, doing tasks of only nominal significance. Some veterans may have been forced out or medically retired involuntarily. Now, feeling betrayed and alienated, and lacking common points of reference, a spiritual disequilibrium may result. This lack of identity may in part be the cause for depression and low self-esteem.

Other helpful instruction and processing should also include helping veterans and active-duty personnel determine which transitional theme (i.e. healing pathways such as forgiveness processing or anger resolution) is appropriate for their spiritual formation and ongoing recovery. Once the transitional theme is acknowledged, reflection disciplines and exercises promote change. Drawing from one's meaning-making system (e.g. life philosophy, religion, etc.), veterans' transformation is thought to be accelerated as they become more aware of their agency (ability) to effect change. As resilience develops, confidence may build as they appropriate their *generalized resistance resources* and reflect on their *sense of coherence* (Antonovsky 1979, 1987).

It should also be brought to their attention that, at some time during these sessions, some discomfort and agitation may result. Sometimes even an intensity of spiritual distress may occur. Normalizing such experiences and providing appropriate explanations may help them maintain treatment focus.

Experiential activity

The moral injury reconciliation model believes helping veterans and servicemembers access stored traumatic memories may be done using displacement stories. Since the homework assigned last week (Chapter 4, Session 1) was to write about the most troublesome morally injurious episode or traumatic event, they are to read their trauma account aloud in the Group. Displacement stories may serve as the lead-in to amplify exposure and corrective processing. Now, these trauma accounts will be put to use in conjunction with the displacement stories.

At this point, the Group leader will present a *displacement story*. It is also acceptable for the experienced provider to make up games, invent role play, or construct demonstrations with various devices (e.g. board game pieces). Telling of personal experiences or stories regarding transitional themes may encourage exposure of the morally injurious experience or trauma. It may also promote *social learning* as well. Such flexibility maintains the modular component (or flexible treatment strategies, intervention menu) (Sauer-Zavala *et al.* 2017) of its transdiagnostic design. Additionally, it also keeps each Group fresh and uniquely fashioned toward reconciliation.

The first excursion into the exposure component will be with Robert (presented earlier). Robert is a fictional 70-year-old U.S. Marine veteran. He struggles with moral injury and accompanying *betrayal* themes. Considering other Group members, the pastoral care provider has selected a ten-minute movie clip that graphically depicts an act of betrayal and its consequences. The Group facilitator notes that a few other Group members seem to become restless too while watching. The abbreviated dialogue may sound similar to what facilitators may encounter when conducting reconciliation treatments. A condensed transformation sequence dialogue is provided as an illustration.

Pastoral caregiver/therapist: Robert, how is that scene you just saw different, the same, or not relevant to the event you shared with the Group earlier?

Robert: Well, it's close, but I was there. I was with them (other squad members). We went to boot camp together, we went to AIT (advanced infantry training) together, we got in trouble together... I was with them when we got hit. They (leadership) knew it was a bad idea, but no! They insisted we do it their way. We were there and knew a better way...we told them, but no! We'd been there before... I don't even know why I'm here (survivor's guilt)... I remember it like it was yesterday; I keep having those dreams. I wake up fighting, my wife gets scared. She's now sleeping in the other room. Those nightmares seem to be getting more intense since I retired. I can't help, but remember that those SOBs knew better (slightly tearful)... They knew, they sold us out (angrily). (*RECOGNITION*—**awareness of the event**; and *REPLY*—**the lament and/or confession**)

Pastoral caregiver/therapist: Robert, keep going... If those leaders were here right now, what would you say, what would you like them to know?

Robert: I'd tell them how wrong they were; how stupid they were. I'd tell them they're all full of sh-t and hope they rot in hell.

Pastoral caregiver/therapist: Okay...and what else would you like to tell them? (At this point, the care provider recognizes that it might be appropriate to introduce the *transitional themes* of *anger resolution* and *forgiveness processing*. Caregiver follow-up questions are designed to provide additional exposure, spiritual awareness, vent for the lament/confession, exploring spiritual healing pathways, assimilating new learning, and corrective behaviors.)

Robert, we talked about our meaning-making systems or philosophies for how we make sense of the world. Even though we'll never change what happened, does *your* meaning-making system help you make sense of what happened? Or, what might it tell you about what you're to do to heal? (If Robert were unable to answer, other Group members may be enlisted for their input. But the provider may need to re-direct the treatment focus to the transitional theme(s) if the Group gets side-tracked.)

Robert: *I know what my faith says*, but I can't go there right now... I just can't... I don't want to... No! I won't. They screwed us, I'll screw them. (*RESPONSE*—**as found in one's meaning-making system**)

Pastoral caregiver/therapist: That's normal, perfectly understandable. But in theory, based on *your meaning-making system* or how you make sense of the world, what possible remedies are available for someone in a situation like yours?

Robert(grudgingly): I guess they'd have to *forgive*, but I won't. (*REMEDY*— **forgiveness, humility, etc.**; and *RECONCILIATION*— **ongoing exposure/extinction through spiritual disciplines, habitualization**)

Pastoral caregiver/therapist (turning to the Group to build the *Group healing culture*): I see. Okay. Good! Very good. Thanks, Robert. What other ideas are out there? (The therapist will come back and revisit Robert's refusal to give up his position of *unforgiveness* and will consolidate other ideas. The clinician may want to review and encourage dialogue for additional exposure opportunities, provide data to support the transitional theme (forgiveness), check for understanding, and end this encounter. *Forgiveness* will be an arena for long-term processing.)

Time will generally permit only two, perhaps three, Group members' presentations. However, as the Group's healing culture develops, it is believed that opportunities will further present themselves for ever-increasing and spontaneous learning and heightened spiritual awareness. As the reconciliation model generally champions Group therapy over one-to-one sessions for its community-building potentiality, it is believed that moral injury and posttraumatic stress injury find substantive healing within the context of community. Since humans attach *meaning* to traumatic events (Charuvastra and Cloitre 2008), the reconciliation model opts for transformation within a Group or religious/spiritual environment.

Additionally, when the group is part of the treatment modality, a favorable factor is the belief that, "to a large extent, *it is the group that is the agent of change.* Herein lies the crucial difference in the basic roles of the individual therapist and the group therapist" (Yalom with Leszcz 2005, pp.120–121; emphasis original). Additionally, since isolation is so often a part of the moral injury syndrome and posttraumatic stress disorder, weight is put on rebuilding veterans' and active-duty members' *identity* and *sense of belonging*, which are believed to be restored through community.

Homework

The standing homework assignment is for the Group to practice (in consultation with their medical provider) the "Big 3." That is: sleep hygiene, activity and recreation, and nutrition. This hopes to create a *spiritual self-care discipline.* Homework will remain an integral part of the moral injury reconciliation process for it is thought to bind the Group learning, subsequent lifestyle change, and an immediate and positive connection with the moral injury reconciliation process.

Homework assignments must be stressed and are what helps keep Group lessons in constant awareness. This is part of the habit-training process. Completed homework assignments can also be used as an assessment feature by the Group leader regarding the relative level of motivation of each Group member. Such tracking may be used with other indicators to make likely prognosis regarding lifelong transformation.

Hand out homework assignments and have a volunteer read the instructions. Close this section by asking if there are questions about any aspect of the program so far. Homework assignments will focus on developing spiritual awareness and stress tolerance. Such assignments will also be selected by the therapist that reinforce the transitional theme of each session. Individual homework assignments are to be accompanied by prayer as each member reconnects with their own faith tradition. Those without denominational ties may recommit to their values.

Community-building ritual

At the end of each session, a voluntary community-building exercise is held to help secure each Group member's individual identity and a sense of belonging to a larger community. This simple verbal or non-verbal activity incorporates *therapeutic touch*. This model suggests therapeutic touch may quicken how one is able to become spiritually aware by noticing and paying attention to *self*: a self or person who is able to actually sense their environment and their relationship to it. Person-to-person contact through a handshake or the Group linking arms can be a powerful metaphor and an objective reality of unity, belonging, and a validation to one's identity.

Ask the Group to join in the circle (voluntarily) and hold hands or link arms shoulder-to-shoulder and recite the common Serenity Prayer or simply have a moment of silent reflection. Then, dismiss the Group with words of encouragement.

INTRODUCTION TO SESSIONS 3 AND 4

Sessions 3 and 4 will be conducted as a continuation of Session 2. While Session 2 encouraged awareness of the depth of pain in one's lament (or chief complaint), Sessions 3 and 4 keep the focus on *self* and the intentional awareness of one's own feelings and reactions. In relation to one's *past* moral injury or trauma, Sessions 3 and 4 seek to provide past trauma correctives through transitional themes and habitualization into new learning and behavior change. These new behaviors will be strengthened by each Group member's engagement with their prayers as they are familiar with their faith traditions. As mentioned, for those without a religious background, a commitment to their *values* is encouraged.

Confronting a past morally injurious episode or traumatic event is an essential element of the reconciliation model. Unlike, say, a *solution-focused approach* that believes it is unnecessary to understand the presenting problem(s) or the past (de Shazer 1988; Nichols and Schwartz 2001), the moral injury reconciliation model seeks the opposite. Goals of the reconciliation model would have to have all clients consider their problems, understand their past (e.g. moral injury or traumatic event), and how they have attempted to solve their problems. Without such knowledge, repeat use of failed strategies may continually be attempted. Thus, clients may be unable to effect change on their own. Solution-focused therapies at best might use *language* and *meaning* to simply shape reality and the significance of events and relationships (Nichols and Schwartz 2001; Gehart and Tuttle 2003). A therapeutic *reframe* would be an example.

To effectively reconcile past trauma, the moral injury reconciliation model believes it is important to comprehend both the nature of the problem and how previous attempts to solve the problem have failed. Not only is awareness (insight) of past issues believed to be of high value, but understanding how the construction of previous problem-solving schemes may (in part) be to blame and lead to additional problems. Such a *solutionless* orientation may produce what has been called "a solution-generated problem" (Fraser and Solovey 2007, p.24), as "failed solutions, it bears emphasizing, will be repeated until interrupted" (p.23).

SESSION 3

Negative spiritual, emotional, and behavioral alterations are likely to worsen should moral injury and traumatic stress go untended. Therefore, direct confrontation with a morally injurious episode is suggested. By acknowledging the past and developing a spirit of "daring," moral injury may be interrupted.

Therapist's objective

Each session has goals for the provider. For Sessions 2–4 the provider's goals are to fortify Group cohesion (build the Group's spiritual healing culture), communicate clearly, identify the transitional theme, engender hope, and define and promote spiritual awareness throughout the reconciliation process. Other goals for the therapist are to continually assess all Group members for socialization into the reconciliation process and evaluate spiritual transformation progress.

For Session 3, the goal is to facilitate the Group's attention to the fact that there is spiritual disequilibrium present. And no matter what they have attempted and/or are attempting to do to rid themselves of the problem, it is probably not working. Therefore, *humility* (or acceptance) is suggested as the transformational theme.

Veteran's or servicemember's objective

Each session of the reconciliation model is designed to have a theme that leads to transitions out of spiritual disequilibrium and into reconciliation. Session 3's goals for Group members are for them to: notice/sense their feeling-state, identify and respond to the transitional theme (humility), and re-order their spiritual economy to accommodate new learning.

Movement I (self) and Session 3 often involve the transitional theme of *humility*. As the Group is assembled as a result of moral injury or trauma, humility to accept the fact that change is needed may be evident. In essence, it is about understanding the limits of one's ability and affirming that help-seeking behaviors are to be commended. This session seeks to open the door to grief/loss issues, as well as spiritual and emotional hurts, and recognizing the limits in their attempts to *control* their thoughts and feelings if triggered.

Environmental preparations and completing the PCL-5 (weekly)

Begin at the appointed time with the Group facilitator having prepared the room with pens/pencils, posttraumatic stress checklist (PCL-5) (Weathers *et al.* 2013) sheets, and pretested and cued media presentation (displacement story video). The PCL-5 weekly will be scored at the end of session. The Group leader should also check the Group room for the quality of the chairs, room temperature, restroom facilities, and lighting.

Have the veteran or servicemember complete the PCL-5. The PCL-5 (weekly) checklist is completed to provide the therapist a snapshot of each member's prevailing level of distress and/or functioning. It is also to help the veteran begin the key discipline of reflection or spiritual awareness through habitualization or habit-training into new, wanted behavior change.

Spiritual awareness and watchfulness (SA/W) exercises

Continue this exercise as outlined in Session 2. Slight variations in procedure are recommended. This should help train the Group to adopt the *habit* of checking and cultivating their level of spiritual awareness. Help them to grow more comfortable by getting everyone to close their eyes during this activity for the greatest benefit.

The SA/W exercises should be slightly progressive. That is to say, the initial exercises should be shorter in duration and general rather than complex. The goals of the SA/W exercises are to condition the body to recognize how it responds and train those involved to continually and intentionally perceive their spiritual nature. Such habits are believed to be part of establishing a sense of agency that strengthens a person's identity and confidence in their abilities to direct their behaviors toward corrective spiritual care interventions.

Moral injury reconciliation didactic

The teaching portion of Session 3 should focus on how some may be bound by their moral injury or traumatic stress. Suggesting that *humility* (a Phase 1 transitional theme) is an oft-used remedy is a helpful reminder. Nevertheless, humility is a theme that should be re-visited in other phases. This simply means that clients' moral injury or trauma is a unique circumstance, and they are trapped until they change the current solution to the problem. Subscribing to new thinking and behaviors may be difficult. It is perhaps amazing that even though distress may be well articulated by the veteran or servicemember, there are occasions where a "known" stressor will be endured and no change will be attempted despite evident dysfunction. As the "known" problem is *predictable* and safe (to the sufferer), the "unknown" promise of relief through "change" can strike fear and keep the client in a continued state of distress. Thus, the safe and predictable may be preferred over the "unknown" change and the promise of new life.

As some veterans and servicemembers have been literally fighting a war, it is of little surprise if some continue to fight their moral injury or traumatic stress using ineffective problem-solving techniques. These may be called *avoidance strategies*. Helping them to at least consider what a change would mean is part of the Group leader's goal. Additionally, how a veteran or warfighter may be *avoiding* is part of the distress the veteran is undergoing to which the transitional theme of humility hopes to resolve. Humility to acknowledge the moral injury or trauma and affirm one's failed remedies to resolve the problem is potentially liberating.

Knowledge of the structure of one's avoiding strategies is part of this session. Understanding how even helpful activities such as rigid dieting, exercising, legal or illegal drugs, or busyness may serve to maintain symptoms is believed useful. As the structure of ineffective problem solving and its consequences are processed, a subsequent softening of one's defenses may be produced (Walser and Westrup 2007).

A continuing discussion on the *push–pull dichotomy* can do much to keep veterans or active-duty personnel abreast of the role strains in making transitions from military life back into the civilian community. Simply said, on the one hand, the intense backward pull of a deeply ingrained military culture may prompt reliance on skills, avoidance, and problem-solving strategies (e.g. convoy driving, hyper-alertness, or other self-defense procedures), yet some are rendered ineffective in a civilian context. On the other hand, the push of living in civilian communities seeks to shape behaviors that conform to established norms of society. Thus, one's *identity* and sense of belonging may be challenged. However, an attitude of humble submission to the challenge may provide several opportunities for transition into spiritual wellness.

Experiential activity

This session's experiential activity is to further process the general nature of the moral injury and trauma. Experiential activities should therefore help Group members openly discuss (*confess*) their issues and acknowledge that they have reached a point of being unable to shake off the morally injurious episode and admit that attempts to adjust (*reconcile*) past events have not worked. Not only that, but in some cases their solutions to the problems have made things worse.

As the transitional theme for this Group at this juncture is humility and acknowledgment of moral injury or trauma, selecting a vehicle to illustrate this intervention is the job of the provider. Such a selection may allow each member to see themselves in relation to other important environmental features such as the military culture, their age, level of maturity, or their sense of helplessness at that time. And since this model's framework is a religious/spiritual orientation, surrender and prayerful requests to higher ideals and the sacred are appropriate.

Video clips, and imaginative or concrete examples, can accurately portray the virtue of humility. Developing an accepting attitude relative to the current state of affairs may bring authenticity and an ongoing healing Group culture. Allowing the Group to resonate as a community with the selected medium (displacement story or social learning activity) should encourage opportunities to acknowledge that spiritual distress is present. Reasoning that previous efforts to date have been ineffectual, the adoption of a humble posture is a positive step. Additional relief may also come through utilizing generalized resistance resources to correct the problem and may be the opening for increasing transformation.

Session 3's displacement story (or activating event) may now be initiated. The following dialogue may result when *humility* and *acceptance* are the transitional themes. We will re-visit Robert where we left off last time.

Pastoral caregiver/therapist: Robert, last week you shared that you "just can't" and "won't forgive," but I'm wondering how this stance has been working for you? What I mean is, what problems do you still have in *your life* that you're trying to get rid of?

Robert: Hell, you name it, I got it: depression, anxiety, can't sleep, my wife's on edge telling me to "just get over it," can't talk to my kids, I'm pissed off most of the time, and the only relief I get is having a few beers. But now my wife says I'm "drinking too much." (Robert's list seems to validate that he currently lacks the resources to overcome his moral injury or trauma alone. A position of humility and acceptance of a failed coping scheme may be his best strategy.)

Pastoral caregiver/therapist: Okay. And what have you tried to get rid of those problems?

Robert: Just not thinking about it...staying away from everybody. Working on my car and *trying to forget* about it all.

Pastoral caregiver/therapist: Hmm? (musing). It doesn't seem like life's going to let you do that. So, I'm wondering what would happen, Robert, if you were to at least temporarily *abandon* the position you now have (i.e. "I won't forgive"). What would happen, hypothetically, if you were to agree that what you've tried before (i.e. avoiding the morally injurious episode, isolation, drinking) isn't working and *endorse* the remedy of your faith tradition— *forgiveness* (the forgiveness process)?

Robert (long pause, staring at the floor): I don't *feel* like going there.

Pastoral caregiver/therapist: Okay, I hear you. But what things have you ever done before, even when you didn't *feel* like it, because there was a bigger payoff? In fact, we do things every day like this, and I'll bet it's more times than you realize. (If the client is unable to come up with examples, you may add that going to work, paying bills, exercising, obeying the law, or taking certain meds may be prime examples.)

Robert (grudgingly): Maybe taking my wife shopping...taking out the trash...changing grandkids' dirty diapers...picking up dog crap...

Pastoral caregiver/therapist: You're absolutely right, Robert. (Turning to the Group) And we can all perhaps understand that just because we forgive doesn't mean we accept what happened as right or that what was done that hurt you was okay. No! Forgiveness is about our spiritual wellbeing, our spiritual nature, and taking care of ourselves and our families. (This segment may provide an opportunity to delve deeper into the forgiveness theme.)

Homework

As stated, the daily spiritual self-care discipline is to make sleep hygiene actionable, pursue some form of activity and recreation, and monitor nutrition. It goes without saying that each individual will be reminded to contact their qualified medical personnel for specific guidance, especially if taking medications or attempting to modify diets or engage in strenuous activity.

Written assignments involve reflecting on past moral injury and trauma. First, they are to identify their meaning-making system (e.g. religious/spiritual heritage, philosophy, or any strategy you use to help you make sense of the world). This is what Antonovsky (1979) referred to as one's *sense of coherence*.

Next, list those who may have caused you hurt or those you may have hurt. Finally, list at least three reasons why you should forgive and why you should not "forgive" based on your meaning-making system (this includes "self-forgiveness" if you have perpetrated an offense). Answer any remaining questions and move to the community-building ritual. Finally, incorporate prayer at least once daily according to each person's faith tradition. Extra time reading religious literature and attending church worship services is also encouraged.

Community-building ritual

Continue this final activity with a quick review, and then assume the position that was agreed upon during past Group sessions (holding hands, linking arms shoulder-to-shoulder, or standing silently). Ask the Group to join in the circle (voluntarily) and hold hands or link arms shoulder-to-shoulder and recite the common Serenity Prayer or simply have a moment of silent reflection.

Before dismissing the Group, the spiritual caregiver will thank the Group for their participation, provide a verbal reminder for next week's scheduled meeting, promote the "Big 3" (sleep hygiene, activity/recreation, and nutrition), and offer a few words of encouragement.

SESSION 4

Session 4 concludes Movement I (*self*) and the thematic interventions of Phase 1. As reconciliation's socialization process continues, so too the spiritual disciplines, for they are determining features in the overall transformation sequence. Therefore, clients are encouraged to develop a sense of "daring," as it will take much effort to systematically undertake the spiritual disciplines that lead to spiritual wholeness. It should be remembered that the moral injury reconciliation model is about a change in thinking and behaviors. It is about developing one's spiritual nature, perhaps for the first time. Nevertheless, for those who "dare" to change, a new creation may emerge.

Negative spiritual, emotional, and behavioral alterations are likely to worsen should moral injury and traumatic stress go untended. Therefore, direct confrontation with morally injurious events is suggested. By acknowledging the past and developing a spirit of "daring," moral injury may be mitigated.

Therapist's objective

Maintaining the spiritual alliance and Group cohesion are the therapist's goal. Other objectives are to keep in mind moral injury reconciliation's methodology and treatment focus. And as *humility* and *acceptance* has been suggested as previous transformational themes (Session 3), forging one's *identity* may be the next thematic intervention for Session 4.

Veteran's or servicemember's objective

Again, each session of the reconciliation model is designed to have a theme that leads to transitions out of spiritual disequilibrium and into reconciliation and spiritual stability. Transitional themes are those religious/spiritual pathways leading to spiritual healing and spiritual formation. Session 4's goals for Group members are for them to: notice/sense their feeling-state, identify and respond to the transitional theme or identity, and re-order their spiritual economy to accommodate new learning.

At this point of early-stage treatment (Movement I, *self,* Session 4), the transitional theme of *identity* is in likely need of processing. As the Group is assembled as a result of moral injury's spiritual upset, one's identity will need to be addressed. In essence, after one accepts the concept of humility and affirms that help-seeking behaviors are to be commended, foundations for self-identity may be necessary. This session seeks to establish individual identity so that opportunity for processing grief/loss issues, and spiritual and emotional hurt, is not overlooked.

Environmental preparations and completing the PCL-5 (weekly)

As before, each session will begin at the appointed time with the Group facilitator having prepared the room with pens/pencils, posttraumatic stress checklist (PCL-5) (Weathers *et al.* 2013) sheets, and pretested and cued media presentation (displacement story video). All sheets should be scored at the end of Group. The Group leader checks the Group room for necessary furnishings, chairs, comfortable room temperature, and lighting. The Group room lighting should offer the appearance of hopefulness.

Begin the session by having each veteran or servicemember complete the PCL-5 as in previous sessions. This facilitates *habitualization* (habit-training) into new, wanted behavior change.

Spiritual awareness and watchfulness (SA/W) exercises

Continue this exercise as outlined in Sessions 2 and 3. Slight variations in procedure are recommended. This should help train the Group to get in the *habit* of checking and cultivating their level of spiritual awareness. Help them to grow more comfortable by getting all to close their eyes for the greatest benefit.

Spiritual awareness/watchfulness should be noticeably progressive. That is to say, the initial exercises should be shorter in duration and general rather than complex. However, the goals of the spiritual awareness exercises are to condition and train those involved to continually and intentionally perceive their spiritual nature and direct their behaviors toward corrective spiritual care interventions.

Moral injury reconciliation didactic

The teaching portion of Session 4 should focus on how they may still be bound by their ineffective moral injury or traumatic stress coping strategies. Suggesting that *identity* (the new transitional theme) is the intervention may be helpful. This simply means that their moral injury or trauma is a condition likely to rob or cause doubt about one's identity. Their cultural transition from military to civilian life may require too much for them to immediately answer. Self-doubt and low self-esteem are indicators. However, subscribing to their new *sense of self* (identity) may be difficult, but here, agency and empowerment to make new choices in light of current under-functioning may greatly impact one's quality of life.

A challenge for the provider is to *coach* the veterans or servicemembers and guide their adjustment to new methods of *coping*. Changing to new coping styles may be extra hard as some may be letting go of techniques they believe kept them alive during combat. So, the question for the client may become: "If I change my way of dealing with stress, will I be the same person? Who will I actually be?" Or: "How can I identify with the civilian world?—I've been through so much."

Helping clients to at least consider what change would mean is part of the Group leader's responsibility. Additionally, instruction in common avoidance (evading of problems) strategies is part of a veteran's change process. This change is further facilitated by the establishment of one's identity.

Knowledge of one's avoiding structure is part of this session. Reflection on lifestyle habits is useful too. As the structure of ineffective problem solving and its consequences are processed, a subsequent softening of one's defenses may be produced.

Experiential activity

As in previous sessions, the provider will select the experiential activity based on the selected transitional theme. In this case, it will involve re-discovering one's identity. Experiential activities should therefore help Group members cultivate their identity from their religious doctrines, their life philosophy, or their *values*. Their efforts to address their spiritual despair have not worked. As the transitional theme for this Group at this time has shifted to *identity-building*, selecting a vehicle to illustrate this intervention is the job of the provider.

Session 4's displacement story (or activating event) may now be initiated. The following dialogue may result when *identity, self-worth,* and *confidence* are this session's transitional themes. Thomas may represent some veterans or active-duty members struggling with self-worth and identity deficits.

Pastoral caregiver/therapist: Thomas, you spoke about the hazing incidents. Can you go a bit deeper into what those incidents meant to you—if anything?

Thomas: I don't know. It just hurt. (*RECOGNITION*) I didn't know what to do... I felt alone, helpless. (*REPLY*)

Pastoral caregiver/therapist: Okay. So, how do you *make sense* of those situations?

Thomas: I didn't know what to do, what to think.

Pastoral caregiver/therapist: Well, does *your meaning-making system* instruct you in any way?

Thomas: Not sure; I felt alone inside, abandoned. (*RECOGNITION* and *REPLY*)

Pastoral caregiver/therapist: What about your *values*? You spoke about how much you love your family and how much they're depending on you. Would you be able to find *self-worth* or significance in your love of your family? Or, that you're a good father? Would you perhaps be able to find *meaning* in your family or what you mean to them; how valuable you are to them? Or, what about your faith and how God values you, protects you? It's in *your* Scripture, isn't it? Reflect on the 23rd Psalm for a moment. What's it saying?

Thomas (reflecting): The Lord is watching over me, protecting me... He comforts me, and even if I walk through the valley of the shadow of death "Thou are with me" and that "goodness and mercy will follow me all the days of my life..." (*RESPONSE* and *REMEDY*)

Pastoral caregiver/therapist: So, sounds like you're not alone after all. It even sounds like you've memorized it.

Thomas: Yes. Learned it in Sunday School years ago. Sometimes I still recite it. (*RECONCILIATION*)

Pastoral caregiver/therapist: Excellent! Thomas, I'd encourage you to continually reflect (*RECONCILIATION*) on that passage in order to help keep it fresh. Let it help you make sense of (reconcile) those hazing incidents. It may also help your understanding of the *forgiveness process* of the event. (*REMEDY* and *RECONCILIATION*)

Thomas: That sounds fairly easy since I already know most of it.

Pastoral caregiver/therapist: It's important to have a firm foundation about how we're to make sense of this world. This can keep all on firm footing on who we are (identity), what happened, and your new direction. Your daily readings will help reinforce your sense of *identity*, thinking, and actions.

Homework

Again, sleep hygiene should be emphasized and the sleep diary should be completed each day. Also, the daily spiritual self-care discipline is to make sleep hygiene a priority while pursuing some form of activity and recreation, and monitoring nutrition. Written assignments involve reflecting on past moral injury and trauma. Therefore, repeating homework routines may help correct maladaptive behaviors.

Repeat the process you followed in Sessions 2–3. Identify your meaning-making system (e.g. religious/spiritual heritage, philosophy, or any strategy you use to help you make sense of the world). This is what Antonovsky (1979) referred to as one's *sense of coherence*.

Next, list those who may have caused you hurt or those you have hurt. Finally, list at least three reasons why you should forgive and why you should not "forgive" based on your meaning-making system (this includes "self-forgiveness" if you have perpetrated an offense). Answer any remaining questions from the Group and move to the community-building ritual. Finally, encourage the Group to incorporate prayer at least once daily according to each person's faith tradition. Extra time reading religious literature and attending church worship services is also highly approved.

Community-building ritual

Continue this final activity as carried out in Sessions 2 and 3. Recite the Serenity Prayer or simply maintain a moment of silence. Assume the position that was agreed upon during past Group sessions (holding hands, linking arms shoulder-to-shoulder, or standing silently).

POST-SESSION ACTIVITIES

Post-session activities will include tabulating the PCL-5 checklists and making the appropriate clinical note entries. These actions are in preparation for entering Movement II (*world*) and using Phase 2 transitional themes for relationship and community-building in the middle stage of moral injury reconciliation treatment.

SUMMARY

Chapter 5 is the early stage of moral injury reconciliation therapy. It contains the first of three Movements (*self*) and Phase 1 transitional themes. Spiritual awareness, humility, self-worth, and establishing one's identity are the Group's focus. Treating moral injury is thought to be affected by the reconciliation sequence of: *recognition*, *reply*, *response*, *remedy*, and *reconciliation*.

The transitional themes are used according to how moral injury presents within the individual or the Group. The Group facilitator has the responsibility of guiding the Group to express their laments and working through distress. At the conclusion of each session, each PCL-5 checklist will be tabulated, recorded, and compared to the previous week.

Having completed Session 4, this ends Movement I (*self*), and the Phase 1 themes thought necessary to move clients out of a downward trajectory toward spiritual despair. Armed with PCL-5 scores from the past four sessions, the therapist has an idea of the relative level of spiritual distress each Group member is challenged with. With this information the caregiver is ready to begin Movement II (*world*) and use Phase 2 transitional themes. These themes include: communication skills, empathy, emotional intelligence (Goleman 2006), communication stress styles (Satir *et al.* 1991), bonding, trusting, and establishing or re-establishing relationships. Entering into new or recovered intimate or community-building relationship is pivotal, even though some level of *risk* may be present.

CHAPTER 6

MIDDLE-STAGE TREATMENT

SESSIONS 5–7

As a spiritually integrated psychotherapy, the moral injury reconciliation model places high value on relationships and community for their potential to accelerate spiritual growth. Even as moral injury can destroy trust, trust can restore broken relationships and revive one's spiritual signature. One's spiritual signature is their persona—their climate or tell of character qualities that either attracts or repels others. Whatever one's tell, relationships will need to be re-established, though certain risks are involved. The value of others is at such a premium that calculated risks must be taken for the sake of one's spiritual wellbeing.

Since moral injury often produces symptoms akin to posttraumatic stress (Drescher *et al.* 2011; Maguen and Litz 2012; Nash and Litz 2013; Nash *et al.* 2013; Currier *et al.* 2015; Yan 2016) and has unique stressors such as guilt and shame (Litz *et al.* 2009), relationship upset is likely somewhere in life. Movement I sought to reconcile the *past*; it is in transitioning into Movement II that spiritual transformation expands beyond self. This treatment model seeks to now take the self-awareness discovered (or re-discovered) during Movement I and bring the benefits found in relationships and community to assist individual recovery. This process hopes to bring a present-focused vitality to one's immediate environment (world).

The moral injury reconciliation model is a growth-oriented intervention. It is sensitive to family systems and to the anticipated impact one's community life plays on spiritual formation development. For these and other reasons, transition to Movement II (world) and the transitional Phase 2 themes are deemed a necessary part of the course of treatment. As the veterans or servicemembers move out of the past, their new identity, humility, forgiveness processing, and relationship communication skills will be needed for present-day functioning.

Expanding one's sense of identity in relation to others is part of the spiritual growth process despite impending risks. Such growth may be exploited through a basic understanding of emotional intelligence (Goleman 2006) and how one comprehends the self in relationships. Another strategy meant to restore relationships is through understanding the stress styles of communicating (Satir 1976, 1983, 1987; Satir et al. 1991).

TRANSITIONING: SHIFTING FROM MOVEMENT I TO MOVEMENT II

Now that Movement I has been completed, the momentum turns slightly to focus on the advantage of constructing (or re-constructing) the necessary healing community with others. Moving forward in Movement II requires a re-targeting without ever fully neglecting self or one's past. This section appropriates those activities that may enhance how one interacts with the world through relationships. The remaining milestones of the reconciliation model's transformation sequence are now the objective. These last three elements of Figure 6.1 are the: response (using one's faith system or values to direct behaviors), remedy (unique behaviors and activities to resolve issues), and reconciliation (repetitive behaviors to re-code/reorient thinking and behaviors).

As the reconciliation sequence has shifted its specific focus, the interventions are modified as well. This new direction is shown in Figure 6.2. The moral injury reconciliation process is a cumulative endeavor to build on the last treatment session. It hopes to advance each client in their spiritual formation discovery of newness of being and recovery of self in intimate and community relationships. Figure 6.3 is also shown as the clinician's procedural map guiding the overall treatment plan. It displays possible Phase 2 transitional themes to be used during active treatment. These themes/goals are provided to allow the pastoral caregiver the flexibility of choosing a particular emphasis should the Group or individual present with specific challenges throughout Sessions 5 to 7.

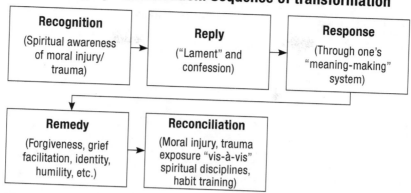

Figure 6.1 Moral injury reconciliation's transformation sequence

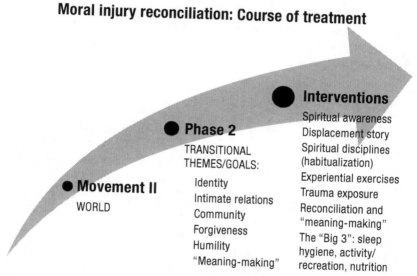

Figure 6.2 Moral injury reconciliation's course of treatment—Movement II

As part of this model's methodology, the therapeutic triad (Figure 6.3) is attempting to eliminate at least one leg of the fire triangle which symbolizes the development and/or maintenance of moral injury or other trauma. It is hypothesized that if one of the components of the triangle is eliminated (e.g. relationship renewal at Movement II), the conditions that maintain the dysfunction may be eliminated, and thus the greater possibility for healing.

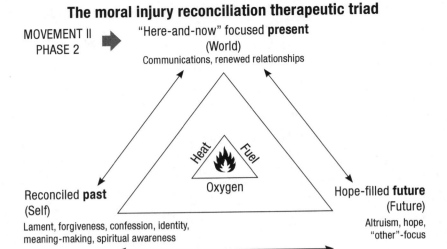

Figure 6.3 The moral injury reconciliation therapeutic triad. Adapted from Beck *et al.* (1979) *Cognitive Therapy of Depression.* Copyright Guilford Press. Adapted with permission of Guilford Press.

SESSIONS 5 THROUGH 7

The reconciliation model believes it is very difficult to heal or grow in a spiritual vacuum. This vacuum is often seen as isolative behaviors. In part, we are who we are in relation to others. Movement II is a continuation of the identity and meaning-making tasks expanding into the veteran's or servicemember's environment.

In some ways, moral codes are part of a community covenant of what we call norms. Should we violate these norms, we have in essence broken a community agreement. This broken treaty may not only affect our individual sense or rightness about a matter, but may bring feelings of being outside the camp of humanity. Such a transgression needs to be mended and a new sense of community-belonging is warranted. Renewal puts us in right with others. This is why isolation is thought to be so harmful to our spiritual nature.

A means for reversing alienation is believed to be provided in Movement II. This may be done through, first, acquiring a correct self-assessment of maladaptive behaviors, and then exploring the possibilities for new coding and adaptation through habitualization of spiritual competencies. The intentional practice of spiritual disciplines is thought to bring community connectedness and reconciliation.

Therapist's objective

As in previous sessions, the caregiver's goals are to maintain the integrity of the spiritual alliance and preserve Group cohesion. Since the Movement has shifted, Group review and reorientation may be necessary. Phase 2's transitional themes are presented so that one who suffers from moral wounds may join (or rejoin) an intimate relationship or community interactions.

The therapist's primary goals are to weld Movement I and Movement II and build a logical thematic progression of treatment as shown in Figure 6.3 above. Other goals are to continue clear communications, identify the transitional theme for the Group, stimulate the need for community and relationship, and promote spiritual awareness throughout the reconciliation process. Ongoing Group safety assessments (e.g. self-harm) and the evaluation of spiritual transformation progress are to be continually noted.

Veteran's or servicemember's objective

Over the course of these sessions, the aim is for the client to understand and recognize that a shift from past to present daily functioning has taken place. Questioning and observation of clients' behaviors may be assessed. Caregivers may also assess through completed homework assignments. While the Group is to carry over Movement I's new learning and behaviors, an emphasis on Movement II's orientation should direct the veterans or servicemembers to adjust their thinking and behaviors toward the community-building progress.

Some of Phase 2's transitional themes are shown in Figures 6.2 and 6.3 above. In addition to meeting these objectives, the goals of the spiritual awareness/watchfulness (SA/W) exercises are to: notice and sense their feeling-state, identify and respond to the transitional theme (relationship), and re-order their spiritual economy. This combination is thought to facilitate reconciliation by adapting their worldview to accommodate new learning and subsequent behavior change. Additional benefits may be found in moral injury and posttraumatic stress symptom reduction.

Environmental preparations and completing the PCL-5 (weekly)

Begin Movement II by having each Group member complete posttraumatic stress checklist (PCL-5 Weekly; Weathers *et al.* 2013) score sheets and tabulate each at the end of session. By reflecting on the previous week's state-of-mind, it is suggested that this may be part of the *shaping* process that begins spiritual disciplines or *habitualization* (habit-training) into new and desired behavior change. This activity leads to the next spiritual awareness activity: the SA/W exercises.

The provider should have already pre-selected the displacement story video or experiential activity that illustrates the significance of relationships and community transitional themes. All aids need to be previewed for content, pretested, and cued for playback at the appropriate time. The Group leader should also check the Group room as previously discussed.

Spiritual awareness and watchfulness (SA/W) exercises

Continue this exercise format as outlined in Session 2. Slight variations in procedure are recommended. This should help train the Group in the adaptation of newness or change in formation of habits (disciplines). Help them to grow more comfortable by getting everyone to close their eyes during this activity for the greatest benefit.

Spiritual awareness/watchfulness activities should be slightly progressive. That is to say, the initial exercises should be shorter in duration and general rather than complex, but duration and complexity should increase. The goals of the spiritual awareness exercises are to condition the body to recognize how it responds and train those involved to continually and intentionally perceive their spiritual nature. Such habits are also designed to establish agency. Agency is thought to be one's confidence in one's ability to self-direct or effect change. It may also be the strength or daring to embrace one's identity. Agency may generate a new confidence in their abilities. Such abilities may turn behaviors toward re-formulating intimate relationships and community involvement.

Moral injury reconciliation didactic

Instruction on the transition from Movement I to Movement II should be discussed. The therapeutic triad should provide a deeper explanation and aid Group members' understanding (see Figure 6.3 above). Nevertheless, the need for others in intimate and community relationships is the central focus of this Movement. Phase 2's transitional themes are shown in Figure 6.2 above. These themes will serve as Sessions 5 through 7's goals as brought about by the specific interventions listed in Figure 6.2 above.

Sacred literature and research data bases are replete with information relative to the value of relationships. The clinician's job is to make the presentation interesting, thought provoking, and relevant to moral injury reconciliation methodology. It is recommended that selection of research literature be congruent with sacred literature which is love-centered and theocentrically grounded. What follows is a suggested topic teaching outline for Sessions 5 through 7.

To develop a well-balanced reconciliation model of care, each clinic can augment their foundational religious/spiritual instruction with a theocentrically based theory of character formation and strategies for enhanced social interaction. Allowing each clinician or clinic to target their Group to a specific theme to meet clients' needs gives this model the modularity that makes it a transdiagnostic therapy. The recommended teaching focus for Sessions 5 through 7 is Goleman's (2006) emotional intelligence presentation. Goleman draws from extensive brain and behavior research to construct a powerful case on how self-awareness, self-discipline, and empathy may prove to be a masterful combination for wholeness and relationship enlargement. Likewise, Satir's communication model of stress styles may help veterans' or servicemember's reflections on their early development of stress-reducing coping strategies which are carried into the adult years. Without knowledge of our manner of stress style (Satir 1967, 1972, 1975; Satir et al. 1991), a continued erosion of essential relationships may result. A review at this point may be of use.

Tying and keeping the facets of the reconciliation model together may be aided by referring back to this model's comprehensive therapeutic structure shown in Figure 6.4. By way of review, the chain of events may be explained as follows. Essentially, a spiritual shock wounds the client; the shock is moral injury or another traumatic stressor. This event is registered and then filtered through one's spiritual economy, which looks for stability through meaning and accommodation of known past events or knowledge which has been coded from childhood. These actions regulate the type and intensity of response. If the event has a register of known experiences and the event does not violate norms, a morally injurious episode or traumatic event is *not* likely to occur. However, should the potentially harmful episode have no registration of previous encounters and transgress moral boundaries, a moral injury and/or posttraumatic stress may occur.

To interrupt this destructive process, the provider facilitates the client's awareness of the event as well as develops the spiritual alliance. Next, the spiritual caregiver hears the lament and begins to fabricate the treatment plan and assess where the client lies on the wellness continuum. Assessing clients for their degree of wellness (despite physical or spiritual–emotional wounds) and for which resources the client uses to maintain functioning is known as a salutogenic orientation.

Teachings on the roots of health (Antonovsky 1979, 1987) are thought to help clients activate their religious/spiritual framework to their healing. This is agency. An evaluation of one's effective use of their generalized resistance resources may preclude *tension* from becoming *stress* (Antonovsky 1979). Thus, the moral injury reconciliation model may be used as an assessment guide and a growth and intervention tool.

After assessment and case conceptualization, the provider now implements the reconciliation model's three Movements with its three thematic phases for spiritual transformation, symptom reduction, and behavior alterations.

Moral injury reconciliation (MIR): Therapeutic structure

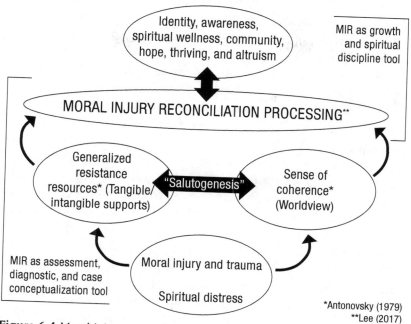

Figure 6.4 Moral injury reconciliation's therapeutic structure

Experiential activity

Each session will have a specific experiential activity where the veteran connects with the activity in relation to the moral injury or traumatic event. Movement II's themes are focused on relationships in the context of one's environment (world). Therefore, the provider has the freedom to develop experiential activities or displacement stories and process these social learning events after their completion. The experiential activities for this session are based on Phase 2's themes, which include humility, finding one's identity, continued forgiveness processing, meaning-making, community, and intimate relationships, as part of Session 5, 6, or 7.

However, there is one exercise that may be substituted during Session 6 or 7. This exercise is called "Eye-2-Eye" (Hayes, Strosahl, and Wilson 1999, p.244). As used in the moral injury reconciliation model, it was selected for its possible usefulness in helping clients better connect with their spiritual nature, recognize and tolerate their own stress response, and show their level of motivation for staying with a stressful encounter. Cultivating one's sense of daring may heighten sensitivity to various feeling-states during interpersonal encounters.

The activity calls for Group members to pair up. If there is an odd number, the provider will pair with the client without a partner. Each pair will then pull chairs to where they are about knee-to-knee and eye-to-eye to each other. When directed, each pair will simply "stare" at one another. The intent is to notice one's internal response to tension. Its design is meant to cause *mild stress* as well as produce the desired results previously listed. Afterwards, the event will be processed. The goal is for each client to *notice* how they respond when under mild stress.

After Session 6's experiential encounter, a post-exercise dialogue is useful (see below). As the Eye-2-Eye exercise induces tension, this may be helpful to bring one's self into conscious awareness apart from a morally injurious episode meaning. In other words, clients should sense: "I have a spiritual nature that is separate from the actual traumatic experience." Additionally, it may also support one's tension tolerance capacity for bearing heavier spiritual demands.

The case example now turns to "Jimmy," who has had difficulties with relationships and transitioning into community life after his discharge.

Pastoral caregiver/therapist: Jimmy, during the Eye-2-Eye exercise, what sensations did you notice?

Jimmy (shaking his head): I hated it... I never want to do that again... I didn't know what to do. One moment I wanted to laugh, then started giggling. I wanted to get up and walk out... I got all tense with different thoughts racing in my head. I could feel my heart pumping and I wanted to look away, but then I thought, "What's he thinking?" "How do I look to him?" "What expressions can he see on my face?" I felt like I was going crazy; flooded with crazy thoughts. It was pretty intense.

Pastoral caregiver/therapist: Jimmy, thanks for working through that exercise. It's important to engage that sense of daring we spoke about. Have you ever felt like that before?

Jimmy: Not exactly, but when I get near crowds, I start getting tense. I know when my heart's pumping really hard... That exercise made me feel like that.

Pastoral caregiver/therapist: I also noticed that you said you wanted to "get up and walk out." What kept you in the activity?

Jimmy (reflecting): Not really sure, but I guess I've been in tougher spots before. Heck, everybody else was hanging-in-there—well, I guess I felt that I could too.

Pastoral caregiver/therapist: Good! Excellent. I'm also wondering if you might be able to use this experience the next time you're near other people, particularly large crowds. I say that because being in relationships and involved with others is very important...so important that it just might be worth the *risk* of some anxiety. (At this point the caregiver may turn to others and follow a similar line of inquiry.)

Homework

Discuss homework and reinforce the importance of the sleep logs and lifestyle issues (the "Big 3": sleep hygiene, activity/recreation, and nutrition). These should be now thought of as lifestyle and spiritual self-care issues. If medical questions arise, clients are directed to seek immediate medical attention follow-up.

Also, part of the Group's homework is their reflection on moving toward wellness. By reflecting on values or by engaging in prayer, the point of focus is the client's individual recovery and agency. Considering higher ideals and making supplications for divine support further advances reconciliation processing. Specific values or life goals may be written down. Prayer requests may also be logged and later discussed in Group; even to the point of asking other Group members to pray for them as well.

Community-building ritual

This final event is designed to reinforce each member's identity, but more importantly their sense of belonging to something larger; all to affirm their sense of humanity. If the Group has agreed to link arm-in-arm, potentially, a beneficial therapeutic touch is inherent in this activity. Continue this final act with a quick session review and end with a recitation of the Serenity Prayer. Otherwise, the Group may simply maintain a moment of silence. Conduct this community-building event in the manner it was agreed upon during past Group sessions (holding hands, linking arms, shoulder-to-shoulder, or standing silently). Now, ask the Group to join in the circle (voluntarily).

Before dismissing the Group, the spiritual caregiver will thank the Group for their participation, provide a verbal reminder for next week's scheduled meeting, promote the "Big 3" (sleep hygiene, activity/recreation, and nutrition), and offer brief words of encouragement.

SUMMARY

Recovery from moral injury and trauma is a painstaking process, but becomes even more difficult in isolation. Using the thematic interventions offered in each of the two Movements, transformation may be possible. Building on the work done in Movement I (Sessions 1–4), Movement II (Sessions 5–7) is thought to offer a strategy to take the next steps toward the ongoing reconciliation of moral injury or other trauma. Transitioning from military to civilian life is important and so too is the shift from Movement I to Movement II. It is so important that certain risks are worth taking.

In the moral injury reconciliation process, the veteran continues the transformation sequence to increase one's "here-and-now" present-day functioning and enjoyment found in relationships. This dimension may take shape as new learning from sacred literature is combined with other knowledge, enhancing relationship bonding. Recommended knowledge includes emotional intelligence and communication stress styles. In large measure, this Movement is concerned with re-sorting one's sense of humanity and self-worth as a vital member of the larger community. Restoration may come through recovery or discovery of intimate relationships, through learning about self, and self in personal or community relationship interactions. Key processes are the use of prayer or values reflection for spiritual growth. Such processes are augmented by lifestyle and habitualization of spiritual disciplines (e.g. prayer, reading sacred literature, self-care).

The next step in the reconciliation process is Movement III, Sessions 8 and 9. This Movement seeks to secure hope for the future. The reconciliation process's final Movement is where the client looks forward to see that there is a tomorrow—a tomorrow that now includes being other-focused. That is the subject of our next chapter.

CHAPTER 7

LATE-STAGE TREATMENT

SESSIONS 8–9

As far back as 1446 B.C.E., sacred literature taught one to "love your neighbor as yourself" (Leviticus 19.18b) and: "The stranger who dwells among you shall be to you as one born among you, and *you shall love him as yourself*" (Leviticus 19.34; emphasis added). Later, this command was summarized to state: "Therefore, love the stranger for you were strangers in the land of Egypt" (Deuteronomy 10.19). Lessons in empathy were to grow from new learning derived from instructions in moral–ethical behavior.

Even though these admonitions were part of the law given to an ancient people, love was a character trait intended to replace the seemingly natural tendency toward selfishness and withdrawal. In this historic instruction to correct an inward self-focus, counterintuitive thinking and behaviors were prescribed. This instruction to "love" provides further insights into the Divine nature and was transmitted through the ages. And the act of ultimate love was personified by the supreme example of selflessness in the person of Jesus of Nazareth around 33 C.E. Even today, the dictum to "love" one's neighbor seems to have evolved into a universal proverb for its proven utility.

In this last Movement, Sessions 8 and 9 promote altruism as a culmination of a veteran's or active-duty member's reconciling their past and their joining relationships for a here-and-now focused present. Practicing altruism is also a method—a spiritual discipline for individual growth and lifelong spiritual formation. Figure 7.1 shows the moral injury reconciliation therapeutic triad's focus on Movement III. It uses Phase 3's thematic guidance to direct each of the two remaining sessions.

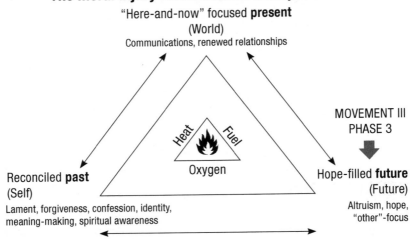

Figure 7.1 The moral injury reconciliation therapeutic triad. Adapted from Beck *et al.* (1979) *Cognitive Therapy of Depression.* Copyright Guilford Press. Adapted with permission of Guilford Press.

Regardless of how one may understand the foundations undergirding the reconciliation model, it is a call for a change of heart and behavior. The moral injury reconciliation paradigm is a new spiritual care entry designed to address diverse mental health issues. Other therapies meant to serve practitioners in the mental health field are acceptance and commitment therapy (ACT) and cognitive processing therapy (CPT). These therapies have full approval and are routinely used at nearly all Veterans Administration facilities.

Acceptance and commitment therapy is founded on centuries-old beliefs and affirms that "mindfulness is an ancient *Buddhist practice* that can have a powerful impact on our lives today" (Walser and Westrup 2007, p.20; emphasis added). It seems that millions worldwide venerate the founder of Buddhism even today. Likewise, CPT treatments have roots in Stoic philosophies (see Chapter 2) which made the case for the following "belief" system: "Control of most intense feelings may be achieved by changing one's ideas." Such beliefs have roots in Stoicism, Taoism, and Buddhism (Beck *et al.* 1979, p.8). Therefore, it is nonetheless believed, then, that the moral injury reconciliation model of therapy should soon be included in this company following clinical trials. To love one's neighbor seems to have grown into no less than a universal directive in its power to transform both the giver and receiver of what is materially (e.g. food, shelter) and spiritually (e.g. intimacy, fellowship) needed to sustain physical life and further spiritual formation. Scripture promotes love, and the true nature of love leads to the Divine, for God is love (1 John 4.8).

The timeless moral code for the benevolent treatment of others may work to transform through new thinking and habit-training. In other words, care for others is the outworking of the transformed heart. It is a heart motivated by the good, and in so doing basic instruction for self-care and community involvement is satisfied. Moral injury reconciliation's course of treatment at this late stage is depicted in Figure 7.2. So important was altruistic behaviors that it rose and became the second Great Commandment (Matthew 22.37–39). In many ways, such displays of altruism was a measure of the degree of transformation of one's heart (Mark 12.33; John 13:34–35; 1 John 2.10; 1 John 3.14). Such a measure may be a barometer of transformed thinking and behavior today.

Moral injury reconciliation: Course of treatment

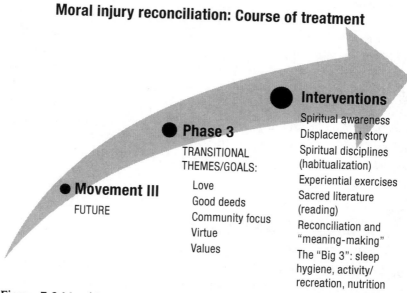

Figure 7.2 Moral injury reconciliation's course of treatment—Movement III

The final Movement rounds out the therapeutic triad in the hopes of moving the client out of the ranks of the morally injured and into a reconciled state. Using counterintuitive interventions, the reconciliation model believes that a spiritual symbiosis exists when one commits to the good of another, but only so long as the giver is fully cognizant of their spiritual deficits (e.g. anger, state of un-forgiveness, isolation) and is actively addressing them. Here, sacred literature provides helpful instruction for changing inwardly focused thinking and behavior patterns. And though it is hoped that war never occurs, moral injury reconciliation's religious/spiritual framework holds that war, moral injury, or traumatic stress cannot be *prevented* under present circumstances as some may suggest (Shay 2003). Nevertheless, sacred literature clearly provides a remedy back to wellness, though traumatic experiences will certainly be a war-effect.

However, through the spiritual disciplines of habit-training and application of new thinking from sacred literature, specific behavior change may be subjectively thought to promote feelings of wellness, community, and demonstrations of love. On the other hand, symptom reduction, improvement in sleep hygiene, good fitness levels, and nutritionally sound food and lifestyle selections may be seen as objective transformation.

Because the moral injury reconciliation model seeks to transform the client and not simply reduce symptoms (as does the traditional medical model), evidence of change should be observed through a genuine concern for others. Whereas a hardness of heart may have developed to successfully perform combat military operations, empathy and serving for the good of others is now part of the veteran's new character. As sufferers of moral injury and trauma may lack a sense of meaning and purpose, being other-focused may afford the veteran or servicemember a new sense of identity and belonging—evidence of transformation.

THE ALTRUISTIC ADVANTAGE

Altruism may be defined as an unselfish regard for others. This degree of service may come at a risk, even to the point of self-sacrifice (goods, services, health) for the sake of another. A strategic intervention of the reconciliation model is being other-focused. Benevolence remains a key tool that helps the spiritually wounded heal and thrive. Perhaps the most well-known story of one helping another is the story of the Good Samaritan. This parable is found in the New Testament (Luke 10.29–37) and provides an example of altruism. It contrasts the true nature of mercy with hearts that are inwardly focused and without compassion. Inconvenience or excuses for withholding aid were unacceptable. This is the new standard of moral–ethical conduct irrespective of longstanding prejudice or ill-feelings. And to the extent moral injury or trauma can wound, altruism can heal. Providing help to others changes things—ourselves, others, and society at large.

Movement III's thematic focus is the spiritual disciplines of doing good intentionally. Interventions assigned to Phase 3 are veterans' or servicemembers' spiritual disciplines that search for opportunities to do good works. This new thinking and behavior may provide a complementary set of skills that empower the morally wounded. But to be clear, no number of good deeds will erase past events or atone for unethical behavior. Nevertheless, the perpetrator can find full relief and forgiveness through the grace and mercy granted by the Divine. Thus, acting from a forgiven spirit and out of profound gratitude, one rejoices in their new, divine nature (2 Peter 1.4b). This is often shown through thankfulness demonstrated as service to others. Such a state is one's true spiritual self. Not only that, but the social sciences and the neuroscience of altruism strongly suggest good works aid in the development of resilience and moral character (Southwick and Charney 2015). Transformation of this type would fully leverage agency that strengthens contributions to humankind while regaining a new spiritual identity.

TRANSITIONING: SHIFTING FROM MOVEMENT II TO MOVEMENT III

The transitional themes for Sessions 8 and 9 are to produce good deeds, great and small, that facilitate spiritual formation trajectories to secure hope for the future. Movement III's final two sessions should be the natural progression out of Movement II. These sessions are the capstone of moral injury reconciliation therapy. The transitional themes will hopefully drive the direction of the course to its end-state and produce the sought-after symptom reduction and relationship renewal. This final Movement will be conducted in much the same way as the previous seven sessions. Sustained hopefulness and altruistic activity are thought to serve as protective factors, potentially warding off depression, spiritual disequilibrium, or self-harms.

Moral injury reconciliation is a religious/spiritual framework for second-order change. Habit-training in good works is commendable and can provide self-confidence and purpose for one who was once thought "worthless." By performing "good works," evidence is manifest that, by their own hands, they are being changed—transformed by this new thinking and conduct. This progression may be hopefully seen and the reconciliation process continues.

SESSIONS 8 AND 9

Movement III's structure lends itself to consolidating the gains that may have been made during earlier sessions. This movement provides opportunities to put into practice those virtues that promote spiritual formation. In this case it is altruism or being other-focused as a result of habitualization. This movement is also an opportunity for the provider to be both coach and cheerleader of client gains and symptom reduction.

Therapist's objective

At this point in the process, it may be instructive to discuss feeling versus thinking. All to say that as the spiritual awareness/watchfulness (SA/W) exercises have been engaged, one's feelings may be distinguished from one's thinking. This differentiation is part of the spiritual differentiation mentioned in Chapter 5—distinguishing one's essence from a general psychological conscious awareness. Spiritual differentiation is so much more than being alert and oriented. Should one become spiritually aware, additional choices are made available, as potential for donning one's divine nature is now possible. This competency allows the client to remain aware of self and the Divine, and be in relation to others.

It is also worth noting that clients may not feel like doing good deeds. This response however should be normalized as an honest reaction of true feelings and that the SA/W exercises may be actually working. That is to say that a client who previously lacked sensitivity of self and emotion toward others may now no longer be psychically numb. It should also be remembered that initial learning generally has fits-and-starts to which a natural clumsiness or resistance prevails. Still, the pastoral care provider may need to be somewhat directive and gently push them to further examine feelings and consequent behaviors. And through the daring of the will and habit-training, good works may manifest.

The therapist's objective is to help veterans or servicemembers transition into spiritual wellness. And even though the formal treatment process is ending, spiritual formation and lifelong habit-training may be now just beginning. For this reason, much encouragement is in order. Phase 3's transitional themes (e.g. love, good deeds, community focus) may also provide the platform to use self as therapist. Here, while using clinical judgment, the caregiver may selectively share strategic personal examples to reinforce or clarify various points the veterans or servicemembers may have questioned.

Finally, additional objectives for the provider are the continued maintenance and cohesion of the Group while attending to the high quality of the spiritual alliance. A final discussion of the sequences of the moral injury reconciliation process is encouraged. This would include the continuous Group safety assessment and the evaluation of spiritual transformation progress.

Veteran's or servicemember's objective

The veteran's and servicemember's goals are to practice and develop spiritual awareness and competence capable of perceiving one's emotions and sensations while engaging in virtuous acts. Such activity should be in keeping with one's values and/or religious/spiritual precepts. These events are to be done in the context of second-order change (i.e. the client seeking whole-life transformation and not simply symptom reduction). The knowledge that virtuous acts are in contradistinction to any previous morally injurious episodes should reinforce the moral order in one's world and provide remedies for correction.

Clients should note that, after intentional acts of kindness, such acts may then become spontaneous—even second-nature. And out of this response to their divine nature, satisfaction, self-worth, and a sense of joy may emerge.

Environmental preparations and completing the PCL-5 (weekly)

Sessions 8 and 9 start as usual with the completing of the posttraumatic stress checklist (PCL-5) weekly (Weathers *et al.* 2013) sheets and scoring at the end of session. Recall of prior states and how one responds to stressors is one aspect of spiritual awareness.

Spiritual awareness and watchfulness (SA/W) exercises

Continue as described in previous sessions. Newness of the encounters may be sensed if the provider is able to vary the dialogue with each successive reading. Hopefully, at this late stage of therapy, everyone is able to feel safe enough to close their eyes during the activity. As the Group becomes more comfortable in the spiritual community constructed and maintained by the pastoral care provider, slighter longer sessions may be conducted too.

Moral injury reconciliation didactic

Instruction on altruism is the teaching topic for these sessions. Clients should be able to articulate how they may be transitioning from Movement I (past) into Movement II (present-day functioning), and looking forward with hopeful expectations through Movement III's future-focused orientation. Hopefulness may be augmented by reading and reflecting upon sacred literature. The transitional themes of each phase are supported in the ancient Biblical text for the sake of a congruent and comprehensive framework. Additional teaching on differentiation of self, current events, or human interest stories provides thematic teaching content. For example, as I am finishing the writing of this book, numerous stories are being broadcast of neighbors and strangers from across the country bringing aid to the hurricane-damaged Gulf coast. Share or illustrate through displacement story or other social learning examples.

Teaching at this stage should also include instructing Group members on the importance of the continuation of the spiritual disciplines irrespective of one's immediate feeling state. Training in perceiving one's mood and processing both feelings and thinking are thought to be dynamic practices in resilience strategies. Other teaching points are left to the competent pastoral care provider to direct the clients while staying within the treatment methodology. Here is where the full practice of the thematic vehicles are put to work for continual habitualization.

Experiential activity

Having an other-focused life means holding others in such high regard that self-sacrifice and intentional efforts to provide either material, emotional, or spiritual support are given. This also means that evidence that one's spiritual equilibrium has been restored may be demonstrated objectively. An in-session experiential activity may be a live animal exhibit.

Many Veterans Administration facilities have vetted volunteer organizations with pre-screened pet therapy animals trained to visit veterans at the hospital bedside. These animals are well groomed and good natured and would make excellent metaphors for being other-focused. Such an activity may allow the handlers to bring the dogs to Group and have a ten-minute interaction as veterans pat, view, and interact with the pets and/or their handlers. Advanced scheduling and facility clearances may be required. Nevertheless, this activity may provide an introduction into altruistic thinking and subsequent selfless behaviors.

Therefore, Sessions 8 and 9 should use experiential illustrations or examples of others who model such qualities. Many video clips (displacement stories), autobiographies, and/or creative role play may be put to use for reflection and processing. Creativity is encouraged so long as the moral injury reconciliation methodology is honored. Examples that make things personal may serve best especially when the example is someone with military service. A fictional account follows of what may happen when embarking on a habit-training homework assignment as part of one's spiritual formation profile.

Joseph is a 94-year-old World War II member of a bomber crew who earlier expressed feelings of remorse and guilt over wartime action. Although residing in an assisted living facility, he selected homework assignments that would at least bring a smile to someone every day. Surprisingly, his small effort delivered more than he anticipated.

Pastoral caregiver/therapist: Joseph, what homework assignments did you choose to demonstrate *altruism?*

Joseph: Well, I don't get around too much anymore, but I decided to do something. So, I thought that I can at least "smile" and speak kind words to at least one person every day. It wasn't always easy, because some days I just hurt, but somehow I don't notice the pain as much when I do it from the heart. I mean I can manage a smile, but then it seems to open a door. People sometimes just start talking, then we're in a conversation. The things I learned from those exercises and filling out the sheets (PCL-5) each week about "noticing" how I'm feeling seem to work; maybe not all the time, but I think more times than not. It's kind of strange (smiling), but when I get into a conversation, I feel a bit different. I still have problems, but something's changed. I don't know what it is, but I'll keep doing it.

Pastoral caregiver/therapist: Good observations, Joseph. Anything else?

Joseph: Well, I've been attending church a little. I can't do much, but I'm planning to get involved and be on the "prayer" ministry team. There I find out who needs help, and this group prays for them. I can't do much, but I can do that.

Pastoral caregiver/therapist: That's great, Joseph. Good work, excellent. That's the spirit of altruism. Doing what you can for another with just what you have.

Homework

Homework is the continued journey for spiritual formation and behavior change. Session 9 is the official termination of the Group. At this point and if they have not already done so, they may share a Group list with individual contact information to perhaps form another spiritually healing community. The provider may also supply additional sleep logs and PCL-5 checklists (to track their own progress in symptom reduction). Currently, the pastoral care provider's encouragement to continue lifestyle focus for physical resilience is suggested. And as a spiritual self-care discipline, highlight the importance of consulting with medical providers regarding lifestyle, medication needs, or nutritional issues.

As a final but daily homework assignment, the *Good Driver Exercise* is selected. It is a simple and lifelong activity in the habitualization of patience, self-control, and altruistic behavior. And as the name implies, it is to be a good driver. The assignment is geared more for known rush hour or peak driving times. The task is to first prepare yourself by accepting the fact that a stressful event is about to happen (i.e. driving). However, you are prepared and know you have the capacity and the choice of how you will respond (agency).

Therefore, the following steps guide the homework activity. It is to: 1) obey all posted speed limits and written regulations; 2) be a *courteous* and *polite* driver by allowing others to merge into your lane; 3) *signal* all lane changes and, when you notice oncoming traffic giving way, *wave politely* and *noticeably* as a show of thanks; 4) give way to the faster drivers in the fast lane if you are not driving at the higher speeds; and 5) when/if you are cut off or need to take emergency action to avoid a collision, do so, but after recovery do not give chase, follow, or pull alongside to stare or otherwise intimidate the offender. However, disengage, self-soothe, and forgive the transgression as it is likely everyone will offend someone on the road more often than they might think. Use other acquired spiritual awareness competencies too. For instance, peace or gentleness may be called for when you arrive at your destination. Finally, find a trusted person and process the event with someone and do not neglect the *Big 3* (sleep hygiene, activity/recreation, and nutrition) throughout the week.

These are only a few of the character-shaping skills that may further train one in the spiritual disciplines for change. All are encouraged to use the skills learned for ongoing spiritual formation and moral injury reconciliation.

Community-building ritual

Community ritual is a practical exercise and metaphor to demonstrate the value of others. As the Group disbands, their efforts to find and/or cultivate their own community may act as a measure of their spiritual formation plan. It may also show what value they place on belonging. For the morally injured, regaining a sense of identity and belonging could prove the difference between healing and further spiritual distress. Reciting the Serenity Prayer en masse may also be an antidote for aloneness, especially for someone like Joseph introduced earlier.

Such rituals may even have an especially powerful effect as advanced age settles in.

SUMMARY

Movement III is the final segment of this methodology. And of all the character traits, the moral injury reconciliation model chooses love as the greatest of all. Love is the doing of good deeds from a decided heart and a behaviorally congruent new self. And for lasting change to be effective, such change must come to be demonstrated continually from a regenerated heart. Love originates not from authoritarian edits, but from an inward passion to serve another, for it is believed that, absent a heart-felt desire to serve others on its own merits, it is likely the sheer force of one's will can only grow weary.

However, a future orientation is one where hopefulness abounds. Such hope is often found where meaning and purpose in life is clear: where a social support network is in place, and where the Divine is in relationship through prayer. On its face, serving others may be thought to be unviable due to its counterintuitive approach. However, through shaping, a progressive spiritual formation may be found even where just an intentional goal of smiling may change thinking. Future-oriented actions may account for lifelong expectations in hopefulness.

Continued acts of altruism have been found to possess resilience qualities in the lives of those that practice humanitarian service. The ancient instruction in sacred literature commands to "love" one's neighbor. When practiced, such a moral and ethical standard has a transformative quality such that empathy can develop. Thus, the command to love which served as a tutor is no longer in force as the second-order change has transformed the heart. Love is now demonstrated in word and deed and originating from a pure heart of service to others.

Conclusion

A methodology for treating moral injury and posttraumatic stress has been presented. Yet there is much left undone. Life's uncertainties tax our resources and confusion may often rule. Thus, the meaning-making system we embrace will help or hinder our quality of life. Changing circumstances and setbacks must be met with hard work. Subscribing to life's basics is thought to bring resilience and achievement.

Even so, what has been respectfully presented is a workable, well-founded strategy for *hope*. The moral injury reconciliation model has as its core a religious/spiritual framework. And since war, disaster, and pain are the vagaries of the day, a belief system strong enough to meet this distress is found in the ancient wisdom of biblical literature. And though it is practical in its application, it is nevertheless challenging for its counterintuitive approach to problem solving.

A theological context was selected for its ability to connect the three world religions that subscribe to the imperative to "love" one's neighbor. Despite the difficulties of life, there are ways to achieve resonance and comprehensive answers to life's most challenging encounters.

One way is to start with the basics. The basics are simple life principles that pay handsomely when consistently practiced. This practice is more than a moral ascent to do good or a desire to change. It is a committed determination to change one's mind followed by the appropriate actions in the correct proportion. Action is needed to remain spiritually stable and steadfast when resolve is required. Our capacity to overcome life's stressors and problem-solve will affect our quality of life should we have a "basic plan" of action. A basic plan has fundamental patterns of thinking and behaving that generally remain consistent no matter the impediment.

Contentment is a basic. Likewise, gratitude and a spirit of thanksgiving may be the remedy for the restless spirit. Nevertheless, while "love" is the greatest of virtues, it is a basic that guides imperceptibly toward good works and a lifelong spiritual growth. Further, *love* is the keystone for all other virtues and good deeds.

This book opened with a brief biography of how my life was transformed by my surroundings and the desire to serve. Helping another by getting involved was a basic I learned early on. However, I learned this basic through religious/spiritual guidance. The introduction listed numerous research findings affirming the validity of faith practices relative to positive health outcomes. Such evidence is hard to ignore. Since life is full of pain, the case was made that moral injury and all pain is principally a spiritual issue. Thus, through spiritual interventions, relief may be found. We are spiritual by nature and transformed by new thinking and behavior alterations.

Still, as we are buffeted by war and strife, we may comprehend the costs and challenges of moral injuries and traumatic stress. Such invisible wounds take a toll on veterans, military personnel, their families, and society at large. Unfortunately, war may be occasionally necessary. However, religious and spiritually informed remedies to treat moral injury must be available. Such remedies may be effected through transitional themes to address such issues as anger, guilt, shame, isolation, or grief. This is accomplished by taking the vertical (the existential and the divine) and horizontal (interpersonal, community) realities into reconciliation. And since trauma symptoms are quite variable in their presentation, the reconciliation model's structure appears to be a genuine transdiagnostic (or unified) approach to care. The reconciliation model's methodology may be capable of treating a host of mental health concerns.

The reconciliation model uses three Movements and three variable thematic phases to treat moral injury through a reconciliation sequence of: recognition, reply, response, remedy, and reconciliation. Systematically, each overarching Movement addresses: self (past), world (present), and future expectations in hopefulness. Effective second-order change is hypothesized to take place as the spiritual economy transacts moral injury and trauma with new thinking. And with the new thinking, accommodation takes place, as the new coding, orientation, and behavior patterns emerge from the spiritual crucible.

While there is much work left, no one need fear moving forward. Cherishing loved ones, enjoying simple pleasures, or putting committed faith in our meaning-making system empowers one's life for real and lasting transformation. Such new thinking may bring joy, though the past we cannot erase. Finding meaning and purpose in our lives will forever remain an enterprise that brings about a sense of coherence.

Finally, I end with a short story of one Charles Foster Kane. Kane grew up poor, but enjoyed great fun with his friends, especially during the winter. Nevertheless, he was later raised apart from his birth parents, but he grew very successful nonetheless. So successful that he accumulated great wealth, prestige, and a desire for power beyond anyone's measure. Yet such power brought a corresponding despair that he never seemed to shake. But after his death, the custodians were ordered to burn his great holdings of furniture and things perhaps never used. Others inquired about his last spoken word. Old and feeble, he was found clutching a snow globe and, in a barely audible voice, he was heard to say "Rosebud." News reporters, friends, and the general public wondered too. What or who was "Rosebud"?

As the scene closes with custodians continually burning his overstock of possessions, one man grabs an old sled of a by-gone era and tosses it into the inferno of "stuff" that never brought authentic pleasure. And as the flame ignited the dry wooden sled, the paint bubbled and the image of a "Rosebud" could be seen on the sled of Citizen Kane's old play toy.

References

Acosta, J., Becker, A., Cerully, J.L., Fisher, M.P., *et al.* (2014) 'A literature review on mental health stigma reduction.' Available at www.dtic.mil/get-tr-doc/pdf?AD=ADA610275, accessed on October 19, 2017.

Adams, J. (1776) Letter to Zabdiel Adams. Available at https://founders.archives.gov/documents/Adams/04-02-02-0011, accessed on October 19, 2017.

Adams, J. (1798) Letter to Massachusetts Militia. Available at https://founders.archives.gov/documents/Adams/99-02-02-3102, accessed on October 19, 2017.

Adler, A. (1932/2010) *What Life Should Mean to You.* Mansfield, CT: Martino Publishing.

American Psychiatric Association (1994) *Diagnostic and statistical manual of mental disorders American Psychiatric Association.* Washington, DC: American Psychiatric Association.

American Psychiatric Association (2000) *Diagnostic and Statistical Manual of Mental Disorders: DSM-IV-TR, 4th Edition.* Washington, DC: American Psychiatric Association.

American Psychiatric Association (2013) *Diagnostic and Statistical Manual of Mental Disorders (DSM-5®), 5th Edition.* Washington, DC: American Psychiatric Association.

Antonovsky, A. (1979) *Health, Stress, and Coping.* San Francisco, CA: Jossey-Bass.

Antonovsky, A. (1987) *Unraveling the Mystery of Health: How People Manage Stress and Stay Well.* San Francisco, CA: Jossey-Bass.

Antonovsky, A. (1996) 'The salutogenic model as a theory to guide health promotion.' *Health Promotion International 11,* 1, 11–18.

Augustine, S. (397 C.E) Rotelle, J.E. (1997) *The Works of Saint Augustine: A Translation for the 21st Century* (Vol. 20). New York: New City Press.

Bandura, A. (2002) 'Selective moral disengagement in the exercise of moral agency.' *Journal of Moral Education 31,* 2, 101–119.

Bandura, A., Barbaranelli, C., Caprara, G.V., and Pastorelli, C. (1996) 'Mechanisms of moral disengagement in the exercise of moral agency.' *Journal of Personality and Social Psychology 71,* 2, 364.

Barlow, D. H., DiNardo, P. A., Vermilyea, B. B., Vermilyea, J., and Blanchard, E. B. (1986). 'Co-morbidity and depression among the anxiety disorders: Issues in diagnosis and classification.' *The Journal of Nervous and Mental Disease, 174,* 2, 63–72.

Beck, A.T., and Alford, B.A. (2009) *Depression: Causes and Treatment.* Philadelphia, PA: University of Pennsylvania Press.

Beck, A.T., Rush, A.J., Shaw, B.F., and Emery, G. (1979) *Cognitive Therapy of Depression.* New York: Guilford Press.

Beck, J.S. (2011) *Cognitive-Behavior Therapy: Basics and Beyond.* New York: Guilford Press.

Begić, D., and Jokić-Begić, N. (2001) 'Aggressive behavior in combat veterans with post-traumatic stress disorder.' *Military Medicine, 166,* 8, 671.

Benjamins, M.R. (2004) 'Religion and functional health among the elderly: is there a relationship and is it constant?' *Journal of Aging and Health 16,* 3, 355–374.

Berges, I.M., Kuo, Y.F., Markides, K.S., and Ottenbacher, K. (2007) 'Attendance at religious services and physical functioning after stroke among older Mexican Americans.' *Experimental Aging Research 33*, 1–11.

Bilmes, L.J. (2011) 'Current and projected future costs of caring for veterans of the Iraq and Afghanistan wars.' Unpublished manuscript, Department of Economics, Harvard University, Massachusetts, USA. Available at https://research.hks.harvard.edu/publications/workingpapers/citation.aspx? PubId=8956&type=FN&PersonId=177

Blevins, C.A., Weathers, F.W., Davis, M.T., Witte, T.K., and Domino, J.L. (2015) 'The posttraumatic stress disorder checklist for DSM-5 (PCL-5): Development and initial psychometric evaluation.' *Journal of Traumatic Stress 28*, 6, 489–498.

Blosnich, J.R., Dichter, M.E., Cerulli, C., Batten, S.V., and Bossarte, R.M. (2014) 'Disparities in adverse childhood experiences among individuals with a history of military service.' *JAMA Psychiatry 71*, 9, 1041–1048.

Bowlby, J. (1973) *Attachment and Loss: Separation* (Vol. 2). New York: Basic Books.

Bowlby, J. (1982) 'Attachment and loss: Retrospect and prospect.' *American Journal of Orthopsychiatry 52*, 4, 664.

Boyd-Franklin, N. (2006) *Black Families in Therapy: Understanding the African American Experience* (2nd ed.). New York: Guilford Publications.

Braš, M., Lončar, Z., Boban, M., Gregurek, R., *et al.* (2007) 'Self-inflicted burns in patients with chronic combat-related post-traumatic stress disorder.' *Collegium Antropologicum 31*, 4, 1173–1177.

Bretherton, I. (1992) 'The origins of attachment theory: John Bowlby and Mary Ainsworth.' *Developmental Psychology 28*, 5, 759.

Britt, T.W., Greene-Shortridge, T.M., Brink, S., Nguyen, Q.B., *et al.* (2008) 'Perceived stigma and barriers to care for psychological treatment: Implications for reactions to stressors in different contexts.' *Journal of Social and Clinical Psychology 27*, 4, 317–335.

Brodsky, B.S., and Stanley, B. (2008) 'Adverse childhood experiences and suicidal behavior.' *Psychiatric Clinics of North America 31*, 2, 223–235.

Brown, T.A., Campbell, L.A., Lehman, C.L., Grisham, J.R., and Mancill, R.B. (2001) 'Current and lifetime comorbidity of the DSM-IV anxiety and mood disorders in a large clinical sample.' *Journal of Abnormal Psychology 110*, 4, 585.

Bruffaerts, R., Demyttenaere, K., Borges, G., Haro, J.M., *et al.* (2010) 'Childhood adversities as risk factors for onset and persistence of suicidal behaviour.' *British Journal of Psychiatry 197*, 1, 20–27.

Bryan, C.J., Clemans, T.A., Hernandez, A.M., Mintz, J., *et al.* (2016) 'Evaluating potential iatrogenic suicide risk in trauma-focused group cognitive behavioral therapy for the treatment of PTSD in active duty military personnel.' *Depression and Anxiety 33*, 6, 549–557.

Charuvastra, A., and Cloitre, M. (2008) 'Social bonds and posttraumatic stress disorder.' *Annual Review of Psychology 59*, 301–328.

Clark, D.A., and Taylor, S. (2009) 'The transdiagnostic perspective on cognitive-behavioral therapy for anxiety and depression: New wine for old wineskins?' *Journal of Cognitive Psychotherapy 23*, 1, 60–66.

Collier, R. (1961) *The Sands of Dunkirk*. London: Collins.

Colvonen, P.J., Masino, T., Drummond, S.P., Myers, U.S., Angkaw, A.C., and Norman, S.B. (2015) 'Obstructive sleep apnea and posttraumatic stress disorder among OEF/OIF/OND veterans.' *Journal of Clinical Sleep Medicine: JCSM: Official Publication of the American Academy of Sleep Medicine 11*, 5, 513.

Craske, M.G. (2012) 'Transdiagnostic treatment for anxiety and depression.' *Depression and Anxiety 29*, 9, 749–753.

Currier, J.M., Holland, J.M., Jones, H.W., and Sheu, S. (2014) 'Involvement in abusive violence among Vietnam veterans: Direct and indirect associations with substance use problems and suicidality.' *Psychological Trauma: Theory, Research, Practice, and Policy 6*, 1, 73–82.

Currier, J.M., Holland, J.M., and Malott, J. (2015) 'Moral injury, meaning making, and mental health in returning veterans.' *Journal of Clinical Psychology 71*, 3, 229–240.

Department of Defense (DoD) (2010) 'Overview of the VA/DoD 2010 clinical practice guideline for PTSD.' Available at https://www.healthquality.va.gov/ptsd-full-2010c.pdf, accessed on January 2, 2018.

de Shazer, S. (1988) *Clues: Investigating Solutions in Brief Therapy*. New York: W.W. Norton.

Drescher, K.D., and Foy, D.W. (1995) 'Spirituality and trauma treatment: Suggestions for including spirituality as a coping resource.' *National Center for PTSD Clinical Quarterly 5*, 1, 4–5.

Drescher, K.D., Foy, D.W., Kelly, C., Leshner, A., Schutz, K., and Litz, B. (2011) 'An exploration of the viability and usefulness of the construct of moral injury in war veterans.' *Traumatology 17*, 1, 8.

Dudik, L. (2012) *I Once Was…: A World War II Transformation*. San Diego, CA: Linda Dudik (self-published).

Enright, R.D. (2001) *Forgiveness is a Choice: A Step-by-Step Process for Resolving Anger and Restoring Hope*. Washington, DC: APA Life Tools.

Fergusson, D.M., McLeod, G.F., and Horwood, L.J. (2013) 'Childhood sexual abuse and adult developmental outcomes: Findings from a 30-year longitudinal study in New Zealand.' *Child Abuse and Neglect 37*, 9, 664–674.

Figley, C., and Nash, W. (eds) (2007) *Combat Stress Injury: Theory, Research, and Management*. New York: Routledge.

Fletcher, S.K. (2004) 'Religion and life meaning: Differentiating between religious beliefs and religious community in constructing life meaning.' *Journal of Aging Studies 18*, 2, 171–185.

Fontana, A., and Rosenheck, R. (2004) 'Trauma, change in strength of religious faith, and mental health service use among veterans treated for PTSD.' *The Journal of Nervous and Mental Disease 192*, 9, 579–584.

Foy, D.W., Drescher, K.D., and Smith, M.W. (2013) 'Addressing Religion and Spirituality in Military Settings and Veterans' Services.' In K.I. Pargament (ed.) *APA Handbook of Psychology, Religion, and Spirituality (Vol. 2): An Applied Psychology of Religion and Spirituality*. Washington, DC: American Psychological Association.

Frankl, V.E. (1978/2011) *The Unheard Cry for Meaning: Psychotherapy and Humanism*. New York: Simon and Schuster.

Fraser, J.S., and Solovey, A.D. (2007) *Second-Order Change in Psychotherapy: The Golden Thread that Unifies Effective Treatments*. Washington, DC: American Psychological Association.

Freud, S. (1918) *Reflections on War and Death*. Trans. by A. A. Brill and Alfred B. Kuttner. New York: Moffat, Yard & Co., 1918; Bartleby.com, 2010.

Freud, S. (1929/2015) *Civilization and its Discontents*. Peterborough, Ontario: Broadview Press.

Gehart, D.R. (2010) *Mastering Competencies in Family Therapy: A Practical Approach to Theory and Clinical Case Documentation* (1st ed.). Belmont, CA: Brooks/Cole.

Gehart, D.R., and Tuttle, A.R. (2003) *Theory-based treatment planning for marriage and family therapists: Integrating theory and practice*. Baltimore, MD: Brooks/Cole Publishing Company.

Gehrman, P., Harb, G., and Ross, R. (2016) 'PTSD and sleep.' *PTSD Research Quarterly 27*, 4, 2–3.

Goleman, D. (2006) *Emotional Intelligence*. New York: Bantam.

Grame, C.J., Tortorici, J.S., Healey, B.J., Dillingham, J.H., and Winklebaur, P. (1999) 'Addressing spiritual and religious issues of clients with a history of psychological trauma.' *Bulletin of the Menninger Clinic 63*, 2, 223.

Granqvist, P., Mikulincer, M., and Shaver, P.R. (2010) 'Religion as attachment: Normative processes and individual differences.' *Personality and Social Psychology Review 14*, 1, 49–59.

Gray, M.J., Schorr, Y., Nash, W., Lebowitz, L., *et al.* (2012) 'Adaptive disclosure: An open trial of a novel exposure-based intervention for service members with combat-related psychological stress injuries.' *Behavior Therapy 43*, 2, 407–415.

Greene-Shortridge, T.M., Britt, T.W., and Castro, C.A. (2007) 'The stigma of mental health problems in the military.' *Military Medicine 172*, 2, 157–161.

Griswold, C. (2007) *Forgiveness: A Philosophical Exploration*. Cambridge: Cambridge University Press.

Guerin Jr, P.J. (1976a) *Family Therapy—Theory and Practice*. Gardner Press, Inc.

Guerin Jr, P.J. (1976b) 'The use of the arts in family therapy: I never sang for my father.' *Family Therapy: Theory and Practice*, 480–500.

Gutner, C.A., Galovski, T., Bovin, M.J. and Schnurr, P. (2016) 'Emergence of transdiagnostic treatments of PTSD and posttraumatic distress.' *Current Psychiatry Reports 18*, 95.

Haskell, S.G., Gordon, K.S., Mattocks, K., Duggal, M., *et al.* (2010) 'Gender differences in rates of depression, PTSD, pain, obesity, and military sexual trauma among Connecticut war veterans of Iraq and Afghanistan.' *Journal of Women's Health 19*, 2, 267–271.

Hayes, S.C., Strosahl, K.D., and Wilson, K.G. (1999) *Acceptance and Commitment Therapy: An Experiential Approach to Behavior Change.* New York: Guilford Press.

Heifetz, R.A. (1994) *Leadership Without Easy Answers* (Vol. 465). Harvard, MA: Harvard University Press.

Henriksen, T. (2012) *WHAM: Winning Hearts and Minds in Afghanistan and Elsewhere.* Kindle edition, Special Operations Command.

Hill, P.C. and Pargament, K.I. (2003) 'Advances in the conceptualization and measurement of spirituality and religion: Implications for physical and mental health research.' *American Psychologist 58*, 64–74.

Hoge, C. (2010) *Once a Warrior—Always a Warrior: Navigating the Transition from Combat to Home—Including Combat Stress, PTSD, and mTBI.* Lanham, MD: Lyons Press.

Hoge, C.W., Grossman, S.H., Auchterlonie, J.L., Riviere, L.A., Milliken, C.S., and Wilk, J.E. (2014) 'PTSD treatment for soldiers after combat deployment: Low utilization of mental health care and reasons for dropout.' *Psychiatric Services 65*, 8, 997–1004.

Holland, J.M., Currier, J.M., Coleman, R.A., and Neimeyer, R.A. (2010) 'The Integration of Stressful Life Experiences Scale (ISLES): Development and initial validation of a new measure.' *International Journal of Stress Management 17*, 4, 325.

Hufford, D.J., Fritts, M.J., and Rhodes, J.E. (2010) 'Spiritual fitness.' *Military Medicine 175*, 8S, 73–87.

Idler, E. (1987) 'Religious involvement and the health of the elderly: Some hypotheses and an initial test.' *Social Forces 66*, 226–238.

Idler, E. (1995) 'Religion, health, and nonphysical senses of self.' *Social Forces 66*, 683–704.

Idler, E. (1997) 'Religion among disabled and nondisabled persons II: Attendance at religious services as a predictor of the course of the disability.' *Journal of Gerontology 52B*, 6, S306–S316.

Imiola, B., and Cazier, D. (2010) 'On the road to articulating our professional ethic.' *Military Review: The Professional Journal of the U.S. Army.* [Special edition.]

Jordan, A.H., Eisen, E., Bolton, E., Nash, W.P., and Litz, B.T. (2017) 'Distinguishing War-Related PTSD Resulting from Perpetration- and Betrayal-Based Morally Injurious Events.' *Psychological Trauma: Theory, Research, Practice, and Policy.* Advance online publication. http://dx.doi.org/10.1037/tra0000249

Kang, H.K., Bullman, T.A., Smolenski, D.J., Skopp, N.A., Gahm, G.A., and Reger, M.A. (2015) 'Suicide risk among 1.3 million veterans who were on active duty during the Iraq and Afghanistan wars.' *Annals of Epidemiology 25*, 2, 96–100.

Kar, N. (2011) 'Cognitive behavioral therapy for the treatment of post-traumatic stress disorder: A review.' *Neuropsychiatric Disease and Treatment 7*, 167–181.

Kashdan, T.B., Uswatte, G., and Julian, T. (2006) 'Gratitude and hedonic and eudaimonic well-being in Vietnam war veterans.' *Behaviour Research and Therapy 44*, 2, 177–199.

Keane, T.M., Fairbank, J.A., Caddell, J.M., Zimering, R.T., Taylor, K.L., and Mora, C.A. (1989) 'Clinical evaluation of a measure to assess combat exposure.' *Psychological Assessment 1*, 1, 53–55.

Kessler, R.C., Sonnega, A., Bromet, E., Hughes, M., and Nelson, C.B. (1995) 'Posttraumatic stress disorder in the national comorbidity survey.' *Archives of General Psychiatry 52*, 12, 1048–1060.

Kim, L. (2010) *Homer between History and Fiction in Imperial Greek Literature.* Cambridge: Cambridge University Press.

Koenig, H.G., Berk, L.S., Daher, N.S., Pearce, M.J., *et al.* (2014) 'Religious involvement is associated with greater purpose, optimism, generosity and gratitude in persons with major depression and chronic medical illness.' *Journal of Psychosomatic Research 77*, 2, 135–143.

Koenig, H.G., King, D., and Carson, V.B. (2012) *Handbook of Religion and Health.* New York: Oxford University Press.

Koenig, H.G., McCullough, M.E., and Larson, D.B. (2001) *Religion and Health.* New York: Oxford University Press.

Kohlberg, L. (1984) *The Psychology of Moral Development: Essays on Moral Development* (Vol. 2). San Francisco, CA: Harper and Row.

Koyn, B. (2015) 'Religious participation: The missing link in the ready and resilient campaign.' *Military Review 95*, 5, 2–12.

Krupnick, J.L., Sotsky, S.M., Simmens, S., Moyer, J., *et al.* (1996) 'The role of the therapeutic alliance in psychotherapy and pharmacotherapy outcome: Findings in the National Institute of Mental Health Treatment of Depression Collaborative Research Program.' *Journal of Consulting and Clinical Psychology 64*, 3, 532.

Kubany, E. S., Abueg, F. R., Kilauano, W. L., Manke, F. P., and Kaplan, A. S. (1997) 'Development and validation of the sources of trauma-related guilt survey—war-zone version.' *Journal of Traumatic Stress*, 10, 2, 235–258.

Kyle, C., McEwen, S., and DeFelice, J. (2012) *American Sniper*. New York: William Morrow.

Lambert, M.J., and Barley, D.E. (2001) 'Research summary on the therapeutic relationship and psychotherapy outcome.' *Psychotherapy: Theory, Research, Practice, Training* 38, 4, 357.

Lessem, R., and Schieffer, A. (2008) *Integral Research: A Global Approach Towards Social Science Research Leading to Social Innovation*. Geneva: TRANS4M Publishing.

Lewis, H.B. (1971) 'Shame and guilt in neurosis.' *Psychoanalytic Review* 58, 3, 419.

Lipka, M. (2015) 'Americans' faith in God may be eroding.' Available at www.pewresearch.org/fact-tank/2015/11/04/americans-faith-in-god-may-be-eroding, accessed on October 19, 2017.

Litz, B.T., Lebowitz, L., Nash, W.P., and Gray, M.J. (2016) *Adaptive Disclosure: A New Treatment for Military Trauma, Loss, and Moral Injury*. New York: Guilford Press.

Litz, B.T., Stein, N., Delaney, E., Lebowitz, L., *et al.* (2009) 'Moral injury and moral repair in war veterans: A preliminary model and intervention strategy.' *Clinical Psychology Review* 29, 8, 695–706.

Lyons, J.A. (1991) 'Self-mutilation by a man with posttraumatic stress disorder.' *Journal of Nervous and Mental Disease* 179, 505–507.

Maguen, S., and Burkman, K. (2013) 'Combat-related killing: Expanding evidence-based treatments for PTSD.' *Cognitive and Behavioral Practice* 20, 4, 476–479.

Maguen, S., and Litz, B. (2012) 'Moral injury in the context of war.' *Department of Veterans Affairs*. Available at www.ptsd.va.gov/professional/pages/moral_injury_at_war.asp accessed on December 17, 2017.

Maguen, S., Luxton, D.D., Skopp, N.A., Gahm, G.A., *et al.* (2011) 'Killing in combat, mental health symptoms, and suicidal ideation in Iraq war veterans.' *Journal of Anxiety Disorders* 25, 4, 563–567.

Mansell, W., Harvey, A., Watkins, E., and Shafran, R. (2009) 'Conceptual foundations of the transdiagnostic approach to CBT.' *Journal of Cognitive Psychotherapy* 23, 1, 6–19.

Mattis, J.S. (2002) 'Religion and spirituality in the meaning-making and coping experiences of African American women: A qualitative analysis.' *Psychology of Women Quarterly* 26, 4, 309–321.

McCraven, W. (2017) *Make Your Bed: Little Things that Can Change Your Life...And Maybe the World*. New York: Grand Central Publishing.

McGoldrick, M., Giordano, J., and Garcia-Preto, N. (eds) (2005) *Ethnicity and Family Therapy*. New York: Guilford Press.

McLaughlin, S.S., McLaughlin, A.D., and Van Slyke, J.A. (2010) 'Faith and religious beliefs in an outpatient military population.' *Southern Medical Journal* 103, 6, 527–531.

Meagher, R.E. (2014) *Killing from the Inside Out: Moral Injury and Just War*. Eugene, OR: Wipf and Stock Publishers.

Melchior, A. (2011) 'Caesar in Vietnam: Did Roman soldiers suffer from post-traumatic stress disorder?' *Greece and Rome* 58, 2, 209–223.

Mental Health Advisory Team (2006) 'Final report.' Available at http://i.a.cnn.net/cnn/2007/images/05/04/mhat.iv.report.pdf, accessed on October 19, 2017.

Miggantz, E.L. (2013) 'Stigma of mental health care in the military.' *Naval Center for Combat and Operational Stress Control*. Available at www.archive.org/details/StigmaWhitePaper, accessed on October 3, 2017.

Miller, I. W., Norman, W. H., Keitner, G. I., Bishop, S. B., and Dow, M. G. (1989). 'Cognitive-behavioral treatment of depressed inpatients.' *Behavior Therapy*, 20, 1, 25–47.

Miller, K.E., Omidian, P., Quraishy, A.S., Quraishy, N., *et al.* (2006) 'The Afghan symptom checklist: A culturally grounded approach to mental health assessment in a conflict zone.' *American Journal of Orthopsychiatry* 76, 4, 423.

Miller, L., Bansal, R., Wickramaratne, P., Hao, X., *et al.* (2014) 'Neuroanatomical correlates of religiosity and spirituality: A study in adults at high and low familial risk for depression.' *JAMA Psychiatry* 71, 2, 128–135.

Mitchell, S.A., and Black, M. (2016) *Freud and Beyond: A History of Modern Psychoanalytic Thought*. New York: Basic Books.

Mohr, S., Brandt, P.Y., Borras, L., Gilliéron, C., and Huguelet, P. (2006) 'Toward an integration of spirituality and religiousness into the psychosocial dimension of schizophrenia.' *American Journal of Psychiatry 163*, 11, 1952–1959.

Murguia, E., and Díaz, K. (2015) 'The philosophical foundations of cognitive behavioral therapy: Stoicism, Buddhism, Taoism, and Existentialism.' *Journal of Evidence-Based Psychotherapies 15*, 1, 37.

Nash, W. (2017) 'Moral injury: A mechanism of harm' [Web log post, June 29]. Available at www.pdhealth.mil/news/blog/moral-injury-mechanism-harm, accessed on October 3, 2017.

Nash, W.P., and Litz, B.T. (2013) 'Moral injury: A mechanism for war-related psychological trauma in military family members.' *Clinical Child and Family Psychology Review 16*, 4, 365–375.

Nash, W.P., Marino Carper, T.L., Mills, M.A., Au, T., Goldsmith, A., and Litz, B.T. (2013) 'Psychometric evaluation of the moral injury events scale.' *Military Medicine 178*, 6, 646–652.

Newport, F. (2012) *God is Alive and Well: The Future of Religion in America.* New York: Simon and Schuster.

Nichols, M.P., and Schwartz, R.C. (2001) *The Essentials of Family Therapy.* Boston, MA: Allyn and Bacon.

Norman, S., Hamblen, J., Schnurr, P., and Eftekhari, A. (2017) 'Overview of psychotherapy for PTSD.' *National Center for PTSD.* Available at www.ptsd.va.gov/professional/treatment/overview/overview-treatment-research.asp, accessed on October 19, 2017.

Obama, B. (2010) Nobel Peace Prize acceptance speech, Oslo, Norway, December 10, 2009.

Olson, M., and Hergenhahn, B. (2013) *An Introduction to Theories of Learning.* Boston, MA: Pearson.

Otto, R. (1958) *The Idea of the Holy.* Oxford: Oxford University Press.

Pargament, K.I. (1997) *The Psychology of Religion and Coping.* New York: Guilford Press.

Pargament, K.I. (2011) *Spiritually Integrated Psychotherapy: Understanding and Addressing the Sacred.* New York: Guilford Press.

Park, C.L. (2010) 'Making sense of the meaning literature: An integrative review of meaning making and its effects on adjustment to stressful life events.' *Psychological Bulletin 136*, 2, 257.

Park, C.L., Moehl, B.M., Juliane, R., Fenster, J.R., Suresh, D., and Bliss, D. (2008) 'Religiousness and treatment adherence in congestive heart failure patients.' *Journal of Religion, Spirituality & Aging 20*, 4, 249–266.

Pattakos, A. (2010) *Prisoners of Our Thoughts: Viktor Frankl's Principles for Discovering Meaning in Life and Work.* San Francisco, CA: Berrett-Koehler Publishers.

Peery, B. (2012) 'Outcome Oriented Chaplaincy: Intentional Caring.' In S. Roberts (ed.) *Professional Spiritual and Pastoral Care: A Practical Clergy and Chaplain's Handbook.* Woodstock, VT: Skylight Paths.

Pew Research Center (2015a) 'Chapter 1: Importance of religion and religious beliefs.' Available at www.pewforum.org/2015/11/03/chapter-1-importance-of-religion-and-religious-beliefs/#belief-in-god, accessed on October 19, 2017.

Pew Research Center (2015b) 'America's changing religious landscape.' Available at www.pewforum.org/2015/05/12/americas-changing-religious-landscape, accessed on October 19, 2017.

Pitman, R.K. (1990) 'Self-mutilation in combat-related PTSD.' *The American Journal of Psychiatry 147*, 1, 123–124.

Richards, P., and Bergin, A.E. (2005) *Casebook for a Spiritual Strategy in Counseling and Psychotherapy.* Washington, DC: American Psychological Association.

Roberts, S. (ed.) (2012) *Professional Spiritual and Pastoral Care: A Practical Clergy and Chaplain's Handbook.* Woodstock, VT: Skylight Paths.

Ross, R.J., Ball, W.A., Sullivan, K.A., and Caroff, S.N. (1989) 'Sleep disturbance as the hallmark of posttraumatic stress disorder.' *The American Journal of Psychiatry 146*, 6, 697.

Sadler, A.G., Booth, B.M., Mengeling, M.A., and Doebbeling, B.N. (2004) 'Life span and repeated violence against women during military service: Effects on health status and outpatient utilization.' *Journal of Women's Health 13*, 7, 799–811.

Satir, V. (1967) *Conjoint Family Therapy.* Palo Alto, CA: Science and Behavior Books.

Satir, V. (1972) *Peoplemaking.* Palo Alto, CA: Science and Behavior Books.

Satir, V. (1976) *Making Contact.* Millbrae, CA: Celestial Arts.

Satir, V. (1983) *Blended Family with a Troubled Boy.* Kansas City, MO: Golden Triad Films.

Satir, V. (1987) *Audiotaped Presentations at Avanta Process Community VII, Module I, in Crested Butte, CO. Blue Moon Cassettes, Recordings 5.* Santa Barbara, CA: Virginia Satir Archives, Special Collection, Davison Library, University of California.

Satir, V., Banmen, J., Gerber, J., and Gomori, M. (1991) *The Satir Model: Family Therapy and Beyond.* Palo Alto, CA: Science and Behavior Books.

Satir, V., Stachowiak, J., and Taschman, H.A. (1994) *Helping Families to Change.* Jason Aronson, Incorporated. New York: Rowman & Littlefield Publishers, Inc.

Sauer-Zavala, S., Gutner, C.A., Farchione, T.J., Boettcher, H.T., Bullis, J.R., and Barlow, D.H. (2017) 'Current definitions of "transdiagnostic" in treatment development: A search for consensus.' *Behavior Therapy 48,* 1, 128–138.

Schiraldi, G. (2016) *The Post-Traumatic Stress Disorder Sourcebook, Revised and Expanded Second Edition: A Guide to Healing, Recovery, and Growth.* New York: McGraw-Hill.

Schneiders, S.M. (2003) 'Religion vs. spirituality: A contemporary conundrum.' *Spiritus: A Journal of Christian Spirituality 3,* 2, 163–185.

Schnurr, P.P., and Spiro III, A. (1999) 'Combat exposure, posttraumatic stress disorder symptoms, and health behaviors as predictors of self-reported physical health in older veterans.' *The Journal of Nervous and Mental Disease 187,* 6, 353–359.

Schuster, M.A., Stein, B.D., Jaycox, L.H., Collins, R.L., *et al.* (2001) 'A national survey of stress reactions after the September 11, 2001, terrorist attacks.' *New England Journal of Medicine 345,* 20, 1507–1512.

Shay, J. (1993) *Achilles in Vietnam: The Undoing of Character.* New York: Scribner.

Shay, J. (2003) *Odysseus in America: Combat Trauma and the Trials of Homecoming.* New York: Simon and Schuster.

Shay, J. (2016) Moral Injury—VA-Military Chaplains Webinars 1/12/16, Air Force Reserve Chaplains 1/15/16, Northampton, Massachusetts Veterans Administration. Available at https://chapvaco. adobeconnect.com/p1ltuzq2t6w/?launcher=false&fcsContent=true&pbMode=normal, accessed on October 19, 2017.

Shay, J., and Munroe, J. (1999) 'Group and milieu therapy for veterans with complex posttraumatic stress disorder.' *Posttraumatic Stress Disorder: A Comprehensive Text,* 391–413. Needham Heights, MA: Allyn & Bacon.

Sher, L. (2009) 'A model of suicidal behavior in war veterans with posttraumatic mood disorder.' *Medical Hypotheses 73,* 2, 215–219.

Shephard, B. (2001) *A War of Nerves: Soldiers and Psychiatrists in the Twentieth Century.* Harvard, MA: Harvard University Press.

Sherman, N. (2015) *Afterwar: Healing the Moral Wounds of Our Soldiers.* Oxford: Oxford University Press.

Skrabski, Á., Kopp, M., Rózsa, S., Réthelyi, J., and Rahe, R.H. (2005) 'Life meaning: An important correlate of health in the Hungarian population.' *International Journal of Behavioral Medicine 12,* 78–85.

Sloan, L., and Friedman, M. (2009) *After the War Zone: A Practical Guide for Returning Troops and Their Families.* Cambridge, MA: Da Capo Press.

Smith, J.C., Hyman, S.M., Andres-Hyman, R.C., Ruiz, J.J., and Davidson, L. (2016) 'Applying recovery principles to the treatment of trauma.' *Professional Psychology: Research and Practice 47,* 5, 347.

Soothill, K., Morris, S.M., Harman, J.C., Thomas, C., Francis, B., and McIllmurray, M.B. (2002) 'Cancer and faith. Having faith—does it make a difference among patients and their informal carers?' *Scandinavian Journal of Caring Sciences 16,* 3, 256–263.

Southwick, S.M., and Charney, D.S. (2015) *Resilience: The Science of Mastering Life's Greatest Challenges.* Cambridge: Cambridge University Press.

Southwick, S.M., Pietrzak, R.H., Tsai, J., Krystal, J.H., and Charney, D. (2015) 'Resilience: An update.' *PTSD Research Quarterly 25,* 4, 1050–1835.

Stanford Encyclopedia of Philosophy (2017) Available at https://plato.stanford.edu/contents.html, accessed on October 3, 2017.

Steenkamp, M.M., and Litz, B.T. (2013) 'Psychotherapy for military-related posttraumatic stress disorder: Review of the evidence.' *Clinical Psychology Review 33,* 1, 45–53.

Steenkamp, M.M., Nash, W.P., and Litz, B.T. (2013) 'Post-traumatic stress disorder: Review of the Comprehensive Soldier Fitness program.' *American Journal of Preventive Medicine 44,* 5, 507–512.

Tangney, J.P., and Dearing, R.L. (2002) *Shame and Guilt*. New York: Guilford Press.

Thielman, S.B. (2011) 'Religion and Spirituality in the Description of Posttraumatic Stress Disorder.' In J. Peteet, F. Lu, and W. Narrow (eds) *Religious and Spiritual Issues in Psychiatric Diagnosis: A Research Agenda for DSM-V.* Washington, DC: APA Publishing.

Tick, E. (2005) *War and the Soul: Healing Our Nation's Veterans from Post-Traumatic Stress Disorder.* Wheaton, IL: Quest Books.

Tutu, D. (1999) *No Future without Forgiveness*. New York: Doubleday.

U.S. Department of Veterans Affairs (2017) 'Dissemination of evidence-based psychotherapy for PTSD in veterans affairs.' Available at www.ptsd.va.gov/professional/treatment/overview/dissemination-ebp-ptsd-va.asp, accessed on October 19, 2017.

VanderWeele, T.J., Li, S., Tsai, A.C., and Kawachi, I. (2016) 'Association between religious service attendance and lower suicide rates among US women.' *JAMA Psychiatry 73*, 8, 845–851.

van Wees, J.G.B. (2004) *Greek Warfare: Myths and Realities*. London: Duckworth.

Walser, R.D., and Westrup, D. (2007) *Acceptance and Commitment Therapy for the Treatment of Post-Traumatic Stress Disorder and Trauma-Related Problems: A Practitioner's Guide to Using Mindfulness and Acceptance Strategies.* Oakland, CA: New Harbinger Publications.

Weathers, F.W., Litz, B.T., Keane, T.M., Palmieri, P.A., Marx, B.P., and Schnurr, P.P. (2013) *The PTSD Checklist for DSM-5 (PCL-5)*. Scale available from the National Center for PTSD at www.ptsd.va.gov.professional/assessment/documents/PCL-5_Standard.pdf, accessed on January 2, 2018.

Winnicott, D.W. (1960) 'The theory of the parent–infant relationship.' *The International Journal of Psycho-analysis 41*, 585.

Yalom, I.D. with Leszcz, M. (2005) *The Theory and Practice of Group Psychotherapy*. New York: Basic Books.

Yan, G.W. (2016) 'The invisible wound: Moral injury and its impact on the health of Operation Enduring Freedom/Operation Iraqi Freedom veterans.' *Military Medicine 181*, 5, 451–458.

Yehuda, R., Vermetten, E., McFarlane, A.C., and Lehrner, A. (2014) 'PTSD in the military: Special considerations for understanding prevalence, pathophysiology and treatment following deployment.' *European Journal of Psychotraumatology 5*, 1, 25322.

Zinnbauer, B.J., Pargament, K.I., Cole, B., Rye, M.S., *et al.* (1997) 'Religion and spirituality: Unfuzzying the fuzzy.' *Journal for the Scientific Study of Religion 36*, 4, 549–564.

Zinnbauer, B.J., Pargament, K.I., and Scott, A.B. (1999) 'The emerging meanings of religiousness and spirituality: Problems and prospects.' *Journal of Personality 67*, 6, 889–919.

Subject Index

Author Index